Learn Visio® 2000

For users of
Visio 2000 Standard Edition
Visio 2000 Technical Edition
Visio 2000 Professional Edition
Visio 2000 Enterprise Edition

by Ralph Grabowski

Wordware Publishing, Inc.

Library of Congress Cataloging-in-Publication Data

Grabowski, Ralph
    Learn Visio 2000 / by Ralph Grabowski.
      p. cm.
    Includes index.
    ISBN 1-55622-673-X (pbk.)
    1. Computer graphics. 2. Visio. I. Title.
    T385.G6927 1999
    604.2'0285'5369--dc21   99-057134
                                    CIP

ISBN 1-55622-673-X
10 9 8 7 6 5 4 3 2
9911

All inquiries for volume purchases of this book should be addressed to:
Wordware Publishing, Inc.
2320 Los Rios Boulevard, #200
Plano, Texas 75074
Telephone inquiries may be made by calling: (972) 423-0090

Contents

	Acknowledgments	xi
	Introduction	xii
Module 1	**Starting a New Drawing**	**1**
	Uses	1
	Starting with a New Drawing	2
	Beginning with a Solution	3
	Creating a New Drawing with a Wizard	7
	Procedures	7
	Starting a New Drawing	7
	Starting a New, Blank Drawing	8
	Starting a New Drawing with a Wizard	8
	Hands-On Activity	9
Module 2	**Saving Files**	**13**
	Uses	13
	Save As	14
	File Properties	14
	File Dialog Boxes	15
	Procedures	19
	Saving a Drawing for the First Time	19
	Saving a Drawing the Next Time	19
	Saving a Drawing as a Template	19
	Hands-On Activity	20
Module 3	**Opening Existing Drawings**	**23**
	Uses	23
	Importing Non-Visio Files	25
	Visio Drawing Viewer	26
	Procedures	28
	Opening a Visio Drawing	28
	Importing a Non-Visio File	28
	Hands-On Activity	29
Module 4	**Setting Up Pages and Layers**	**31**
	Uses	31
	Drawing Pages	32
	Inserting a Page	32

Background Pages 33
Other Page Parameters 35
Drawing Scale 37
Layers 38
Procedures 40
Setting the Drawing Size and Scale 40
Changing the Drawing Size Interactively 40
Creating New Layers 41
Changing Layer Properties 41
Renaming a Layer 42
Removing a Layer 42
Creating a New Page 43
Hands-On Activity 43

Module 5   **Views, Zooms, and Pans** **51**
Uses 51
The Pan & Zoom Window 52
Procedures 54
Zoom in on a Detail 54
Return to Previous Zoom Level 54
Hands-On Activity 55

Module 6   **Rulers, Grids, Guidelines, and Page Breaks** **59**
Uses 59
Horizontal and Vertical Rulers 59
The Grid Lines 60
Guidelines and Guide Points 61
Snap Distance 61
Shape Extensions 63
Dynamic Grid 64
Page Breaks 65
Procedures 65
Setting the Snap 65
Setting the Ruler and Grid 65
Toggling the Snap 66
Toggling the Glue 66
Creating a Guideline 67
Repositioning a Guideline 67
Removing a Guideline 67
Creating and Removing Guide Points 68
Toggling the Display of Guidelines and Points 68
Toggling the Grid Display 68
Relocating the Ruler Origin 68
Hands-On Activity 69

Module 7   **Opening Existing Stencils** **71**
Uses 71

Shape Explorer 73
Procedures. 76
    Opening a Stencil File 76
    Adjusting the Stencil Window. 77
Hands-On Activity. 79

Module 8   **Dragging Masters into the Drawing.** **85**
Uses 85
Procedures. 85
Hands-On Activity. 86

Module 9   **Sizing and Positioning** **89**
Uses 89
    Size & Position Window. 90
Procedures. 92
    Resizing the Shape. 93
    Changing the Height of the Shape 93
    Changing the Wall Thickness 93
    Rotating the Shape. 94
    Free Rotating the Shape. 94
    Flipping the Shape. 94
    The Size & Position Window 95
    Bring to Front and Send to Back 95
    Center Drawing. 95
Hands-On Activity. 95

Module 10   **Placing Multiple Shapes** **99**
Uses 99
Procedures. 99
    Making a Copy. 99
    Duplicating More Than One Copy 100
    Making an Offset Copy 101
Hands-On Activity. 102

Module 11   **Connecting Shapes Together** **105**
Uses 105
    Connection Points 106
    Glue 107
    Variations on Connectors 109
    Creating Connections 111
Procedures 112
    Connecting Shapes Automatically During Dragging. 112
    Connecting Existing Shapes Automatically 112
    Connecting Shapes Automatically. 113
    Connecting Shapes Manually 113
    Adding a Connection Point 113
Hands-On Activity 114

Module 12 **Cutting, Copying, and Pasting** **117**
Uses 117
Procedures 119
    Cutting Text and Graphic Objects 119
    Copying Text and Graphic Objects 119
    Pasting Text and Graphic Objects 120
    Paste Special 121
Hands-On Activity 122

Module 13 **Formatting Shapes** **125**
Uses 125
    Formatting Lines 125
    Formatting Areas 127
    Shadow Casting 129
Procedures 131
    Formatting Lines 131
    Applying a Fill Color and Pattern 133
    Quick Formatting 135
Hands-On Activity 136

Module 14 **Formatting Text** **139**
Uses 139
    Text Blocks 139
    Text Format Bar 141
Procedures 141
    Selecting All Text in a Shape 142
    Selecting a Portion of the Text 143
    Changing the Font 143
    Changing the Justification of a Paragraph 145
    Changing the Vertical Alignment 147
    Setting Tabs 148
    Adding Bullets to Text 149
Hands-On Activity 149

Module 15 **Creating and Applying Styles** **153**
Uses 153
Procedures 155
    Format Painter 155
    Defining a Style 155
    Applying a Style 157
    Text Style List 157
    Line Style List 158
    Fill Style List 158
Hands-On Activity 159

Module 16 **Aligning Shapes** **163**
Uses 163

Procedures 163
    Align Shapes 164
    Distribute Shapes 165
    Lay Out Shapes 166
Hands-On Activity 169

Module 17   **Creating Groups** **173**
Uses 173
Procedures 174
    Create a Group from Shapes 174
    Add to a Group 174
    Remove from a Group 174
    Disband a Group 175
Hands-On Activity 175

Module 18   **Boolean Operations** **177**
Uses 177
Procedures 178
    Union Operation 178
    Combine Operation 178
    Fragment Operation 179
    Intersect Operation 179
    Subtract Operation 179
    Building a Region 180
Hands-On Activity 181

Module 19   **Previewing Before Printing** **187**
Uses 187
Procedures 187
    Print Preview 188
Hands-On Activity 192

Module 20   **Printing Drawings** **195**
Uses 195
Procedures 196
    Printing the Drawing 197
    Tiling Drawings 198
    Transmitting Faxed Drawings 200
    E-mailing Drawing Attachments 201
    Printing to File 202
Hands-On Activity 204

Module 21   **Undoing and Redoing** **205**
Uses 205
Procedures 206
    Undoing an Action 207
    Redoing an Undo 207
    Multiple Undo Levels 207

Hands-On Activity 207

Module 22 **Help** **213**
Uses 213
Procedures 217
Hands-On Activity 217

Module 23 **Drawing Tools** **225**
Uses 225
Procedures 227
Drawing with the Pencil Tool 228
Drawing with the Line Tool 229
Drawing with the Arc Tool 229
Drawing with the Rectangle Tool 230
Drawing with the Ellipse Tool 230
Drawing Closed Objects. 231
Adding Segments to an Object 232
Moving the Vertex 233
Hands-On Activity 234

Module 24 **Placing Text and Fields** **237**
Uses 237
Procedures 238
Placing Text 238
Inserting a Text Field. 240
Hands-On Activity 242
Creating a Dimension Line 244

Module 25 **Spelling** **247**
Uses 247
Procedures 247
Check Spelling 247
Hands-On Activity 249

Module 26 **Finding and Replacing Text** **251**
Uses 251
Procedures 251
Finding Text 252
Replacing Text 254
Hands-On Activity 255

Module 27 **Dimensioning** **257**
Uses 257
Procedures 260
Automatically Dimensioning a Wall Shape. 260
Manually Dimensioning Any Shape 261
Changing the Dimension Line 262
Changing the Extension Line 262

Changing the Dimension Text 264
Hands-On Activity 265

Module 28   **Inserting Objects** **273**
Uses 273
Procedures 276
Inserting a Picture 277
Applying the Crop Tool 279
Inserting a New Object 280
Inserting an Object from a File 282
Placing a Linked Object 284
Editing an Object within Visio 286

Module 29   **Exporting Drawings** **289**
Uses 289
Procedures 293
Export Options 293
Export to AI and EPS 294
Export to BMP and DIB 296
Export to CGM 298
Export to GIF 299
Export to IGES 300
Export to JPEG 301
Export to PICT 303
Export to PCX 304
Export to PNG 305
Export to TIFF 308
Hands-On Activity 310

Module 30   **Special Selections** **311**
Uses 311
Procedures 312
Using Select Special 312
Hands-On Activity 313

Module 31   **Drawing Explorer** **317**
Uses 317
Procedures 317
Navigating the Drawing Explorer 318
Hands-On Activity 321

Module 32   **Double-clicking the Mouse Button** **325**
Uses 325
Procedures 328
Hands-On Activity 328

Module 33   **Behavior** **331**
Uses 331

The Behavior Dialog Box 331
The Placement Tab 334
The Special Dialog Box 335
Hands-On Activity 336

Module 34 **Custom Properties** **339**
Uses 339
Define Custom Properties Dialog Box 341
Editing a Shape's Custom Properties 344
Adding a Custom Property 345
Editing Custom Property Fields 346
Summarizing Custom Property Data 348

Module 35 **Internet Tools** **353**
Uses 353
Procedures 354
Adding a Hyperlink to a Shape or Page 354
Editing a Hyperlink. 357
Jumping to a Hyperlink 358
Hands-On Activity 358

Module 36 **Creating a Web Document** **361**
Uses 361
Procedures 363
Saving as an HTML File 363
Hands-On Activity 368

Module 37 **Importing CAD Drawings.** **371**
Uses 371
Procedures 373
Import a CAD Drawing 373

Module 38 **Toolbar Customization** **377**
Uses 377
Procedures 378
Changing Toolbar Options 378
Creating a New Toolbar 380

Appendix A **Mouse & Keyboard Shortcuts** **383**
Shortcuts by Task. 383
Shortcuts by Keystroke 388

Index 393

Acknowledgments

No author is an island. In that regard, I would like to thank Jim Hill, the publisher of Wordware, for his enthusiasm and support. My wife, Heather, and our three children accepted Dad working evenings and weekends in exchange for taking time off during other peoples' "working hours."

And, as I well know, no author can ever review his own writing. I am grateful for Judy Lemke of Visio Corp., who scanned my manuscript for technical accuracy. Without her help, this would be a poorer book.

Special thanks to Scott Campbell of Visio Corp. for going the extra mile in his support of my Visio books and the Wordware Visio Library.

Finally, thanks to Him who makes all things possible.

Introduction

Getting Started

Visio is software for creating diagrams. Unlike other technical drawing programs, such as computer-aided drawing software, Visio is easy to use. To make a drawing, you don't need to know how to draw! You simply drag shapes from stencils onto the page. Visio also includes a number of tools for drawing lines, circles, boxes, and curves if you prefer to draw freehand.

The shapes are called *SmartShapes* because they know where they connect with each other, resize appropriately, and contain other smarts. All shapes have a mini-spreadsheet hidden behind them, called a *ShapeSheet*. This spreadsheet contains all known information about the shape and can be manipulated directly. The lines that connect shapes, such as in flowcharts, are also smart because they stretch when you move any connected shape.

With SmartShapes and dynamic connectors, Visio creates intelligent drawings. Typical drawings include organization charts, process flowcharts, directional maps, and network diagrams.

Which Visio is for You?

Visio 2000 is available in several flavors: Standard, Technical, Professional, and Enterprise. Which product is best for you?

▶ **Visio 2000 Standard Edition** is for general business diagramming needs. Use this software for creating organization charts, basic network diagrams, Gantt charts, cross-functional flowcharts, and process flowcharts.

▶ **Visio 2000 Technical Edition** is for creating 2D technical drawings without the long learning curve normally associated with CAD software. Use this software for creating space plans, HVAC (heating, ventilating, air conditioning) designs, fluid power schematics, and factory floor layouts, and working with AutoCAD and MicroStation drawings.

▸ **Visio 2000 Professional Edition** is for designing and documenting information systems and business processes.

▸ **Visio 2000 Enterprise Edition** is for designing and documenting networks, modeling and designing databases, and modeling software applications across an enterprise information infrastructure.

About This Book

Learn Visio 2000 covers all versions of Visio 2000: Standard, Technical, Professional, and Enterprise editions. This book discusses only features common to all four programs.

This book is designed to be modular. Instead of chapters, this book has modules. Every module is independent.

Think of this book as a cookbook: you don't need to start at the beginning and work your way though to the end. If you already know how to open and save files, and how to use the Clipboard, you can easily skip those modules.

Once you have mastered the subjects covered in this book, consider *Learn Visio 2000 for the Advanced User,* also by Ralph Grabowski. This book teaches you how to customize Visio for the way you work. You learn how to create templates and custom styles. You go "behind the curtain" to learn how the ShapeSheet operates and find out why it is fundamental to all that goes on in Visio. You also learn how to create diagrams automatically, and how to hook up Visio with database files.

Starting Visio

Visio 2000

To start Visio 2000, either select **Start | Programs | Visio 2000** or double-click the shortcut icon on the Desktop. (To exit Visio at any time, press **Alt+F4** or select **File | Exit**.)

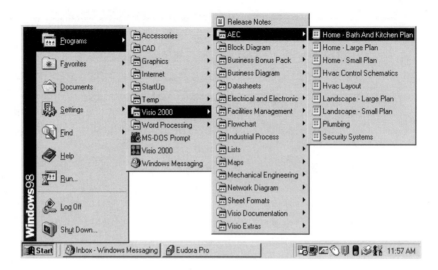

A Guided Tour

When Visio first starts, it displays the Welcome to Visio 2000 dialog box. (This is a vast improvement over earlier versions, where there isn't much to see.) Select **Choose drawing type**.

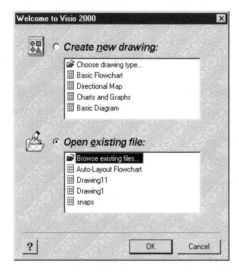

Notice that Visio displays the Choose Drawing Type dialog box. The types of drawings Visio can create are categorized. The drawing types listed under **Category** vary, depending on the edition of Visio 2000 you have. The list shown in the illustration comes with Visio 2000 Technical Edition.

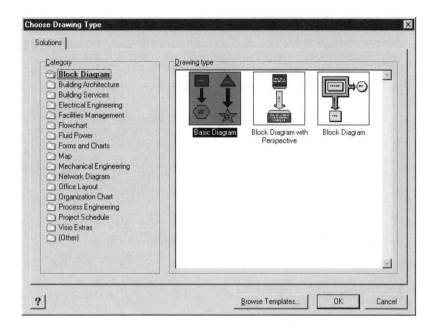

Within each category, Visio 2000 has one or more subcategories. These "subcategories" are called *solutions*. A solution consists of a single drawing page, usually scaled and oriented appropriately for the drawing type. It also includes a set of commonly used stencils. You'll see one such solution shortly.

As you click a category name, such as **Block Diagram** or **Flowchart**, Visio displays previews of drawing types in the right-hand pane. For example, under **Flowchart**, you can select one of several templates, such as the **Audit Diagram**, **Basic Flowchart**, or **Work Flow Diagram** template.

Pause your cursor over one of the drawing previews to see a tooltip describing the drawing type. The *tooltip* is a yellow square of text that floats near your cursor.

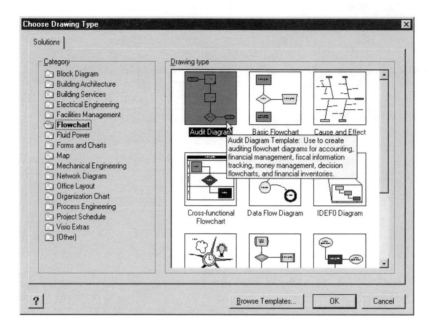

The tooltip describes the drawing type.

Select a solution, such as **Basic Flowchart**, and click **OK**. Once you select a drawing type, the Visio screen comes to life.

Along the top are the toolbar and the menu bar. The menu bar contains most—but not all—of Visio's commands.

Below the menu bar are the *toolbars*. By default, two toolbars are displayed: **Standard** and **Format**. (To simplify the user interface, Visio 2000 displays fewer toolbars than earlier versions.) To add and remove toolbars, right-click on the toolbar and select (or deselect) the name from the shortcut menu.

At the left is a *stencil* with *shapes*. You can open more than one stencil at a time; three stencils are open in the illustration (two are shown just by their title bars). Each stencil in the illustration holds 25 to 35 shapes. To use a shape, simply drag it from the stencil to the page.

The largest part of the Visio window is the drawing area, which displays a *page*. While most of the time you will probably work with a standard 8½ x 11-inch page, Visio accommodates a wide variety of page sizes—all the way up to 36 x 48". You can have up to 200 pages in a drawing, although only one page is displayed at a time.

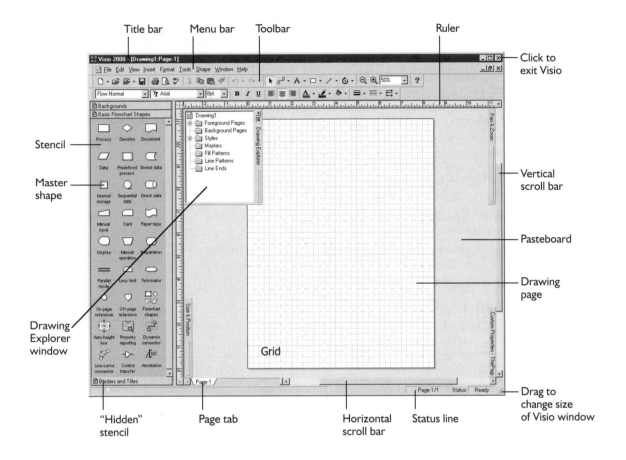

The page tabs, new to Visio 2000, make it easy to switch between pages, as well as add, remove, and reorder pages.

Surrounding the page is the *pasteboard*. You can store shapes there; the pasteboard does not print. *Scroll bars* let you move the page around the window. The *rulers* measure distances.

Diagramming Assistants

Visio uses many visual hints to help you draw quickly and accurately:

Grid: On a blank drawing page, all you see initially are the grid lines. The grid helps you position objects; you can choose to have shapes *snap* to the grid for accurate horizontal and vertical positioning. You may change the grid spacing, including independent x- and y-spacing.

Ruler: The ruler reports the size of the drawing in scaled units. By holding down the **Ctrl** key, you can drag the zero point (from the intersection of the two rulers) to a new zero point. Like the grid, the ruler helps you position objects; you can have shapes *snap* to the ruler increments for accurate horizontal and vertical positioning.

Connection point: Small blue x shapes appear whenever you select a shape that you dragged from a stencil. These indicate the points where you can connect one shape to another.

Selection handle: Perhaps the most important visual clue is the selection handle. Its shape and color change, alerting you to its properties. The most common selection handle is a small, green square. This indicates the points where you can change the size and rotation of the object. Click and hold the square, drag (to change the size or the angle), then let go of the mouse button. In brief, selection handles can take on the following colors and shapes:

- ■ Green square: selection handle.
- ■ Red square: glued connection.
- 🔒 Padlock: shape cannot have its size changed.
- ◎ Round: a rotation handle for rotating the object.
- ◈ Diamond: a vertex point on objects such as arcs.

The red color indicates the object is *glued* to another object. When you move a shape that is glued to another shape, the shapes stay connected.

Drawing with Visio is Better, Faster

You can create a drawing with Visio in exactly the same manner as with other drawing and CAD software: draw lines, circles, and other shapes, then edit them. In addition, Visio offers a much more powerful—faster—method of drawing rarely found in other software. Follow these easy steps:

Step 1:   Start a new drawing.
Step 2:   Open the appropriate template.
Step 3:   Drag shapes into the drawing.
Step 4:   Connect shapes as required.
Step 5:   Save and print the drawing.

Using the pre-drawn shapes saves you the time it takes to draw objects from scratch. If the shape isn't exactly what you need, any shape is easily edited.

Connections between shapes work like magic. Small blue x markers tell you where the connections are located on each shape. When two shapes connect, the connector endpoints turn red. When you move one shape, the connector stays glued to it—until you decide to disconnect it. Visio includes many tools for accurate, automatic positioning and shape manipulation.

Drawings that were created in other software programs can be imported into a Visio drawing. When you have data that resides in database files, you can link the data with Visio drawings, then access the database from within Visio. Visio can export drawings in many vector (CAD) and raster (paint) formats; Visio can also export a drawing as a Web page.

Visio is a powerful program for working with graphics and data. This book will show you how easy it is to harness that power.

A Brief History of Visio

ShapeWare Corp., as Visio Corp. was first called, was founded in 1990 by two of the founders of Aldus Corp. (of PageMaker fame, later merged with Adobe of PostScript fame). When Visio v1.0 was introduced in 1992, the software quickly became popular because it did not present a blank page to the new user. Instead, it invited the user to drag shapes and drop them onto the page.

In 1993, ShapeWare began shipping optional stencils and shapes to Visio called "Visio Shapes." When it was renamed the Visio Solutions Library in 1996, the library included add-ons developed by ShapeWare and third-party vendors. One example is the Visio Business Modeler, which lets you analyze business models found in the SAP R/3 Reference Model.

After shipping Visio v1, v2, v3, and v4, ShapeWare began creating specific releases of Visio. Visio Technical was introduced in 1994 as companion software to CAD products (the first version of Technical was called "version 4.1"). In 1995, ShapeWare Corp. changed its name to Visio Corp. and went public on the NASDAQ stock exchange under the symbol "VSIO".

Visio Professional was released in 1996 for IT professionals (the first version of Professional was called "version 4.5"). In 1997, Visio delivered

Visio Map for GIS users, with mapping technology licensed from ESRI, one of the largest GIS software companies.

In 1998, Visio began shipping IntelliCAD (aka "Phoenix"), an AutoCAD-compatible CAD system Visio obtained by purchasing Boomerang Technology, a former division of Softdesk, which had merged with Autodesk a year earlier. At about the same time, Visio help establish the OpenDWG Alliance (www.opendwg.org) to unravel the mysteries of the AutoCAD DWG file format. Just 18 months later, Visio handed IntelliCAD over to the IntelliCAD Technical Consortium (www.intellicad.org) to market the software as "open source software."

Also in 1998, Visio released Visio Enterprise as an advanced version of Visio Professional, which had replaced Visio Network. Later in the year, Visio Standard and Technical were updated with the Visio Plus editions. Visio opened up its eVisio Web site, where the software and its components can be purchased over the Internet, then couriered to you on CD-ROM.

In 1999, Visio began shipping its more powerful Visio 2000 in four editions: Standard, Technical, Professional, and Enterprise. And, in a surprise move, Microsoft purchased Visio Corp. for $1.3 billion.

For more information about Visio, check the Web site at www.visio.com.

Starting a New Drawing

File | New

Uses

You reach for a piece of blank paper. That's the first step you take when you start a new drawing. In Visio, it is no different: you start with a new drawing *page*.

> **In this chapter you'll learn about:**
>
> ✓ **Starting with a new drawing**
>
> ✓ **Beginning with a solution**
>
> ✓ **Creating a new drawing with a wizard**

A new drawing is like a blank sheet of paper. Visio 2000 lets you start a new drawing in three different ways:

▶ Start with a blank drawing

▶ Begin with a solution

▶ Create a new drawing with a wizard

When you start Visio 2000 for the first time, it displays the Welcome to Visio 2000 dialog box. The dialog box displays the four previously opened solutions and drawings. The upper half, **Create new drawing**, deals with solutions:

▶ **Choose drawing type**: Displays the Choose Drawing Type dialog box, which sorts solutions into categories.

▶ **Blank Drawing**: Opens a new, blank drawing with no stencils (found in the **Other** folder).

▶ *Previously opened templates*: The other files are up to four previously opened solutions. This allows you to quickly access the solution you worked on most recently.

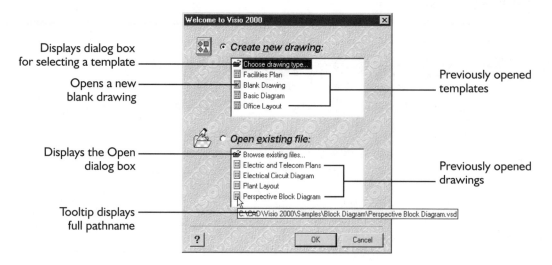

The lower half, **Open existing file**, deals with drawings:

▸ **Browse existing files**: Displays the Open dialog box, which lets
   you open Visio drawing files, as well as a large number of other file
   formats that Visio can read (see Module 28 "Inserting Objects").

▸ *Previously opened drawings*: The other files are up to four previously
   opened drawings. This allows you to quickly access the drawing you
   worked on most recently.

Tip: When you pause the cursor over a template or drawing
name, the tooltip shows the full pathname (drive and folders)
of the drawing. (This feature may not be available in some earlier versions of Windows.)

Starting with a New Drawing

Visio provides two ways to start with a new drawing. When you start Visio,
it displays the Welcome to Visio 2000 dialog box. Double-click **Choose
drawing type**, click **Other**, click **Blank Drawing**, and then click **OK**.

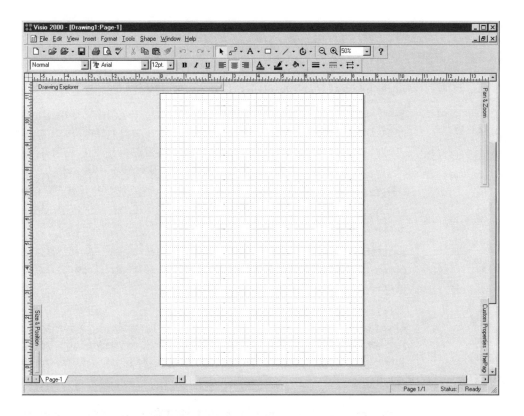

After starting Visio, you can open another blank drawing page. When you press **Ctrl+N** (or select **File | New** from the menu bar), Visio opens a new drawing with the same settings as the current drawing.

To open a truly blank drawing, select **File | New | Blank Drawing** from the menu. Visio opens a blank drawing: an 8½" x 11" sheet of paper in portrait orientation, a scale of 1:1, and no stencils or shapes loaded. Starting with a blank drawing is best when you want to create a new drawing from scratch, with no assistance from Visio stencils or wizards.

Beginning with a Solution

A *solution* is a customized drawing environment for a specific discipline or vertical market, such as flowcharts, electronics, or facilities management. When you open a solution, Visio opens related stencils; configures the drawing page with a suitable size, scale, and orientation; and in some cases may add an item to the menu bar. (Solutions are based on Visio's *.VST template files.)

Each edition of Visio—Standard, Technical, Professional, and Enterprise—comes with a different collection of solutions files:

Standard Edition: Includes block diagrams, flowcharts, maps, office layouts, and project timelines.

Technical Edition: Includes the Standard Edition solutions and technically oriented solutions, such as chemical and petroleum engineering, house and landscape planning, software and network, mechanical and electrical engineering, and space planning solutions.

Professional Edition: Includes the Standard Edition solutions, plus additional solutions for network design, Internet design, database design, and visual modeling (software design).

Enterprise Edition: Includes all of the solutions found in Professional, plus additional templates for networks, software design, and database access.

Visio provides several ways to access solutions. When you start Visio, it displays the Welcome to Visio 2000 dialog box. Select **Choose drawing type** and click **OK**. Visio displays the Choose Drawing Type dialog box. The categories listed in the dialog box vary according to the edition you are using.

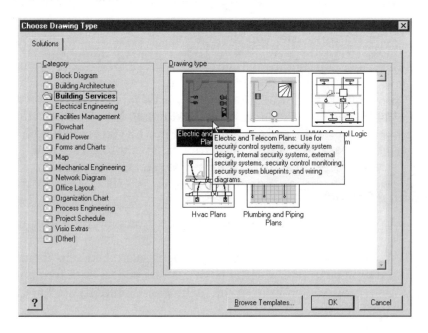

Tip: When you pause the cursor over the template preview image, Visio displays a tooltip describing the solution.

Within Visio, you access the solutions by selecting **File | New** from the menu bar. The menu lists the solution categories. In Visio 2000, click the small arrow next to the **New** icon on the toolbar.

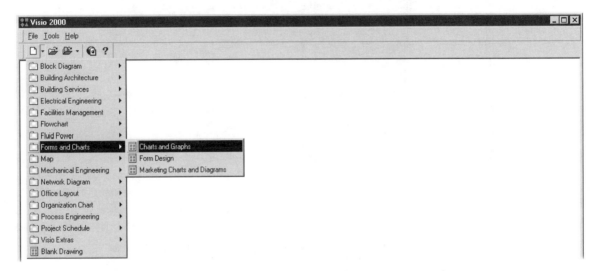

When you choose one of the solutions, Visio opens a new drawing with appropriate stencils and page setup, possibly a toolbar, an additional menu item, a wizard, and sometimes the Project Explorer. For example, when you select the **Process Engineering | Process Engineering** stencil (provided with the Technical Edition), Visio opens the Project Explorer, nine stencils, and a landscape-oriented page that matches your printer's default page size, and adds the **Process Engineering** item to the menu bar.

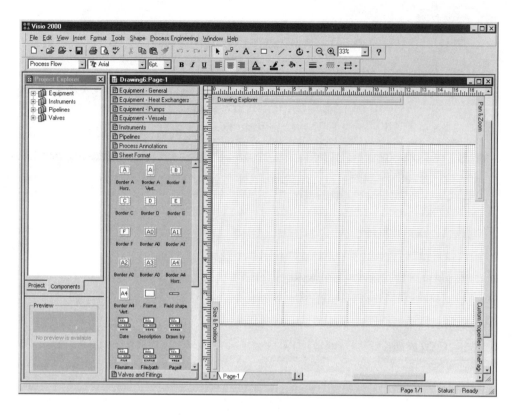

You are not stuck with the solutions that Visio provides. Feel free to modify any solution to suit your needs; just remember to save it as a template drawing (*.VST) with a different name or store it in another folder (see Module 2 "Saving Files").

By creating your own templates, you create a consistent look for all your drawings. Templates are an excellent way to affirm corporate standards. For example, to ensure that the corporate logo and copyright statement appear in every drawing, create a layer with that information, and then save the drawing as a template. The properties you can save in a template drawing include:

▶ Layers, scale, and page settings (see Module 4 "Setting Up Pages and Layers")

▶ Snap and glue settings (see Module 6 "Rulers, Grids, Guidelines and Page Breaks")

▶ Color palette (see Module 13 "Formatting Shapes")

▶ Shape styles and text styles (see Module 15 "Creating and Applying Styles")

▶ Print setup (see Module 20 "Printing Drawings")

▶ Window size and position

You can save a template so that it opens stencils.

Creating a New Drawing with a Wizard

All Visio packages include *wizards* that guide you through the steps of setting up a preliminary drawing. Along the way, you are prompted to fill in information and select options. Wizards are available for creating flowcharts, office layouts, organizational charts, project timelines, and other specialized drawings.

There are two disadvantages to using a wizard: (1) you may find it becomes tedious answering the wizard's many questions, and then waiting for the time it takes the wizard to complete its work; and (2) you sometimes end up doing more work editing the drawing created by the wizard than you would have starting the drawing from scratch.

Procedures

When you start Visio, it automatically displays the Welcome to Visio 2000 dialog box. From this dialog box, you select **Choose drawing type**. Alternatively, you can start a new drawing anytime you are in Visio with the **New** command. The shortcut key is:

Function	Key	Menu	Toolbar Icon
New	Ctrl+N	File | New	▯

Starting a New Drawing

Use the following procedure to start a new drawing:

1. Select **New** from the File menu.
2. Select a solution category, such as **Block Diagram**.
3. Select a solution, such as **Basic Diagram**.
4. Notice that Visio opens a blank, scaled drawing with the appropriate stencils.

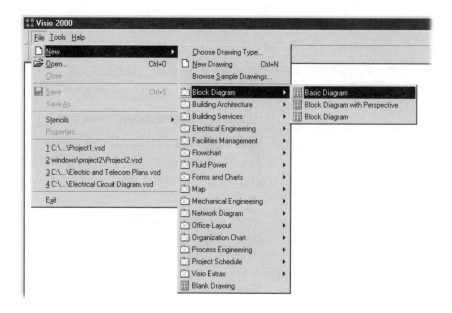

Starting a New, Blank Drawing

Use the following procedure to start a new drawing without a template:

1. Select **File | New | Blank Drawing** from the menu bar.
2. Notice that Visio opens a blank drawing and no stencil.

Starting a New Drawing with a Wizard

Use the following procedure to start a new drawing with a wizard:

1. Select **File | New** from the menu bar.
2. Select a name from the menu, such as **Organization Chart**. (The list of wizards available to you varies, depending on whether you have installed the Standard, Technical, Professional, or Enterprise Edition.)
3. Select a wizard name from the list. For example, under **Organization Chart**, you choose **Organization Chart Wizard**.
4. Notice that Visio opens a scaled, blank drawing with the appropriate stencils, and starts the wizard.
5. Follow the instructions provided by the wizard's dialog boxes.

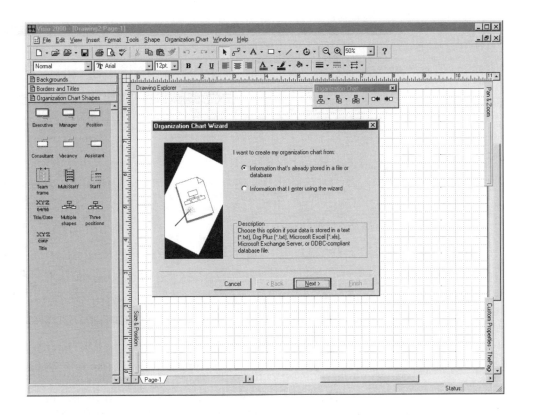

Hands-On Activity

In this activity, you use **File | New** to start a new drawing.

1. Start Visio to begin the activity. Notice that Visio displays the Welcome to Visio 2000 dialog box.
2. Double-click **Choose drawing type**.
3. In the Category list, click **Forms and Charts**.
4. In the Drawing type area, double-click **Charts and Graphs**.

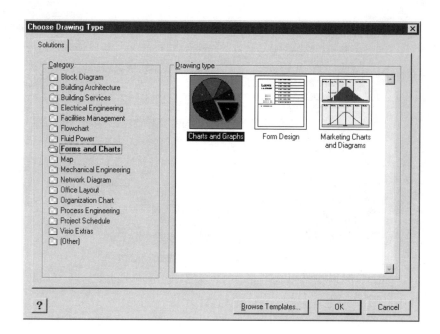

5.   Click **OK**. Visio opens a new drawing that looks like a sheet of graph paper. On the left side is the Charting Shapes stencil.

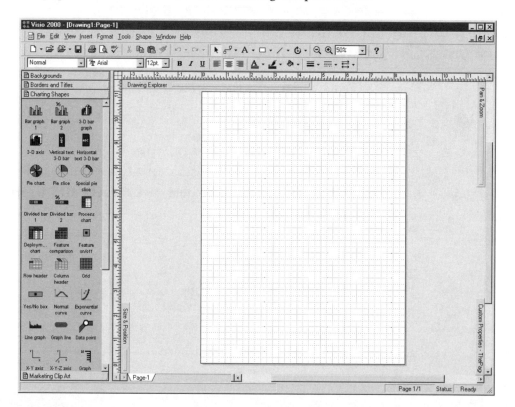

6. To get a feel for how Visio works, drag the **Bar graph 1** symbol from the stencil to the drawing page. Notice the Custom Properties dialog box, which prompts you for the number of bars in the bar chart. See Module 34 "Custom Properties" to learn more about custom properties.

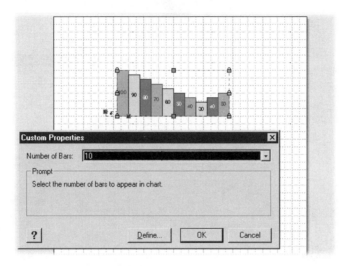

7. Accept the default of 10 bars by clicking **OK**.

8. Enlarge the view of the bar chart to make it easier to see. Right-click the symbol. Choose **View | 100%**. Visio zooms in on the shape.

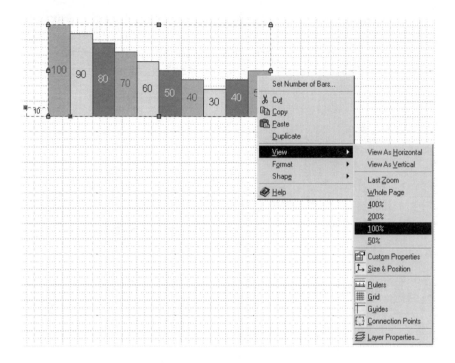

9. Click the first bar of the chart and enter the number **25**. Visio automatically reduces the height of the bar. Enter a negative number, such as **-90**, to make the second bar drop down below the zero line.

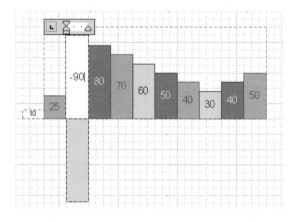

This completes the hands-on activity for opening a new drawing. Do not exit Visio or the drawing because you need both for the next module.

Saving Files

File | Save
Save As
Properties

Uses

In this chapter you'll learn about:

✓ **Using the Save and Save As commands**

✓ **Exploring the File Properties dialog box**

✓ **Saving a drawing as a templaate**

The **Save** command on the File menu saves the current drawing. Saving the drawing to the computer's disk drive lets you work with the drawing again later. If you have more than one Visio drawing opened, you must save each one individually.

Here is how to tell which drawing is current: when the drawing windows are maximized, the current drawing is the one you can see. When the drawing windows are not maximized, the current drawing is the one with the highlighted title bar.

When a drawing is new and unnamed, Visio displays the generic name "Drawing1" on the title bar. The first time you save the drawing, Visio asks you to provide a name for the file. With Windows 95/98/2000 and NT, you type a filename up to 255 characters long. You may want to limit filenames to eight characters if the drawing will be used by an older version of Visio running on a Windows v3.1 system.

After the first time you save the file by name, Save no longer prompts you for the name. Instead, it silently and quickly saves the drawing to disk; the only indication is the hourglass cursor.

When you attempt to exit Visio without saving the drawing, Visio asks, "Save changes to Filename.Vsd?" This gives you one last chance to save the drawing. Click **Yes**.

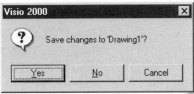

This dialog box saves you from accidentally closing a drawing without saving it.

 Note: You are wise to periodically save (every 15 minutes or so) while you are working on the drawing. That way, you don't lose your work if the power goes out or your computer freezes. Get into the habit of periodically pressing **Ctrl+S** to quickly save your work. A large, 1MB Visio drawing takes only four seconds to save on a slow Pentium. That's a short time to wait for a large investment in your valuable work.

Save As

When you want to save the file with a different name, use the **File | Save As** command, which displays the Save As dialog box. The Save As command also lets you save the drawing in file formats such as AutoCAD, Adobe Illustrator, Corel Draw, and earlier versions of Visio.

File Properties

The first time you save a drawing, Visio displays the Properties dialog box. Its contents are summarized below:

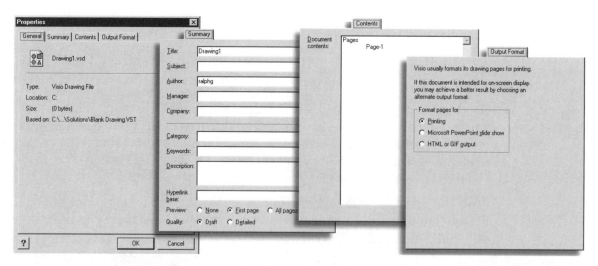

General This tab displays details about the file that comes from the operating system; you cannot edit this data. **Type** describes the class of Visio file, such as "Visio Drawing File." **Location** lists the path to the folder (subdirectory) where the file is located; if the path is too long, an ellipsis (...) truncates the full path name. **Size** indicates the size of the file in bytes and KB (kilobyte = 1,024 bytes). **Based on** tells you the name of the VST template file on which this drawing is based.

Summary This tab records information that describes the drawing file. In most cases, you can type up to 63 characters in each field. You can change the information at any time via File | Properties; use the Field command to automatically modify the information.

Title is a descriptive title of the drawing. **Subject** describes the contents of the drawing. **Author** identifies the author. **Manager** is the name of your boss. **Company** is your firm or client.

Category is a brief description of the drawing, such as map or floorplan. **Keywords** identifies topics related to the file: project name, version number, etc. **Description** allows up to 191 characters. **Hyperlink base** specifies the base URL (uniform resource locator) to be used with the filename. URL is the universal file naming system used by the Internet to identify the location of any file.

Preview determines whether a preview image is saved with the drawing (the only reason you would not save a preview is to save disk space). The preview image of the first page appears in the Open dialog box. **None** doesn't save a preview image. **First page** saves a preview of only the first page, whereas **All pages** creates a preview of all pages in the drawing.

As for **Quality**, **Draft** saves a preview image of Visio shapes; embedded objects, text, and gradient fills are not displayed. **Detailed** saves the preview image with all objects.

Contents This tab displays a list of the pages and *master* shapes in the file. A master shape is the source shape in the stencil.

Output Format This tab allows you to choose an alternative output format, which, Visio says, may improve the output quality. Choose from **Printing** (the default), **PowerPoint slide show**, and **HTML or GIF output**.

To change the file properties at any time, select **File | Properties** from the menu bar.

File Dialog Boxes

All file dialog boxes in Visio allow you to manage files on your computer's disk drives, as well as other drives connected to your computer via a network. To select another folder (subdirectory) or another drive, click the **Save in** list box.

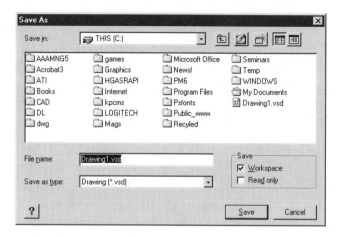

Next to the **Save in** list box are five icons:

Click the **Up One Level** button to move up one level in the folder structure.

Click the **View Desktop** button to display the files and folders at the desktop (topmost) level.

Click the **Create New Folder** button to create a new folder. Windows gives the new folder the default name of "New Folder" and allows you to change the folder name to something more meaningful. Like a filename, a folder name can be up to 255 characters long.

Click the **List** button to display only filenames, the default. Windows attempts to squeeze in as many filenames as it can.

Click the **Details** button to display the name, size, and date for every file. Windows displays the details in three columns but does not ensure that all text is visible. The Details listing allows you to sort the files in several ways: by filename, size of file, and date last modified. To sort, click the column header:

- ▶ Click **Name** to sort the filenames in alphabetical order, from A to Z. Click a second time to reverse the sort, listing filenames from Z to A.
- ▶ Click **Size** to sort the files in order of size, smallest to largest. Click a second time to reverse the sort, from largest to smallest.
- ▶ Click **Modified** to sort the files in order of the date and time stamp, from newest to oldest. This time stamp indicates when the file was last modified. Click a second time to reverse the sort, from oldest to newest.

Note: By default, Windows does not display file extensions. To have Windows 98 display file extensions, start Windows Explorer. From the menu bar, select **View | Folder Options**. When the Folder Options | View dialog box appears, click the radio button next to **Hide file extensions for known file types**. Ensure no check mark appears next to this option. Click **OK** to close the dialog box.

In the Save As dialog box, right-click a filename to display the shortcut menu. This menu lets you perform additional file management functions (your computer system may have additional functions displayed by the shortcut menu).

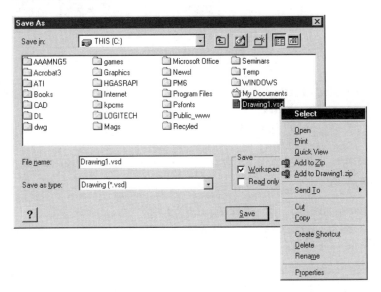

Select: Selects the highlighted filename for the File name text box and saves the drawing.

Open: Opens the selected filename into Visio; same as using the Open command. The Save As dialog box remains open.

Print: Launches a second copy of Visio with the selected filename, and displays the Print dialog box. When printing is complete, the second copy of Visio closes itself. This command fails if the selected drawing is already open in another copy of Visio.

QuickView: Launches the Visio Drawing Viewer (see Module 3 "Opening Existing Drawings").

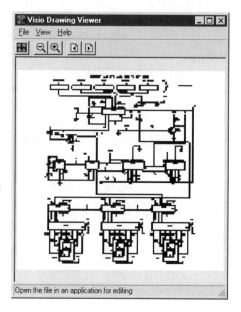

Cut: Copies the file to the Windows Clipboard. This can be pasted into another application. What happens in the other application varies: a word processor pastes the Visio drawing; an e-mail program places the file as an attachment. You may need to cancel the Save As dialog box in Visio for the other program to complete its paste operation. Note that the Cut option does not actually erase the file.

Copy: Works the same as the Cut option.

Create Shortcut: Creates a shortcut to the selected file in the same folder. You can then drag the shortcut to the desktop.

Delete: Sends the file to the Recycle Bin. Windows asks if you are sure.

Rename: Allows you to change the name of the file.

Properties: Displays a tiled dialog box with the properties of the file.

The **Save** area of the Save As dialog box gives you two options for saving the drawing with extra attributes. These come into effect the next time you load the drawing.

Workspace: Saves the drawing, along with the position of windows. This ensures the drawing comes up looking exactly the same way the next time you load it.

Read only: Saves the drawing with the read-only bit set. This means that the next time you load the drawing, you cannot save it. This prevents you (or another user) from making changes to the drawing.

The **Save as type** list box lets you save the drawing in a large number of different file formats. This is also known as *exporting* the drawing. (See Module 29 "Exporting Drawings.") Visio 2000 can export drawings in a variety of formats, which varies according to the edition you are using.

Procedures

Before presenting the general procedure for saving the drawing, it is helpful to know about the shortcut keys. The first two save the drawing, and the last two trigger an option to save the drawing when it has changed:

Function	Keys	Menu	Toolbar Icon
Save As	Alt+FA	File | Save As	...
Save	Ctrl+S	File | Save	💾
Properties	Alt+FI	File | Properties	...
Close	Ctrl+F4	File | Close	☒
Exit	Alt+F4	File | Exit	☒

Saving a Drawing for the First Time

Use the following procedure to save a drawing:

1. Use **File | Save**.
2. Type the filename.
3. Click the **Save** button.
4. When the Properties dialog box appears, fill in as much as you care to, or are required to by corporate policy and procedure manuals.
5. Click **OK** to close the Properties dialog box.

Saving a Drawing the Next Time

Use the following procedure to save a drawing:

1. Use **File | Save** (or press **Ctrl+S** or click the diskette button on the toolbar).
2. Notice that Visio saves the drawing to disk.

Saving a Drawing as a Template

Use the following procedure to save a drawing as a template file:

1. Use **File | Save As**.
2. Type the filename.
3. Click the down-arrow next to the Save as type list box. The list box drops down.

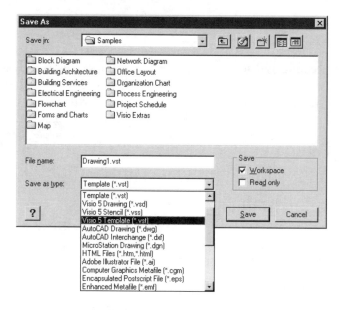

4. Select **Template (*.vst)** from the list.
5. Click **Save**. Visio displays the Properties dialog box.
6. Click **OK**. Visio renames the drawing "Drawing1.Vst". The "t" at the end of Vst is a reminder that you are working with a template drawing.

Hands-On Activity

In this activity, you use the Save As function to save the current drawing. Ensure Visio is running and the drawing you created in Module 1 is displayed.

1. Press **Ctrl+S** to save the drawing.

2. Note that Visio displays the Save As dialog box. The default filename, "Drawing1", is highlighted since this is the first time the drawing is being saved.

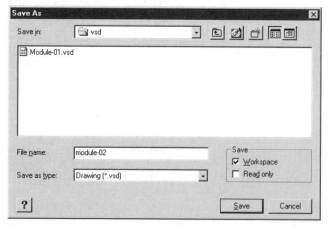

3. Type the filename **module-02**.

4. Click **Save**.

5. Notice that Visio displays the Properties dialog box. Fill in the information requested by this dialog box:

   ▶ Title: **Module-02**

   ▶ Subject: **Learn Visio 2000**

   ▶ Author: *your name*

   ▶ Description: **Sample file for practicing the SaveAs command in Module #2**.

Leave other fields blank.

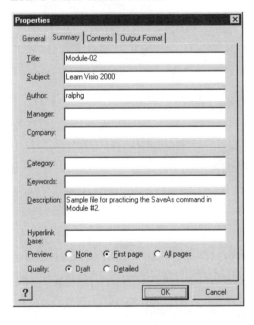

6. Click **OK**. Visio saves the drawing to disk and changes the name of the drawing to "Module-02.vsd" on the title bar.

7. Press **Alt+F4** to exit Visio.

This completes the hands-on activity for saving the drawing.

Opening Existing Drawings

File | Open
Visio Drawing Viewer

Uses

You can open a drawing
in Visio three different
ways:

> **In this chapter you'll learn about:**
>
> ✓ **Importing non-Visio files**
> ✓ **Using the Visio Drawing Viewer**
> ✓ **Opening a Visio drawing**

▶ **Open an
existing file**
when Visio starts.
You can select a drawing from
the Welcome to Visio 2000
dialog box. The dialog box lists
the four drawings most recently
opened; click **Browse existing
files** to look for other files.

▶ **Open a file from within
Visio**. The **Open** selection of
the **File** menu opens an existing
Visio template, drawing, stencil,
or workspace. A *template* file
(extension VST) is a drawing file
that contains custom settings;
new drawings are based on a
template file. A *stencil* file

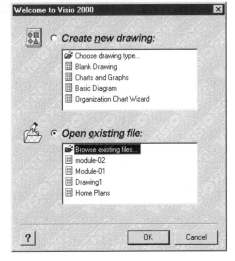

(extension VSS) contains shapes that you dragged onto the drawing
page. A *workspace* file (extension VSW) records the size and
placement of Visio drawing and stencil windows. You have the
option of opening files in three modes. **Original** means that Visio
opens the drawing file that you select. **Copy** means an unnamed
copy is made from the original file; when you save the drawing,
Visio prompts you for a different filename. **Read-only** means that
you cannot save the file.

▶ **Open a file from Windows**. You can double-click a Visio file (files with the VSD, VST, VSS, and VSW extensions) in Explorer; Windows automatically starts Visio and loads the drawing.

You can open more than one drawing at a time in Visio. Simply use **File | Open** for each drawing you want to open. As an alternative, you can select more than one drawing at a time in the Open dialog box: hold down the **Ctrl** key to select more than one file.

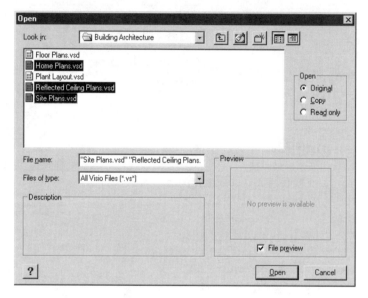

Tip: Visio's Open dialog box displays the contents of the folder defined by the Drawings field of the File Paths tab of the Options dialog box (**Tools | Options**). You can specify the file path for each of the fields listed in this dialog box.

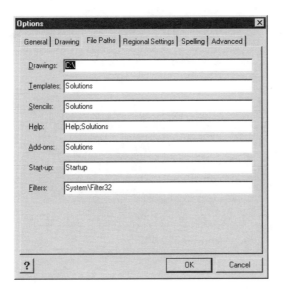

Importing Non-Visio Files

You are not limited to opening files created by Visio; Visio can *import* drawings created by other programs, such as ABC FlowCharter, AutoCAD, CorelDraw, IntelliCAD, MicroGraphx, and MicroStation, as well as raster images created by paint programs.

Vector Formats	Extension
ABC FlowCharter	AF2 or AF3
Adobe Illustrator	AI
AutoCAD and IntelliCAD drawings	DWG
Other CAD software	DXF
Computer Graphics Metafile	CGM
CorelDraw drawing	CDR
CorelFLOW chart	CFL
Corel Clipart	CMX
Encapsulated PostScript	EPS
Enhanced Metafile	EMF
Initial Graphics Exchange Specification	IGS

Vector Formats	Extension
MicroGraphx Designer v 3.1 drawing	DRW
MicroGraphx Designer v6 drawing	DSF
MicroStation drawing	DGN
PostScript	PS
Windows Metafile	WMF

Raster Formats	Extension
Graphics Interchange Format	GIF
JPEG	JPG
Macintosh PICT	PCT
Portable Network Graphics	PNG
Tagged Image File Format	TIFF
Windows Bitmap	BMP or DIB
Z-Soft PC Paintbrush	PCX

Tagged Text Formats	Extension
ASCII text	TXT
Comma-separated value text	CSV

Caution: When any program imports a vector file created by a different program, it must translate the data. In some cases, the translation may not be perfect, resulting in some objects being erased; other objects may look different in Visio than in the originating application.

Visio Drawing Viewer

Visio includes an independent utility program that lets you view a Visio drawing without needing to load Visio itself. The advantages are that the viewer loads itself and the drawing image faster than the full Visio program. The image you see in the viewer is the same image displayed by the Preview area of the Open dialog box.

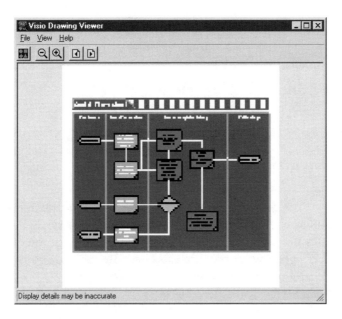

To use the viewer, right-click a Visio file, then select **Quick View**. The Visio Drawing Viewer launches and displays the preview image of the drawing. On the toolbar, the icons have the following meaning:

Open in Visio: Launches Visio and loads the drawing.

Zoom Out: Makes the image smaller so that you can see more of it.

Zoom In: Makes the image larger so that you can see more detail.

Previous Page: Lets you see the preceding page when the drawing contains previews of more than just the first page.

Next Page: Displays the following page when the drawing contains previews of more than the first page.

To view previews of other drawings, drag their filename from Windows Explorer into the Visio Drawing Viewer. Each time you do so, the viewer launches another copy of itself (unless you turn on the toggle in **View | Replace Window**).

The menu bar provides additional options for the Visio Drawing Viewer:

File: **Open in Visio** launches Visio and opens the drawing. **Exit** closes the drawing viewer program.

View: **Toolbar** toggles the display of the toolbar and its icons. **Status Bar** toggles the display of the status bar at the bottom of the viewer.

Replace Window loads new preview images into the current drawing viewer; when turned off (the default), new preview images are loaded into additional copies of the viewer.

Help: **Help Contents** displays the help file. **About Visio Viewer** displays the viewer's copyright information.

Right-click the drawing to display the floating menu. **Open in Visio** starts up Visio and loads the drawing. **Help Contents** displays the help file. **About Visio Viewer** displays the viewer's copyright information.

 Caution: The drawing viewer will not display an image under two conditions: (1) the drawing is already open in Visio; and (2) the drawing was saved with the preview option turned off. To include a preview image, use the **File | Properties** command, and then save the drawing.

Procedures

Before presenting the general procedures for Open, it is helpful to know about the shortcut key. It is:

Function	Keys	Menu	Toolbar Icon
Open	Ctrl+O	File | Open	

Opening a Visio Drawing

Use the following procedure to open a Visio drawing:

1. Start Visio. Notice the Welcome to Visio 2000 dialog box.
2. Select **Browse existing files**.
3. Click **OK**. Notice the Open dialog box displays names of Visio drawings.
4. If necessary, go to the drive and folder where the drawing is located.
5. Double-click the drawing name. Notice that Visio opens the drawing and associated stencils.

Importing a Non-Visio File

Use the following procedure to open a non-Visio file:

1. Start Visio. Notice the Welcome to Visio 2000 dialog box.

2. Select **Browse existing files**.

3. Click **OK**. Notice the Open dialog box displays names of Visio drawings.

4. If necessary, go to the drive and folder where the drawing is located.

5. Click **Files of type**.

6. Select the extension of the file to import.

7. Double-click the filename.

8. Visio opens the file in a drawing.

Hands-On Activity

In this activity, you use the Open function. Begin by starting Visio.

1. From the File menu, click **Open**.

2. Notice the Module-02 filename you saved in Module 2.

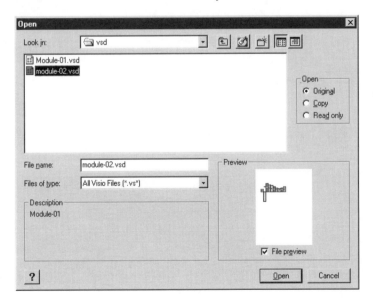

3. Double-click the filename.

4. Visio opens the file in a drawing.

5. Press **Alt+F4** to exit Visio.

This completes the hands-on activity for opening a drawing.

Setting Up Pages and Layers

File | Page Setup
Insert | Page
View | Layer Properties

Uses

A Visio drawing can con-
tain one or more pages.
In that way, Visio is like
having a word processor
and drawing program:
Visio lets you create
pages and pages of draw-
ings. This lets you easily

> **In this chapter you'll learn about:**
> ✓ **Drawing pages**
> ✓ **Inserting pages**
> ✓ **Background pages**
> ✓ **Drawing scale**
> ✓ **Layers**

create multipage documents with mixed text and graphics. Unlike a word
processor, though, text and graphics don't "flow" from one page to the
next. A Visio drawing can have up to 200 pages.

You can view only one page at a time, except for background pages and
when Visio is in print preview mode. Actually, that's not quite true. Visio
has a cumbersome method of displaying all pages in a drawing: the **Edit |
Go To | Page | Open page in a new window** command opens pages
in individual windows. (You may need to follow that with the **Window |
Tile** command.)

Each drawing can also have a set of layers. *Layers* are a way to separate
objects logically, and are common with CAD software. For example, selecting all objects on a page does not select those objects on a locked layer.
Unlike CAD software, though, a shape can be assigned to two or more
layers.

Drawing Pages

Every new Visio drawing contains one page. To create more pages, simply right-click the page tab at the bottom of the drawing; Visio calls this *inserting* a page. The shortcut menu inserts, deletes, renames, and reorders pages.

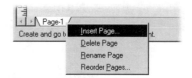

●◆**Tip:** There is one case where Visio creates a page on its own. When you drag a shape from the Backgrounds stencil (found in Visio Extras), Visio automatically creates a new page called "Background" and places the shape on that page.

Pages not in the right order? Visio lets you drag pages around by their tabs. (The Background page cannot be moved.)

Inserting a Page

To add a page to the drawing, right-click any page tab and select **Insert Page**. Visio displays the Page Setup dialog box with the Page Properties tab showing.

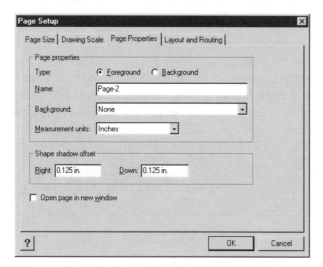

This dialog box can be intimidating, with its many tabs and options. Let's concentrate on just the Page Properties tab:

Type: Specifies whether the page is a foreground or a background page.

Name: Describes the page with a name up to 31 characters long.

Background: Lists the names of the background pages in the drawing, if any.

Measurement units: Specifies the units of measure for the page, if you want it different from the units set for the drawing (see the **Drawing Scale** tab).

Shape shadow offset: Specifies the offset distance for "shadows" applied to shapes; type a negative distance to have the shadow offset to the top or left of the shape.

Open page in new window: When on, the page is opened in a new window; when off, the page is displayed in the current window.

 Tip: You can use pages to give a slide show, as a substitute for PowerPoint. To do this, create your drawing of many pages. From the menu, select **View | Full Screen**; the drawing is displayed all by itself on your computer's screen (background pages are not displayed). To move forward though the pages, press **N**; to move to the previous pages, press **P**. You can right-click to display a shortcut menu, too. Press **Esc** to return to normal mode.

Background Pages

As mentioned earlier, you see only one page at a time, with one exception. The background page shows through to a foreground page (most pages in a Visio drawing are foreground pages). You can use background pages to create a common graphic element, like a background texture, the corporate logo, or a title block. Even though you can see the shapes on the background page, you cannot edit them until you switch to the background page. (If you are a CAD software user, you can think of the background page as a layer or xref common to all pages. If you use PageMaker for desktop publishing, a background page is like a master page.)

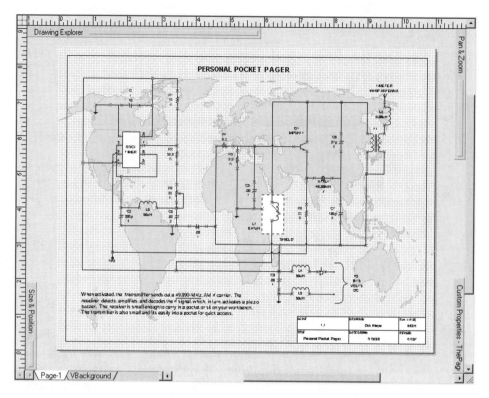

When you create a background page, you have to tell Visio the foreground page(s) with which to associate it. Also, you can assign a background page to another background page. And you can convert a foreground page to background status, and vice versa. To assign a background page to a foreground page:

1. Click the tab of the foreground page.

2. From the menu bar, select **File | Page Setup**.

3. When the Page Setup dialog box appears, click the **Page Properties** tab.

4. From the Background list, select the name of the background page. If you want to disassociate a background page, select **None** from the list.

5. Click **OK**.

In many cases, you must assign the background page to each foreground page individually. If you want all the pages in your drawing to use the same background, set up Page-1 with the correct background; any page you insert after that has the same background page associated with it.

Other Page Parameters

Unlike a word processing document, every page in a Visio drawing can have a different size, scale, and orientation. These items are handled by the **Page Size** tab of the Page Setup dialog box.

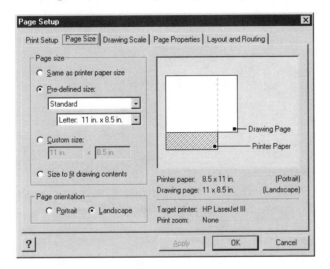

Same as printer paper size: Matches the drawing page size to the printer paper (on the **Print Setup** tab) automatically.

Pre-defined size: Allows you to select a standard paper size. Visio includes sizes that match these standards: Standard, Metric (ISO), ANSI Engineering, and ANSI Architectural up to 34" x 44".

Custom size: Allows you to specify any size for the page. (Contrary to Visio's documentation, the size is not adjusted by the drawing scale.) The horizontal and vertical dimensions can be as big as 1e19" x 1e19"—which is a 1 followed by 19 zeros or ten quintillion inches. That's an area large enough to hold 20,000 copies of our solar system—full size!

Tip: You can change the size of the page interactively, without needing this dialog box. Hold down the **Ctrl** key, then grab the edge of the page with the cursor. Drag the width (or height) wider or narrower.

Not only that, you can also rotate the page interactively. Select the **Rotation** tool, grab the corner of the page, and rotate it. Watch the status line for the angle readout. (If this doesn't work for you, go to **Tools | Options | Drawing** and turn on the **Enable page rotation** option.) You would rotate the page to create an isometric drawing grid using guidelines.

Size to fit drawing contents: This handy option makes the page fit the drawing.

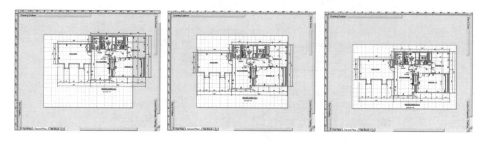

➡️ **Tip:** You can have Visio center the drawing on the page automatically. From the menu bar, select **Tools | Center Drawing**.

Page orientation: Specifies the page as portrait (tall) or landscape (wide); this option is unavailable when **Same as printer paper size** is selected. This option affects only the drawing page: it does not change the orientation of the printer page; the preview window shows how the drawing and printer pages relate to each other. For a square-shaped page, the orientation doesn't matter.

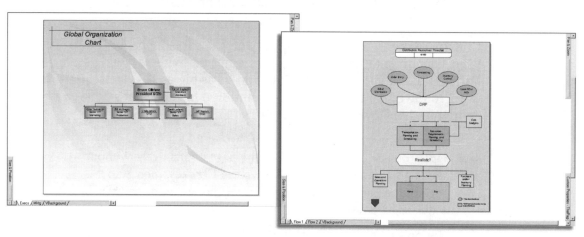

Tip: To force the drawing page to match the printer page, select **Same as printer paper size**.

Drawing Scale

Scale is used to make a large drawing fit a small page. Or, more formally, scale is the relationship between the size of the page and the size of the objects being drawn. For example, when the scale is 1"=10', a 10-foot-wide shape is printed one inch wide. There are two ways that you can scale a drawing:

Scale to fit: If you don't care about the scale, turn on the **Size to fit drawing contents** options in the **Page Size** tab of the Page Setup dialog box.

Specific scale factor: If you require that the drawing be printed at a standard scale, select a scale factor from the **Drawing Scale** tab of the Page Setup dialog box. The table below shows examples of standard scale formats for specific disciplines:

Scale	Example
No Scale	1:1
Metric	1:100
Architectural	3/32" = 1' 0"
Civil Engineering	1" = 10' 0"
Mechanical Engineering	1/32:1
Custom Scale	1" = 12.5' or 1mm = 254m

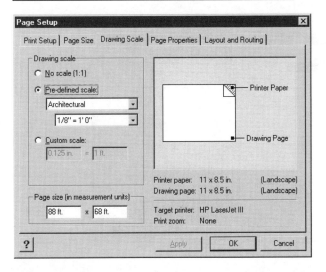

Warning: When you change the scale of a page, it does not affect other pages in the drawing. In particular, be aware that the scale of a page does not affect the scale of the background page; you must set separately the scale of the background page.

No scale (1:1): The page is not scaled.

Pre-defined scale: Allows you to select a standard scale. Visio includes scales that match these standards: Architectural, Civil Engineering, Metric, and Mechanical Engineering.

Custom scale: Allows you to enter any scale factor. The first measurement is the size of the printed page; the second is the size in the Visio drawing.

Page size: Allows you to enter any size of page in "real world" dimensions. For example, if you are drawing a 25' x 50' house, you would enter those dimensions.

Layers

Just as a drawing can have many pages to segregate data, a page can have many layers to further segregate shapes. The difference is that all shapes on different layers can be viewed at the same time; all shapes on different pages (except background pages) cannot be viewed at the same time.

Using layers provides you a powerful tool for controlling the visibility and editability of shapes. You access the Layer Properties dialog box by selecting **View | Layer Properties** from the menu bar. A layer has the following properties:

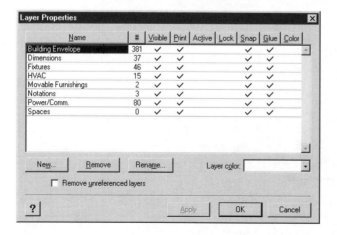

Property	On	Off
Visible	Objects are displayed.	Objects are hidden and do not display.
Print	Objects are printed.	Objects are not printed.
Active	Objects are added to this layer.	Objects are not added to this layer.
Lock	Objects cannot be edited.	Objects are editable.
Snap	Objects snap to other objects.	Objects on other layers cannot snap to objects on this layer.
Glue	Objects glue to other objects.	Objects on other layers cannot glue to objects on this layer.
Color	Objects display in this color.	Objects display their original color.

Tip: A shape rests entirely on one layer; you cannot have part of a shape on one layer, and the remainder of the shape on another layer. This affects text: you cannot have the text of a shape on a separate layer. (If this were possible, you could turn off all the text in the drawing, for example.) The workaround is to create a group: place the shape on one layer, and the separate text on another layer, then group the two together.

Visio creates layers automatically when you drag shapes onto the page because many shapes are preassigned to layers. Unlike CAD software, a Visio object can be assigned to more than one layer at a time.

You can create new layers at any time; you can remove unused layers at a later time. The new layer is added to the current page, not all pages in the drawing. In the same way, a new page does not inherit the layers from existing pages in the drawing.

You can change the layer settings at any time independently for each layer. For example, if you want to display some text but not print it, you place the text on a layer and turn off the **Print** setting.

Tip: Here's the quick way to find out which layer a shape resides on: turn on the **Format Shape** toolbar.

Select the shape. Observe the layer name in the **Layer** list box. If the shape is assigned to more than one layer, the list box reads "(Multiple layers)".

Procedures

Before presenting the general procedures for setting up the page, it is helpful to know about the shortcut keys. These are:

Function	Keys	Menu	Toolbar Icon
Size and Scale	Alt+FU	File | Page Setup	...
Layer Properties	Alt+VL	View | Layer Properties	
Add a Page	Shift+F5	Insert | Page	...
Go to a Page	F5	Edit | Go To	...

Tip: The size, scale, and layer settings are not necessary for some drawings. For example, scale often doesn't matter for flowcharts and graphs. Unless a drawing is complex, it is easier to draw without worrying about layer settings.

Setting the Drawing Size and Scale

Use the following procedure to change the size and scale of a drawing:

1. Select **File | Page Setup** to display the Page Setup dialog box.
2. Select the **Page orientation**.
3. Select the **Page size**.
4. Click the **Drawing Scale** tab to size the drawing.
5. Select a scale factor. Notice that Visio automatically determines the drawing scale.
6. Click **OK**.

Changing the Drawing Size Interactively

Use the following procedure to make the drawing page larger or smaller:

1. Move the cursor over any edge of the drawing page.
2. Hold down the **Ctrl** key, then drag the edge of the drawing inward (for a smaller page) or outward (for a larger page).
3. Let go of the **Ctrl** key. To change the width, grab either side of the page; to change the height, grab either the top or bottom edge; to change both width and height at the same time, grab one of the four corners.

Creating New Layers

Use the following procedure to create a new layer:

1. Select **View | Layer Properties** to display the Layer Properties dialog box.
2. Click **New** to create a new layer. Notice that Visio displays the New Layer dialog box.
3. Type a name for the layer.
4. Click **OK**. Notice that Visio adds the layer to the list of names.
5. Click **OK**.

Changing Layer Properties

Use the following procedure to change the properties of a layer in a drawing:

1. Select **View | Layer Properties** to display the Layer Properties dialog box.
2. Select a layer name.
3. Click **Visible** to change the visibility:
   ▶ Check mark means objects assigned to the layer are displayed.
   ▶ No check mark means the objects are not displayed.
4. Click **Print** to change the printability:
   ▶ Check mark means objects assigned to the layer are printed.
   ▶ No check mark means objects are not printed.
5. Click **Active** to change the layer assignments:
   ▶ Check mark means new objects drawn are assigned to the layer.
   ▶ No check mark means new objects are not assigned to the layer.
   ▶ When more than one layer is active, new objects are assigned to all active layers.
   ▶ Shapes preassigned to a layer go to that layer, not the active layer.
6. Click **Lock** to change the lock setting:
   ▶ Check mark means objects assigned to the layer cannot be selected or edited.
   ▶ No check mark means the layer is not locked.
   ▶ Locked layers cannot change their Visible, Print, Active, Snap, Glue, and Color properties.
7. Click **Snap** to change the snap setting:

▶ Check mark means other objects snap to objects assigned to the layer.

▶ No check mark means other objects do not snap to objects on this layer.

8. Click **Glue** to change the glue setting:

▶ Check mark means other objects glue to objects assigned to the layer.

▶ No check mark means other objects do not glue to objects on this layer.

9. Click **Color** to set the color; select the color from Layer Color.

▶ Check mark means objects assigned to the layer display in the color shown.

▶ No check mark means objects take their preassigned color.

10. Click **Visible**, **Print**, **Active**, **Lock**, **Snap**, **Glue**, or **Color** to reverse the property of all layers at once. This action has no effect on locked layers, except the **Lock** property. The first click changes all layers to the default setting for each property; the second click reverses the setting.

11. Click **#** to have Visio add up the number of objects assigned to each layer.

12. Click **Apply** to apply changes without leaving the dialog box; click **OK** to apply changes and close the dialog box; click **Cancel** to ignore changes and close the dialog box.

Renaming a Layer

Use the following procedure to change the name of a layer:

1. Select **View | Layer Properties** to display the Layer Properties dialog box.

2. Select a layer name.

3. Click **Rename**. Notice the Rename Layer dialog box.

4. Type a new name for the layer.

5. Click **OK**.

6. Click **OK**.

Removing a Layer

Use the following procedure to remove an unused layer:

1. Select **View | Layer Properties** to display the Layer Properties dialog box.

2. Select a layer name.

3. Click **Remove**. Notice the new Layer Properties dialog box. It warns: "Removing this layer will delete all shapes belonging to it. Remove the layer?"

4. Click **Yes** to remove the layer.

5. To remove all unused layers (layers with no objects assigned to them), click **Remove unreferenced layers**.

Creating a New Page

Use the following procedure to create another page:

1. Right-click any page tab.

2. From the shortcut menu, select **Insert Page**. Notice the Page Setup dialog box. In most cases, the default values provided by Visio are appropriate for a new page and you need only click **OK**.

   ▶ **Type: Foreground** (shapes are editable) or **Background** (shapes are seen but cannot be edited).

   ▶ **Name**: Type a name up to 31 characters; **Page-2** is the default name.

   ▶ **Background**: Assign a background page to this new page.

   ▶ **Measurement units**: Select units for the rulers (you may have a different measurement system for each page).

   ▶ **Shape shadow offset**: Applies equally to all shapes on this page that have the shadow option turned on (to cast the shadow up or to the left, use negative values).

   ▶ **Open page in new window**: When on, the page displays in an independent window; when left unchecked, switching to another page replaces the current page.

3. Click **OK**. Notice that Visio displays a new, blank page and states the page number on the title bar.

Hands-On Activity

In this activity, you use the size, scale, and layer functions to set up a new drawing. Begin by starting Visio.

1. In the Welcome to Visio 2000 dialog box, double-click **Choose drawing type**, click **Other**, and then select **Blank Drawing** to create a new empty document.

2. Click **OK**. Visio displays an upright 8½" x 11" page with grid lines. At one inch apart, the grid lines are somewhat heavier. This is important, since we will observe the grid lines to notice changes in scale.

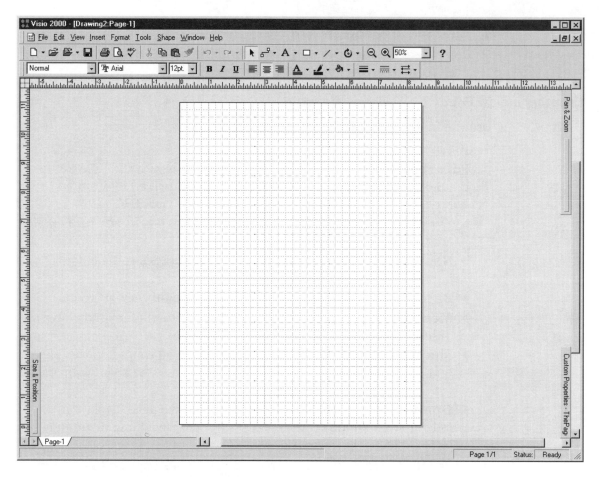

3. Select **File | Page Setup**.
4. In the Page Setup dialog box, select the **Print Setup** tab:
   ▶ Select **Landscape**.

   Click **Apply**. Notice—underneath the dialog box—Visio changes the page from vertical to horizontal orientation.

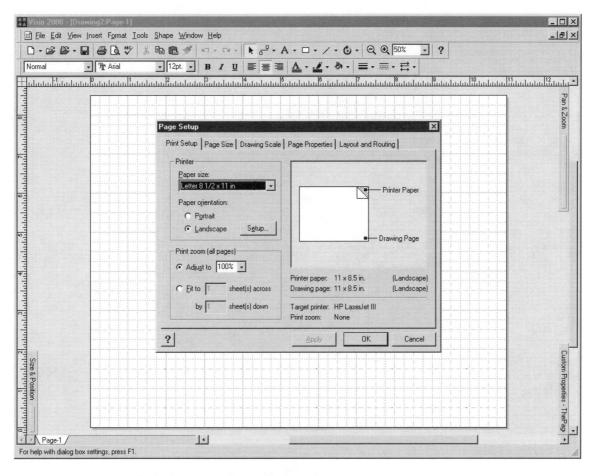

5. Click the **Drawing Scale** tab:

   ▶ Select **Pre-defined scale**.

   ▶ Select **Architectural** in the Drawing scale area of the dialog box.

   ▶ Select **Scale** of **1/2" = 1' 0"**.

   Click **Apply**. Notice how Visio adjusts the **Page Size** to 22 ft. 0 in. x 17 ft. 0 in.

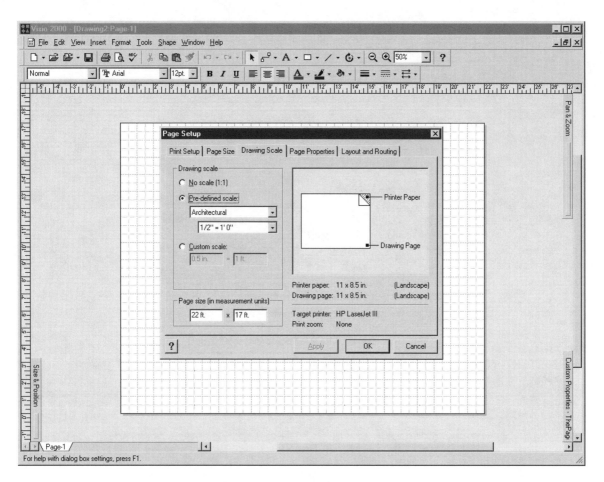

6. Click **OK** to close the dialog box. Notice that the rulers now show the distance as feet, such as 4' 6".

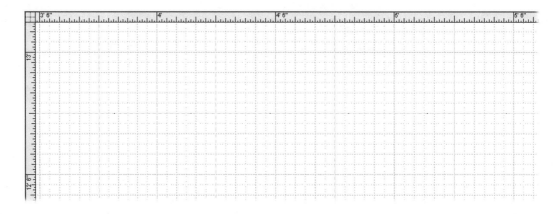

7. Select **View | Layer Properties**. Notice the Layer Properties dialog box has no layer names since this is a brand new drawing.

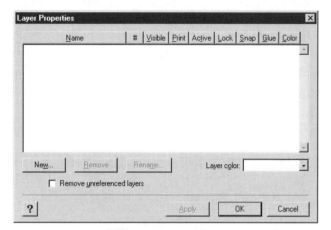

8. Click **New** to create a new layer. Notice the New Layer dialog box.

9. Type **Non-printing text** in the Layer Name box.

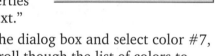

10. Click **OK**. Notice that the Layer Properties dialog box lists layer "Non-printing text."

11. Click **Layer color** at the bottom of the dialog box and select color #7, cyan (light blue). You may need to scroll though the list of colors to find # 7.

12. Uncheck **Print** to make this a non-printing layer.

13. Check **Active** to make this layer the active layer. The next object created will be placed on this layer.

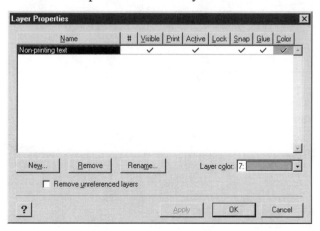

14. Click **OK** to close the dialog box.

15. Select the **Text** tool **A** to place text on the newly created layer.

16. Click near the upper-left corner of the page.

17. Type **Drawing for**. The text is placed on layer Non-printing text and appears in cyan (light blue) color.

18. Notice that Visio enlarges the page and places a boundary box (the dashed lines) around the text.

19. Press **Enter**.

20. Type **Module-04**.

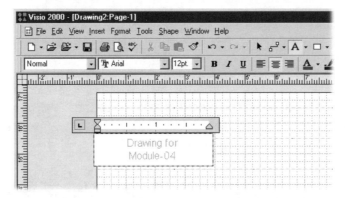

21. Click anywhere else on the page. Notice that Visio returns the page to its original size.

22. Select the **Pointer** tool.

23. Click the text. Notice the handles (green squares).

24. Right-click the text. Notice the shortcut menu.

25. Select **View | Layer Properties**.

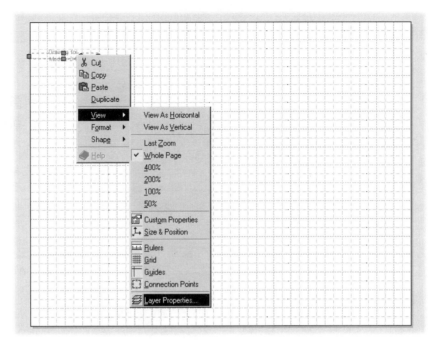

26. Click **OK** to close the dialog box.

27. Use **File | Save As** and save this drawing as **Module-4.Vsd**.

Do not exit Visio or the drawing because you need both for the next module. This completes the hands-on activity for setting up the drawing's size, scale, and layers.

Views, Zooms, and Pans

View

Uses

The zoom selections of the **View** menu enlarge and reduce your view of the page within the Visio window. The term *zoom* comes from the camera zoom lens, which brings objects in a scene closer.

> **In this chapter you'll learn about:**
>
> ✓ **The Pan & Zoom window**
>
> ✓ **Zooming in on a detail**
>
> ✓ **Returning to previous zoom level**

The scroll bars along the edge of the Visio window pan the page. *Pan* means to move the view of the page around without changing the zoom level.

Visio enlarges and reduces by a percentage of the actual size. Actual size is 100%. Smaller than actual size is less than 100 percent. For example, 50% is half-size: objects on the page are half their full-drawn size and you see twice as much of the page. The minimum zoom level is 1%, which makes the page 100 times smaller than actual size. This is useful for seeing a very large drawing on the computer's relatively small screen.

Larger than actual size is more than 100 percent. For example, 400% is four times larger: objects in the page are four times their full-drawn size and you see one-quarter of the page. The maximum zoom is 3098%, which makes the page 31 times larger than actual size.

The **View** menu also adjusts the zoom according to the page area:

> ▶ **Page Width** means the page is zoomed so that its width fits the Visio window.
> ▶ **Whole Page** means the entire page is zoomed to fit the window.
> ▶ **Last Zoom** returns to the previous zoom level.

▶ **Full Screen** removes the toolbars and other user interface accoutrements, showing the entire drawing. You can draw and edit in full-screen mode using function and control keys. Press **Esc** to return to Visio's normal screen.

By using a combination of the Ctrl and Shift keys and the mouse buttons, Visio performs quick zooms and real-time pans. When you hold down the Ctrl and Shift keys, Visio displays a magnifying glass cursor to remind you it is now in zoom mode. By holding down both the Ctrl and Shift keys, you change the view as follows:

View Action	*Mouse Action*
Zoom in	Click left mouse button; each click doubles the zoom percentage.
Zoom out	Click right mouse button; each click halves the zoom percentage.
Zoom window	Drag left mouse button; windowed area becomes new view.
Pan	Drag right mouse button; view pans until button is released.

Real-time pan means that Visio pans the page as quickly as you move the mouse. As you hold the Ctrl and Shift keys and drag with the right mouse button, the view pans around the page; the cursor changes to the hand cursor. An alternative to zooming in is the *windowed* zoom. By holding the Ctrl and Shift keys, you draw a rectangle with the left mouse button; that rectangle becomes your new view.

The Pan & Zoom Window

Visio 2000 introduces a new way to pan and zoom around the drawing. The Pan & Zoom window provides an overview of the entire drawing. A heavy red border indicates the current zoomed-in view. (This window is known in CAD software as the "bird's-eye view" or the aerial view.)

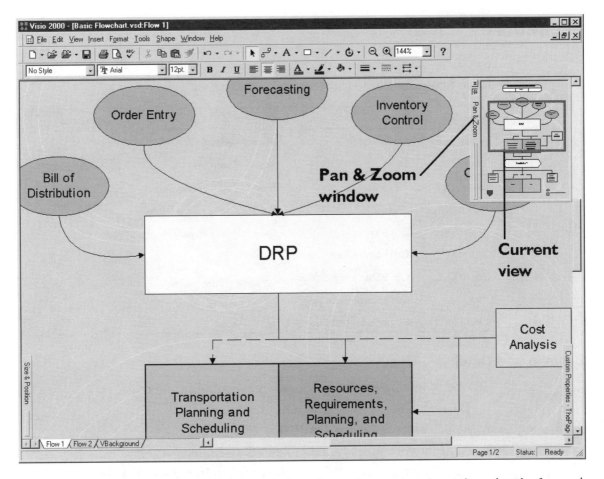

To see the Pan & Zoom window, from the menu select **View | Windows | Pan & Zoom**:

▶ To zoom into the drawing, click and drag the cursor. Notice the heavy red rectangle, which outlines the zoomed-in view.

▶ To pan the view, grab inside the red rectangle and move it around.

▶ To change the zoom level, grab a corner or an edge of the red rectangle and stretch it. As an alternative, you can once again click and drag a new rectangle.

Procedures

Before presenting the general procedures for setting zoom levels, it is helpful to know about the shortcut keys. These are:

Function	Keys	Menu	Toolbar Icon
Actual Size	Ctrl+I	View | Actual Size	...
Zoom	F6	View | Zoom	150%
Last Zoom	Alt+VZL	View | Zoom | Last Zoom	...
Page Width	Alt+VZP	View | Zoom | Page Width	...
Whole Page	Ctrl+W	View | Whole Page	...
Zoom In	Ctrl+Shift+Left-click	...	🔍
Zoom Out	Ctrl+Shift+Right-click	...	🔍
Pan	Ctrl+Shift+Right Drag	...	...
Zoom In	Ctrl+Shift+Left Drag	...	...

Zoom in on a Detail

Use the following procedure to enlarge a detail in the page:

1. Click an object to zoom in on.
2. Select **View | Zoom | 400%**.
3. Alternatively, press function key **F6** and select **400%**.
4. Alternatively, right-click the object and select **View | 400%**.
5. Alternatively, select **400%** zoom from the toolbar.

Return to Previous Zoom Level

Use the following procedure to return to the previous zoom level:

1. Select **View | Zoom | Last Zoom**.
2. Alternatively, right-click and select **View | Last Zoom**.
3. Alternatively, select **Last Zoom** from the toolbar.

Hands-On Activity

In this activity, you use the zoom functions. Ensure Visio is running and the Module-4.Vsd drawing is displayed.

1. Click the text to select it.

2. Notice that Visio surrounds the selected text with a dashed green line and green handles. That's Visio's way of giving you feedback. Notice also that Visio tells you the width, height, and rotation angle of the selected object on the status bar.

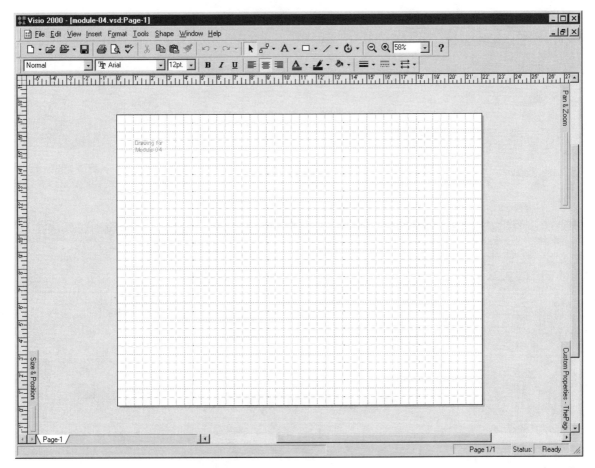

3. Hold down the **Ctrl** and **Shift** keys. Notice that Visio changes the cursor to a magnifying glass with a + (plus) sign in it.

4. Move the cursor to the upper left of the text.

5. Press the left mouse button.

6. With the **Ctrl** and **Shift** keys and the left mouse button all held down, move the cursor down and right.

7. Notice how Visio draws a rectangle, which stretches as you move the mouse.

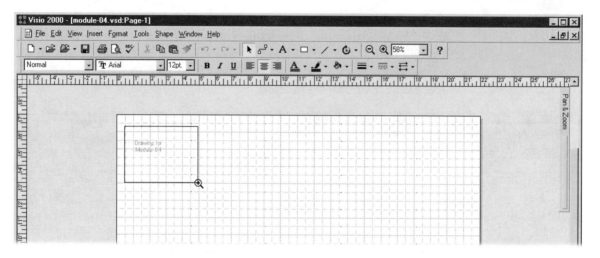

8. Let go of the mouse button. Notice how Visio zooms in and enlarges the text.

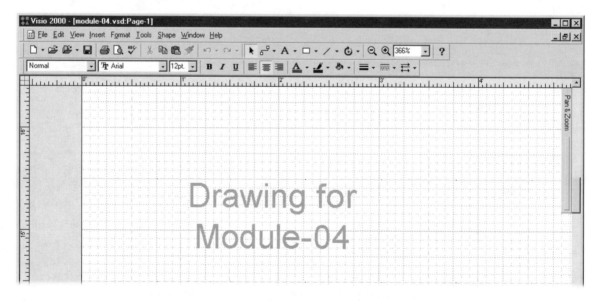

9. Glance at the Zoom Percentage list box. It should be higher than 100%.

10. Hold down the **Ctrl** and **Shift** keys, and press and hold down the right mouse button.

11. Move the mouse. Notice how the cursor changes from the magnifying glass to an open hand. Notice, too, how the entire drawing moves as you move the mouse.

12. Hold down the **Ctrl** and **Shift** keys, and press the right mouse button repeatedly. As you do, notice how the text becomes smaller as Visio zooms out.

13. In the Zoom list box, select **Page** to see the entire page again. Alternatively, press **Ctrl+W**.

14. Press **Alt+F4** to exit Visio.

This completes the hands-on activity for zooming in and out of the page.

Rulers, Grids, Guidelines, and Page Breaks

View | Ruler, Grid, Guides
Tools | Rulers and Grids
Tools | Snap and Glue

Uses

The **Ruler**, **Grid**, **Guides**, and **Page Breaks** selections of the **View** menu toggle the display of the rulers, grid lines, guidelines, and page breaks. The term *toggle* comes from the light switch that turns the lights on and off. You can change the ruler, grid, ruler, snap, and page breaks settings at any time without affecting shapes already placed in the drawing.

> **In this chapter you'll learn about:**
>
> ✓ **Horizontal and vertical rulers**
> ✓ **Grid lines**
> ✓ **Guidelines and guide points**
> ✓ **Snap distance**
> ✓ **Shape extensions**
> ✓ **Dynamic grid**
> ✓ **Page breaks**

Horizontal and Vertical Rulers

The *ruler* runs along the top and left edges of the drawing window. It helps you measure distances. The ruler's measurement system matches that of the units selected for the drawing scale (see Module 4 "Setting Up Pages and Layers"). You select the number of tick marks to display between Fine, Normal, and Coarse.

You can move the ruler's origin (zero point) to anywhere in the page. The horizontal ruler's zero point is normally at the upper-left corner of the page; the vertical ruler's zero point is normally at the lower-left corner of the page.

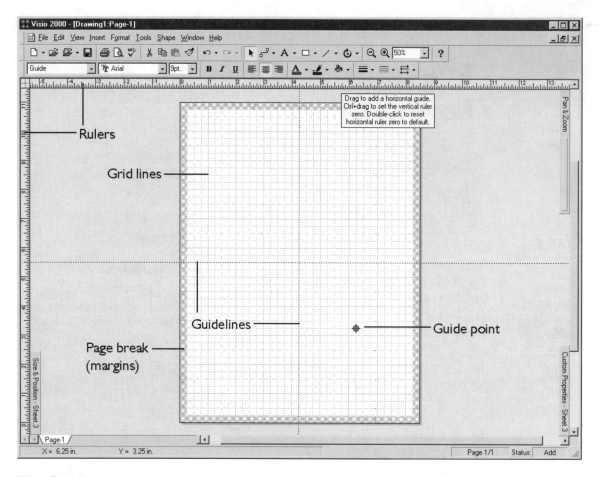

The Grid Lines

The *grid* consists of the horizontal and vertical lines on the page. It helps you line up objects as you draw. The grid has four settings: Normal, Fine, Coarse, and Fixed. You specify how far apart the grid lines are. You can move the origin of the grid to align with an object on the page.

Grid lines do not print, nor are they copied to the Clipboard.

Note: The ruler and grid settings of Fine, Normal, and Coarse are relative terms. In *normal* spacing, the ruler and grid spacing change as you zoom in or out; *fine* displays twice as many grid lines as normal spacing, while *coarse* displays half as many grid lines.

The Fixed setting establishes the grid at a constant distance. When you zoom in and out, the spacing between grid lines doesn't change. This is more similar to the type of grid IntelliCAD users are familiar with.

Guidelines and Guide Points

The *guideline* is like a customizable grid line. You create a guideline by dragging the guideline from the ruler (horizontal or vertical) over onto the page. Guidelines help you align shapes; shapes can be "glued" to the guideline (see Module 11 "Connecting Shapes Together"). Pause the cursor over the ruler to view a tooltip regarding guidelines. CAD users may be familiar with guidelines by the name of "construction line" or xline.

A *guide point* is a small cross marking a point. You create it by dragging from the intersection of the two rulers. Pause the cursor over the rules' intersection to view a tooltip regarding guide points.

> **Tip:** A page can have as many guidelines and guide points as you need, although too many begin to obscure the drawing. Guidelines and guide points do not print. As well, they do not show up when you copy and paste the drawing from Visio into another application.

Snap Distance

Snap is the ability of Visio to cause objects to line up. Snap makes it easier to create an accurate drawing. Think of snap as making shapes magnetic, so that they attract each other. Via the Snap & Glue dialog box's **General** tab, you can specify that Visio snap a shape to:

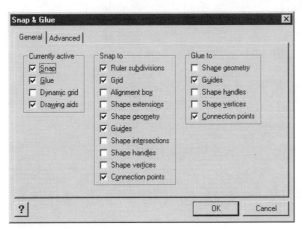

▶ **Ruler subdivisions**: Snaps to tick marks on the ruler.

▶ **Grid**: Snaps to the grid lines.

▶ **Alignment box**: Snaps to the shape's alignment box (the green, dashed rectangle that surrounds every shape).

▶ **Shape extensions**: Snaps to a shape's extension; this option works only with the Line, Arc, Freeform, Pencil, Ellipse, Rectangle, and Connection Point tools.

▶ **Shape geometry**: Snaps to the visible edges of the shape.

▶ **Guides**: Snaps to guidelines and guide points.

▶ **Shape intersections**: Snaps to intersection of two shapes; to the intersection of a shape extension and a shape; and to the intersection of a shape edge and a grid line.

▶ **Shape handles**: Snaps to shape selection handle.

▶ **Shape vertices**: Snaps to a shape's vertex.

▶ **Connection points**: Snap to a shape's connection point.

You can adjust the snap's strength. For example, you set the snap "strength" to five. When the cursor is within four pixels of a grid line, the snap takes place. Visio's other default values are within three pixels of a ruler tick mark, and 10 pixels of a guideline or a guide point. (Snap is not the same as *glue*, which is the ability of shapes to stay together when moved or stretched.) To change the strength of the snap, select the **Advanced** tab of the Snap & Glue dialog box.

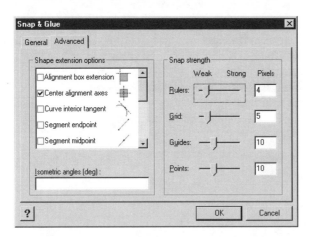

Shape Extensions

Also in the **Advanced** tab of the Snap & Glue dialog box are *shape extensions*. Shape extensions display a dashed line that extends from some portion of a shape's geometry. For example, Curve interior tangent causes a dashed line to appear when the cursor is over an arc or curve. The dashed line is called an *extension line*, and shows you the tangency to the curve's midpoint. In some cases, the extension is an arc or ellipse.

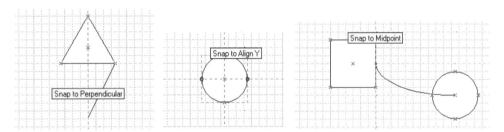

This option works only with the Line, Arc, Free-form, Pencil, Ellipse, Rectangle, and Connection Point tools. Visio 2000 includes a long list of shape extensions:

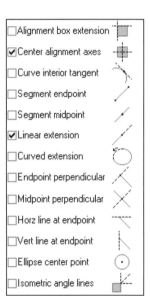

Alignment box extension displays the extension line from the shape's alignment box.

Center alignment axes displays the extension line from the center of the shape's alignment box.

Curve interior tangent displays the extension line from the curve's tangent at the midpoint of the arc segment.

Segment endpoint displays the extension line from the endpoint of a line segment or arc; the line segment include the lines that make up a polygon.

Segment midpoint highlights the midpoint of a segment.

Linear extension displays the extension line from the nearest endpoint of the line.

Curved extension displays the extension ellipse of an arc segment or freeform shape.

63

Endpoint perpendicular displays the extension line perpendicular to the nearest endpoint of a line or an arc.

Midpoint perpendicular displays the extension line perpendicular to the line or arc's midpoint.

Horz line at endpoint displays the extension line horizontal to a line or an arc's endpoint; the line is considered "horizontal" when horizontal to the screen, not the page.

Vert line at endpoint displays the extension line vertical to a line or an arc's endpoint; the line is considered "vertical" when vertical to the screen, not the page.

Ellipse center point highlights the center of an ellipse or a circle.

Isometric angle lines displays the extension line from vertex at the angle specified in the Isometric Angles (Deg.) field.

Isometric angles (deg.) allows you to specify up to ten angles (in degrees), each separated by a comma. For example, angles in 15-degree increments are commonly used: 15, 30, 45, 60, 75, and 90.

Dynamic Grid

In addition to the many drawing aids discussed above, Visio 2000 also displays a *dynamic grid*. Although Visio calls it a grid, it looks the same as a shape extension—a dashed gray line. It is called dynamic because it is not static, as is the drawing grid.

When turned on, the dynamic grid shows you the center of adjacent shapes. This makes it very easy to line up shapes. For example, you can easily center a potted plant on a table. Curiously, dynamic grid is turned off by default, so you need to turn it on in the Snap & Glue dialog box before you can use this helpful tool.

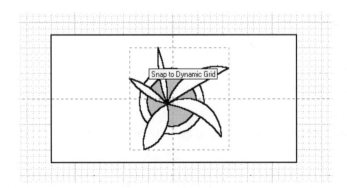

Page Breaks

Page break is Visio's non-standard term for displaying the margin around the edge of the page. The *margin* is the unprintable area along the edges of the page; the printer needs this thin strip (usually 0.5" or less) to feed the paper through the printer.

Procedures

Before presenting the general procedures for ruler, grid, ruler, snap, and page break settings, it is helpful to know about the shortcut keys. *Toggle* means to turn on and off. These are:

Function	Keys	Menu	Toolbar Icon
Snap toggle	Shift+F9	...	🔲
Ruler toggle	Alt+VR	View | Rulers	...
Guides toggle	Alt+VU	View | Guides	🔲
Grid toggle	Alt+VG	View | Grid	🔲
Ruler & Grid dialog box	Alt+TR	Tools | Ruler & Grid	...
Snap & Glue dialog box	Alt+F9	Tools | Snap & Glue	...

Setting the Snap

Use the following procedure to set the snap:

1. Select **Tools | Snap & Glue**. Notice the Snap & Glue dialog box.
2. Select the items you want Visio to snap to in the Snap to section.
3. Click the **Advanced** tab.
4. Move the slider bars in the Snap strength section:
   ▶ **Weak**: the cursor is as close as 1 pixel from the point.
   ▶ **Strong**: the cursor is as far away as 30 pixels from the point.
5. Click **OK**.

Setting the Ruler and Grid

Use the following procedure to set the ruler and grid:

1. Select **Tools | Ruler & Grid**. Notice the Ruler & Grid dialog box.

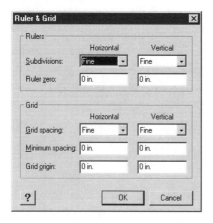

2. Select settings for the ruler from the Rulers section:
    ▸ **Subdivisions**: select from Fine, Normal, or Coarse.
    ▸ **Ruler zero**: specify a horizontal and vertical scale distance from the default point.
3. Select settings for the grid from the Grid section:
    ▸ **Grid spacing**: select from Fine, Normal, Coarse, or Fixed. Fine spacing displays two times as many grid lines as the normal setting; coarse displays half as many grid lines as normal spacing.
    ▸ **Minimum spacing**: for fine, normal, or coarse spacing, specifies the minimum distance between grid lines. For fixed spacing, specifies the distance between grid lines. Visio always displays the fixed grid lines, despite the zoom level.
    ▸ **Grid origin**: specify a horizontal and vertical grid distance from the default origin.
4. Click **OK**.

Toggling the Snap

Use the following procedure to turn the snap on and off:
1. Press function key **Shift+F9**.
2. Alternatively, press the **Snap** button on the toolbar.

Toggling the Glue

Use the following procedure to turn off and on the glue:
1. Press function key **F9**.
2. Alternatively, press the **Glue** button on the toolbar.

Creating a Guideline

Use the following procedure to create one or more guidelines:

1. Move the cursor to the horizontal or vertical ruler. Notice that you can create guidelines at any time.
2. Click the mouse button, and then drag into the drawing. Notice the blue line moving with the cursor; this is the guideline.
3. Release the mouse button once the guideline is in position. Notice that the guideline turns green, indicating that it is selected.

> ●◐ **Tip:** You can drag as many guidelines into the drawing as you require.
>
> Dragging from the horizontal ruler results in a horizontal guideline.
>
> Dragging from the vertical ruler results in a vertical guideline.
>
> Guidelines respect the setting of snap, grid, ruler, connection points, etc. To position the guideline accurately, make use of the positioning aids. An unselected guideline is colored blue.

Repositioning a Guideline

Use the following procedure to reposition a guideline:

1. To reposition a guideline, select the **Pointer** tool.
2. Select the guideline. Notice that its color changes from blue to green.
3. Drag the guideline to a new position.
4. To move more than one guideline at a time, hold down the **Shift** key while selecting guidelines. The first guideline you select turns green; the additional guidelines you select turn cyan (light blue).

Removing a Guideline

Use the following procedure to remove one or more guidelines:

1. To remove a guideline, select the **Pointer** tool**.**
2. Select the guideline. Notice that it turns green.
3. Press the **Delete** key. Visio deletes the guideline.
4. To delete more than one guideline at a time, hold down the **Shift** key while selecting guidelines, then press the **Delete** key. To erase all guidelines and guide points, select **Edit | Select Special**. In the dialog box, click **None**, then select **Guides**. Click **OK**, then press **Delete**.

Creating and Removing Guide Points

Use the following procedure to create and remove guide points:

1. Move the cursor to the intersection of the rulers (upper left corner of Visio's drawing area).
2. Click and drag the guide point into the drawing. Notice the two blue lines moving with the cursor.
3. Let go of the mouse button when the guide point is in position. The guide point looks like a small green plus sign.
4. To delete the guide point, select it and press the **Delete** key.

Toggling the Display of Guidelines and Points

Use the following procedure to turn the display of guidelines and points on and off:

1. Select **View | Guides**. The check mark indicates guide display is on; no check mark means guides are not displayed.
2. Alternatively, press the **Guides** button on the toolbar.
3. Alternatively, create a new layer and place guides on that layer. Toggle the visibility of the guidelines and points by turning the visibility of that layer off and on.

Toggling the Grid Display

Use the following procedure to turn the display of grid lines on and off:

1. Select **View | Grid**. The check mark indicates grid display is on; no check mark means the grid is not displayed.
2. Alternatively, press the **Grid** button on the toolbar.

Relocating the Ruler Origin

Use the following procedure to move the zero setting of the ruler:

1. Move the cursor over the vertical or horizontal ruler.
2. Hold down the **Ctrl** key.
3. Hold down the left mouse button.
4. Drag into the drawing. Notice that a black line moves with the mouse into the drawing.
5. Let go of the **Ctrl** key and mouse button. Notice that the zero point on the ruler has moved.
6. To reset the ruler's zero point back to its default position, double-click the *other* ruler.

To change both rulers at the same time, press **Ctrl** and drag the intersection of the two rulers. Double-click the intersection point to reset the rulers.

Hands-On Activity

In this activity, you use the rule and grid functions. Ensure Visio is running and start a new drawing.

1. Select **Tools | Ruler & Grid**. Notice the Ruler & Grid dialog box. All settings are either **Fine** or **0**.
2. Select **Fine** for the Horizontal and Vertical ruler Subdivisions.
3. Select **Coarse** for the Horizontal and Vertical Grid spacing.
4. Click **OK**. Notice the coarse ruler tick mark spacing and the fine grid line spacing.

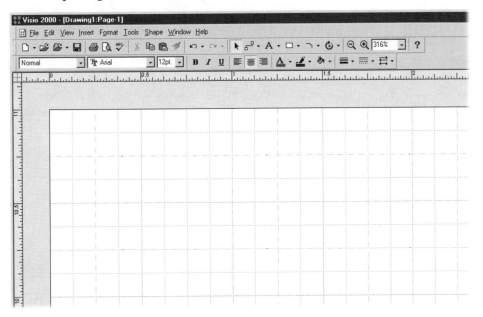

5. To place a vertical guideline, move the cursor to the vertical ruler (located at the left edge of the Visio drawing area). Notice that the cursor becomes a horizontal double-ended arrow.
6. Hold down the left mouse button.

7. Drag the mouse into the drawing. Notice the blue vertical line moving with the mouse.

8. Let go of the mouse button. Notice that the guideline changes from blue to green.

9. Exit Visio by pressing **Alt+F4**.

This completes the hands-on activity for setting the ruler and grid.

Opening Existing Stencils

File | Stencils

Uses

The **Stencils** selection of the **File** menu lets you open one or more stencil files, which are used to place shapes in the page. The term *stencil* comes from the green plastic stencils used by drafters to quickly draw commonly used shapes.

> **In this chapter you'll learn about:**
> ✓ **The Shape Explorer**
> ✓ **Opening a stencil file**
> ✓ **Adjusting the Stencil window**

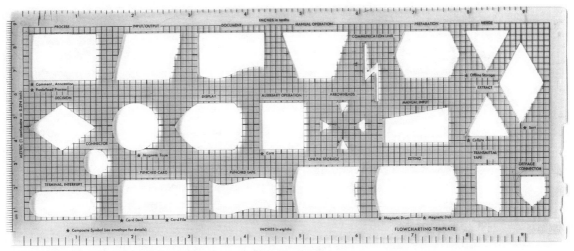

In Visio, stencils contain predrawn objects, called *shapes*. Visio shapes have more intelligence than the shapes cut out of the green plastic. The shapes know their logical connection point and are automatically assigned a layer name. Unlike the plastic stencil shapes, Visio shapes are easy to resize, easy to modify, and are in full color.

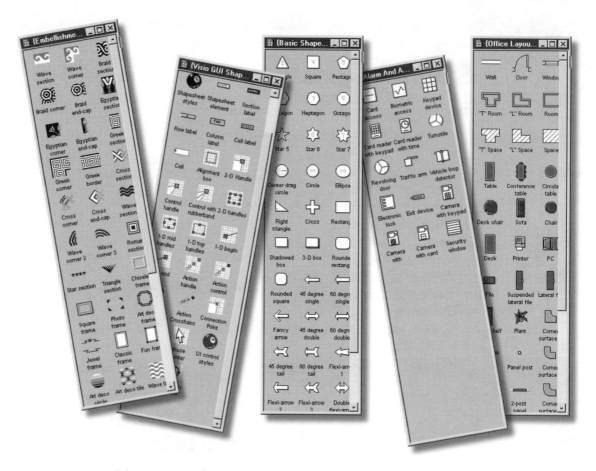

Visio comes with many stencil files, which are files with extension .VSS found in the \Solutions folder. Each stencil file typically includes 10 to 45 shapes. Additional specialized stencil files are available from Visio Corp. and third-party developers. To help you find stencil files, whether on your computer or your firm's network or on the Internet, Visio includes the Shape Explorer.

You use a shape in two steps: (1) open the stencil file; and (2) drag the shape from the stencil to the page. In this module, you learn the first step, opening the stencil file.

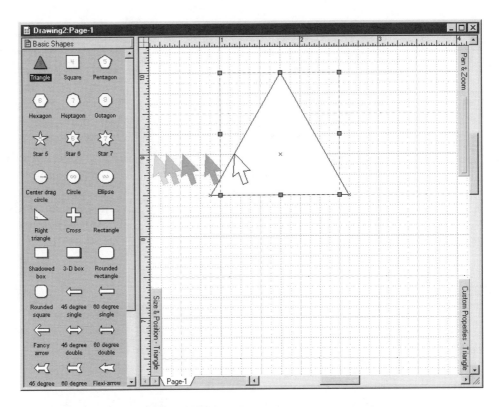

 Note: The shape in the stencil is called the *master shape* because Visio makes a copy of the master when you appear to drag the shape into the drawing.

Shape Explorer

Since Visio includes thousands of shapes, it can get tough looking for a specific shape: which stencil is it stored in? To solve this problem, Visio provides two ways to search for a shape. One solution is to categorize the shapes. Click the small arrow next to the **Open Shape** button on the toolbar; Visio displays a list of stencil categories (which correspond to folders in the \Solutions folder). The exact contents of the list varies, depending on which edition of Visio you are operating.

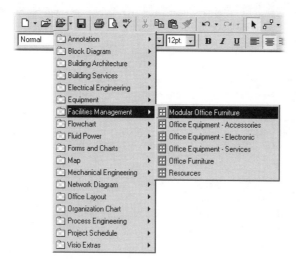

The second solution is the Shape Explorer. This utility searches for shapes, stencils, templates, and wizards on your computer. You can have it search for all of these by leaving the Search for field blank (ignore the warning message about the search taking a long time: it takes just ten seconds on a 400MHz Pentium computer).

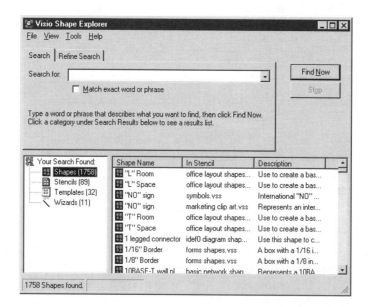

Or, you can type a word that describes the shape. For example, when I entered "map," the Shape Explorer returned 406 shapes, 9 stencils, 3 templates, and 0 wizards.

Match exact word or phrase: Shape Explorer searches for an exact match to the words you type. This is equivalent to using quotation marks, such as "Blocks with Perspective." When you type a single word, Shape

Explorer searches for items that contain only that word. For example, typing "block" returns "Block Diagram" but not "Blocks Raised."

When this option is turned off, Shape Explorer searches for items that have those words, such as "blocks," "with," and "perspective." This could include "Block Diagram," "Blocks Raised," and "Blocks with Perspective."

To search the lists alphabetically, you can click the headers: Shape Name, In Stencil, and Description. The first time you click a heading, the list is sorted alphabetically; the second time you click the heading, the list is sorted in reverse alphabetical order (starting with Z). To further refine the search, click the **Refine Search** tab, and choose (or unchoose) options.

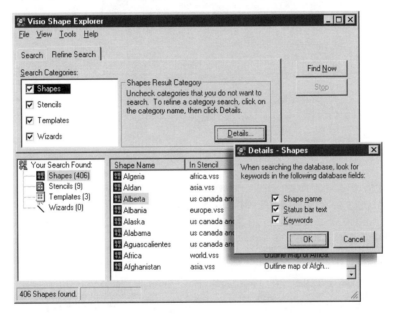

Once you find the shape you are looking for, right-click its name to see a shortcut menu:

- ▶ **Add to Drawing**: Places the shape in the center of the current drawing.
- ▶ **Open Containing Stencil**: Opens the stencil file in Visio.
- ▶ **Create New Stencil**: Opens a blank stencil, and adds the shape.
- ▶ **Properties**: Displays a dialog box that describes the shape and previews the image.

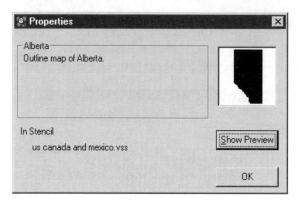

Procedures

Before presenting the general procedures for opening a stencil file, it is helpful to know about the shortcut keys. These are:

Function	Shortcut	Menu	Toolbar Icon
Open stencil file	Alt+FTO	File | Stencils | Open Stencil	☞ ▾
Open blank stencil	Alt+FTN	File | Stencils | New Stencil	...
Shape Explorer	...	Tools | Macros | Shape Explorer	...

Opening a Stencil File

Use the following procedure to open a stencil file:

1. Select **File | Stencils | Block Diagram | Basic Shapes**. Notice how Visio groups the stencil files in this menu selection.

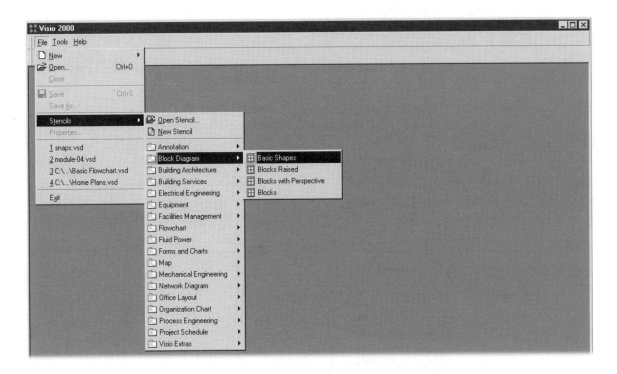

2. You can load more than one stencil file by repeating the procedure and selecting a different stencil name.

Adjusting the Stencil Window

Use the following procedure to change a stencil window:

1. Click the icon on the stencil's title bar. Notice the options:

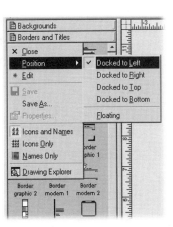

   ▶ **Close**: Closes (removes) the stencil.

   ▶ **Position**: Moves the stencil to another position.

   ▶ **Edit**: Makes stencil editing commands available (right-click a shape to view shortcut menu with editing options).

   ▶ **Save**: Saves changes made to the stencil in Edit mode.

   ▶ **Save As**: Saves the stencil to another filename.

▶ **Properties**: Displays the Properties dialog box for the stencil (available only in Edit mode).

▶ **Icons and Names**: Displays the shapes with icons and names (the default, as illustrated).

▶ **Icons Only**: Displays the shapes with icons only.

▶ **Names Only**: Displays the shapes by name only (takes up less space).

▶ **Drawing Explorer**: Displays the Drawing Explorer window within the stencil window (see Module 31 "Drawing Explorer").

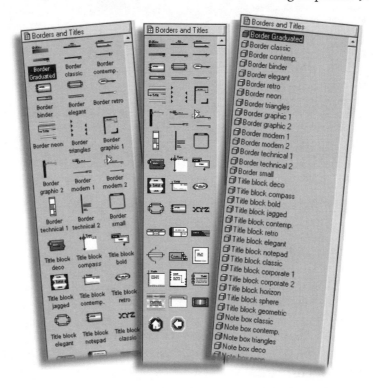

2. Drag the slider bar to see more shapes in the lower part of the stencil.

3. Right-click on a shape in the stencil. Notice the options; most are grayed out, unless **Edit** is turned on (as noted earlier):

- ▶ **Cut**: Cuts (removes) the shape from the stencil and copies it to the Clipboard.
- ▶ **Copy**: Copies the shape to the Windows Clipboard in picture (WMF) format.
- ▶ **Paste**: Pastes a shape from the Clipboard into the stencil; this option is available only when the Clipboard contains a shape.
- ▶ **Paste Shortcut**: Pastes a shape from the Clipboard into the stencil as a master shortcut. Shortcuts allow several stencils to refer back to a single master.
- ▶ **Delete**: Erases the shape from the stencil.
- ▶ **Select All**: Selects all stencils in the shape.
- ▶ **Duplicate**: Makes a copy of the stencil.
- ▶ **Create Shortcut**: Creates a shortcut to the shape.
- ▶ **New Master**: Creates a new, blank shape.
- ▶ **Master Properties**: Displays the Master Properties dialog box.
- ▶ **Edit Master**: Opens the master in a window so that the master can be graphically edited.
- ▶ **Edit Icon**: Opens the master's icon in an icon editor.
- ▶ **Help**: Displays help that answers the following questions: "Where is this shape located?," "How do I use this shape?," "How do I use Visio shapes?" and "How do I find other shapes?".

Modifying masters and creating new stencils is beyond the scope of this book. See *Learn Visio 2000 for the Advanced User*, also from Wordware Publishing.

Hands-On Activity

In this activity, you open two stencil files. Ensure Visio is running.

1. Select **File | New | Office Layout | Office Layout Shapes** from the menu bar. Notice that Visio sizes the page window to accommodate the Office Layout Shapes stencil file.

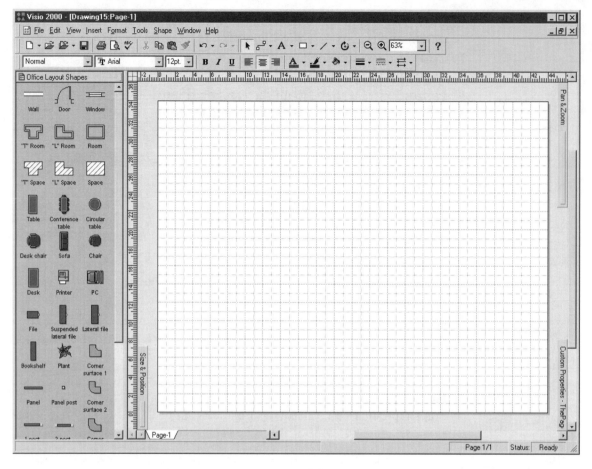

2. Drag the stencil's scroll bar to look at the 35 shapes in the stencil.

3. Open a second stencil by selecting **File | Stencils | Forms and Charts | Marketing Diagrams**. Notice how the newly opened stencil covers up the first stencil. (In case you don't see it, the title bar of the Office Layout Shapes stencil is at the bottom of the Visio window.)

4. To bring the first stencil back into view, click the **Office Layout Shapes** title bar. Notice how it appears to slide up, covering the **Marketing Diagrams** stencil.

5. To see both stencils at the same time, right-click the stencil's title bar. Visio displays a shortcut menu. Select **Position | Docked to Right**. Notice how both stencils are visible, one on either side of the drawing area.

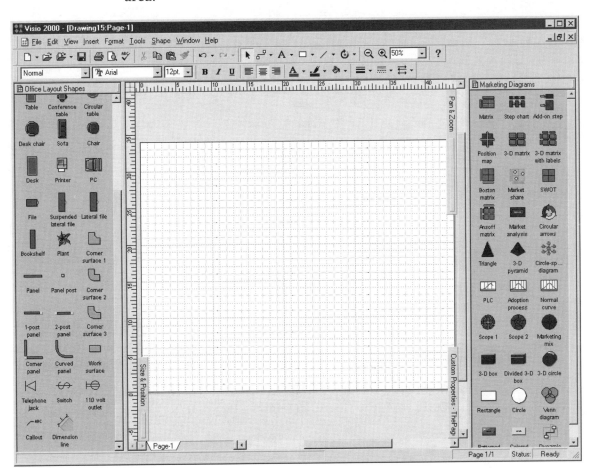

6. To make more room for the drawing area, you have three options:

▶ Drag the side of the stencil to make it narrower.

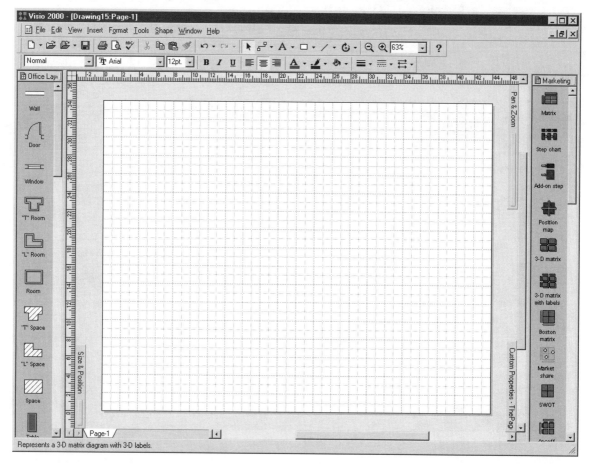

▶ Right-click on either stencil's title bar. Select **Icons Only** or **Names Only** from the floating menu. Notice that both stencils change.

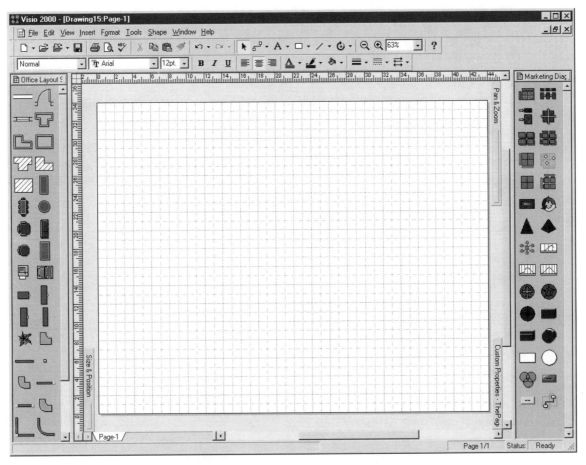

▶ Right-click the title bar and select **Float**. Notice that the stencil becomes an independent window and can be placed anywhere on your screen, even outside of Visio.

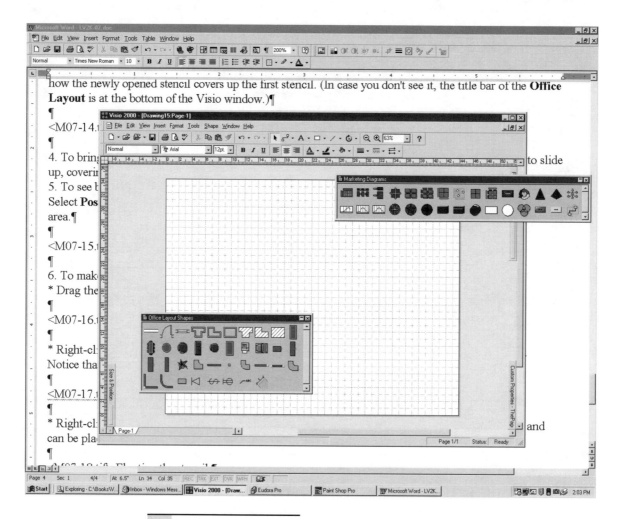

Tip: To move a floating stencil, drag it by the title bar. To prevent a stencil from docking, hold down the **Ctrl** key as you move the stencil. To resize a stencil, drag it by one of its four corners.

7. Exit Visio with **Alt+F4**.

This completes the hands-on activity for opening and positioning a stencil file.

Dragging Masters into the Drawing

In this chapter you'll learn about:

✓ *Dragging shapes into a drawing*

Uses

To use a shape, you drag it from the stencil to the drawing. There are no menu selections, toolbar icons, or shortcut keys for placing shapes in the drawing.

▲ **Note:** While in the stencil, the shape is called a *master*. When you drag the master into the drawing, Visio makes a copy of the master and places an *instance* in the drawing. The instanced master is the shape.

Procedures

Use the following procedure to drag a shape into the drawing. Ensure Visio has at least one stencil file open and a drawing page displayed.

1. Move the cursor over a master in the stencil.

2. Drag the master to the drawing. You *drag* by holding down the left mouse button, then moving the master into the drawing, and letting go of the mouse button.

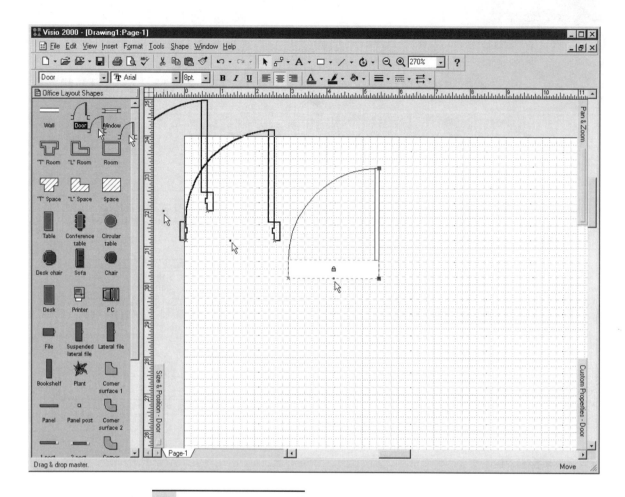

Tip: You can drag the master from the stencil to the page many times. A Visio stencil does not "run out" of shapes. You delete a shape by dragging it back onto the stencil.

Hands-On Activity

In this activity, you start to create an office drawing by dragging shapes onto the page. Ensure Visio is running, and is displaying the Office Layout Shapes stencil file.

1. Move the cursor over the **Room** master shape in the stencil.
2. Click the mouse button. Notice that Visio highlights the shape by changing its color. Notice also that, after a second or two, Visio displays a tooltip that helps you use the shape.

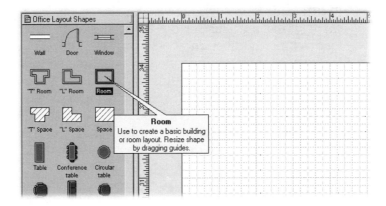

3. Drag the **Room** shape to the drawing. Notice that Visio adds walls to the room.

4. Right-click the shape to display the shortcut menu. The options found on the menu vary, depending on the shape. The first several options are specific to the Room shape; the following options are common to all shapes:

   ▶ **Cut** cuts the shape from the drawing and places it in the Windows Clipboard.

   ▶ **Copy** copies the shape to the Clipboard. It is available to Visio and other Windows applications in different formats: Visio drawing, Visio drawing data, Picture (WMF), Enhanced Picture (EMF), and ANSI text of the shape name. See Module 12 "Cutting, Copying, and Pasting."

   ▶ **Paste** pastes whatever is currently in the Clipboard into the center of the drawing.

   ▶ **Duplicate** makes a copy of the selected shape, slightly offset.

   ▶ **View** lets you change the zoom level and toggle the display of drawing aids, such as grids and rulers.

   ▶ **Format** lets you change the formatting of the lines and text that make up the shape. See Modules 13 and 14 "Formatting Shapes" and "Formatting Text."

   ▶ **Shape** lets you change the position of the shape, such as flipping it. See Module 9 "Sizing and Positioning."

   ▶ **Help** displays the same help box we saw earlier.

▶ **Properties** varies with the shape you select. For this particular wall shape, it displays the Custom Properties dialog box that lets you type an inventory number and owner name. Filling in this information is completely optional; the data can be extracted to a database to help you create an inventory listing. Other shapes have other custom properties. For example, the Cray computer shape has text fields for ID, Location, Manufacturer, Product Name, Model Number, and Description. In some cases, the fields are filled in for you, but you can edit them. See Module 34 "Custom Properties."

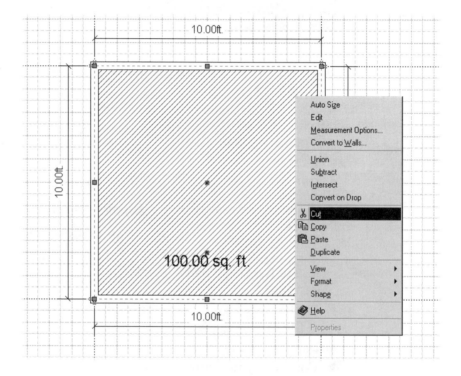

5. Exit Visio with **Alt+F4**.

This completes the hands-on activity for placing a shape in the drawing.

Sizing and Positioning

Shape | Rotate
Flip
Bring to Front
Send to Back
Tools | Center Drawing
View | Windows | Size & Position

Uses

The **Size & Position** selection of the **View | Windows** menu is used to change the size and position of the selected shape. Most of the time, you will probably use the shape's handles (the green squares) to size and position the shape. The term *handle* comes

> **In this chapter you'll learn about:**
> ✓ **The Size & Position window**
> ✓ **Resizing the shape**
> ✓ **Changing the wall thickness**
> ✓ **Rotating the shape**
> ✓ **Flipping the shape**
> ✓ **Bring to Front and Send to Back**
> ✓ **Centering the drawing**

from handles on suitcases and mugs that help you carry and hold them. Via the handles, you change the size of a shape. You can perform the following actions with the handles on a 2D shape:

▶ Corner handles: size the shape proportionally.
▶ Top handles: size the shape horizontally.
▶ Bottom handles: size the shape vertically.

You can perform the following actions with the handles on a 1D shape:

▶ Begin and end handles: change the length of the shape.
▶ Center handle: widen the shape relative to its base.

When you see small gray padlocks instead of green squares, it means the shape cannot be resized. (The small blue x markers are connection points.)

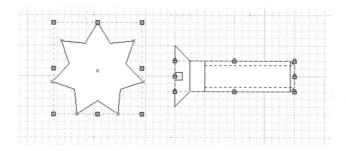

The **Rotate** selections of the **Shape** menu rotate the shape at right angles (90 degrees) each time you use the command. **Rotate Left** rotates the shape 90 degrees counterclockwise; **Rotate Right** rotates the shape 90 degrees clockwise. In addition, Visio has the **Rotation** tool that lets you rotate the shape by any angle.

The **Flip** selections of the **Shape** menu transpose the shape. **Flip Horizontal** transposes the left and right halves, while **Flip Vertical** reverses the top and bottom halves.

The **Bring to Front** selection of the **Shape** menu moves a shape in front of an overlapping shape; the **Send to Back** selection moves the overlapping shape behind the underlying shape. When three or more shapes overlap, the **Bring Forward** and **Send Backward** selections move the selected shape by one shape at a time.

The **Center Drawing** selection of the **Tools** menu centers the entire drawing on the page. This command is useful after changing the size or orientation of the page.

Size & Position Window

The **Size & Position** window allows you to interactively change the position of the shape. The data listed in the window varies according to the shape. Two examples are illustrated on the next page:

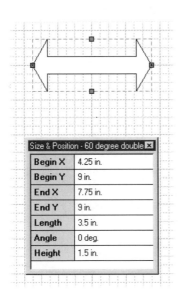

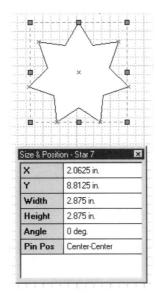

Size & Position - 60 degree double ☒	
Begin X	4.25 in.
Begin Y	9 in.
End X	7.75 in.
End Y	9 in.
Length	3.5 in.
Angle	0 deg.
Height	1.5 in.

Size & Position - Star 7 ☒	
X	2.0625 in.
Y	8.8125 in.
Width	2.875 in.
Height	2.875 in.
Angle	0 deg.
Pin Pos	Center-Center

For the 1D shape, the parameters have the following meaning:

Begin X: The x-coordinate of the shape's begin point; x is measured from the ruler's zero point.

Begin Y: The y-coordinate of the shape's begin point.

End X: The x-coordinate of the shape's end point.

End Y: The y-coordinate of the shape's end point.

Length: The length of the shape.

Angle: The angle of the shape; the angle is measured in degrees from the x-axis.

Height: The height of the shape.

You can click a data field and change the value. For example, click the field next to **Height** and change the value to **3**; Visio changes the width of the shape to 3.0 inches. Conversely, you can size the shape via its handles, and you will see the data updating in the Size & Position window.

For the 2D shape, the parameters have the following meaning:

X: The x-coordinate of the shape's pin position.

Y: The y-coordinate of the shape's pin position.

Width: The width of the shape's alignment box.

Height: The height of the shape's alignment box.

Angle: The angle of the shape's alignment box, relative to the pin.

Pin Pos: The location of the pin relative to the shape's alignment box.

The *pin* of the 2D shape is used by Visio to measure the distance from the page's origin (0,0). Think of sticking a pin through a memo on a bulletin board. When you click the field next to Pin Pos, Visio displays a list of other pin positions, such as Top-Left.

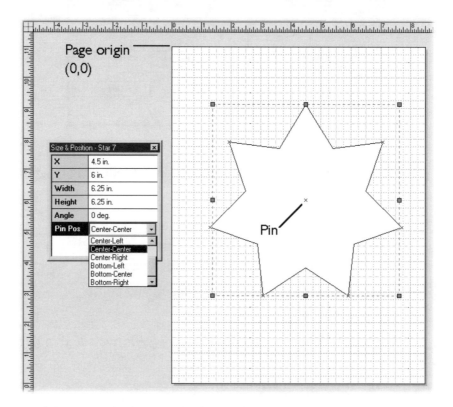

Procedures

Before presenting the general procedures for sizing and positioning, it is helpful to know about the shortcut keys. These are:

Function	Keys	Menu	Toolbar Icon
Size & Position window	Alt+VWS	View | Windows | Size & Position	...
Flip horizontal	Ctrl+H	Shape | Flip Horizontal	
Flip vertical	Ctrl+J	Shape | Flip Vertical	
Free rotation	Ctrl+0	Shape | Size & Position	
Rotate left	Ctrl+L	Shape | Rotate Left	
Rotate right	Ctrl+R	Shape | Rotate Right	
Bring to front	Ctrl+F	Shape | Bring to Front	
Send to back	Ctrl+B	Shape | Send to Back	
Center drawing	Alt+TW	Tools | Center Drawing	...

Resizing the Shape

Use the following procedure to resize the shape:

1. Select the shape.
2. Move the cursor over a corner handle. Notice that the cursor changes to a diagonal double arrow.
3. Drag the corner handle away from the shape. Notice the shape getting larger.
4. Release the mouse button. The shape is larger.

Changing the Height of the Shape

Use the following procedure to stretch the shape:

1. Select the shape.
2. Move the cursor over the bottom, middle handle. Notice that the cursor changes to a double arrow.
3. Drag the handle away from the shape. Notice the thin outline of the shape stretching.
4. Release the mouse button. The shape is taller.

Changing the Wall Thickness

Use the following procedure to change the thickness of the walls:

1. Select the shape.

2. Move the cursor over an outside corner handle. Notice that the cursor changes to a four-headed arrow and a small hint box explains the function of the handle ("Wall Thickness").

3. Drag the corner handle away from the shape. Notice the thin line stretching out. The length of the line indicates the new width of the two walls connected to the handle. Move diagonally to change the width of both the horizontal and vertical walls.

4. Release the mouse button. The wall is thicker.

5. Repeat the steps above to change the thickness of the other two walls.

Rotating the Shape

Use the following procedure to rotate the shape by 90 degrees:

1. Select the shape.

2. Select **Shape | Rotate Left**. Notice the shape has rotated counter-clockwise by 90 degrees. The status line reports "Angle = 90 deg."

3. Repeat to rotate another 90 degrees.

Free Rotating the Shape

Use the following procedure to free rotate the shape:

1. Select the shape.

2. Select the **Rotation** tool button on the toolbar. Notice the shape has new handles that look like green circles:

   ▶ **Center of Rotation**: The center handle is a green circle with a small cross; the shape rotates around this handle. This handle can be moved to change how the shape is rotated.

   ▶ **Rotation Handle**: The other green circle handles are used to rotate the shape around the center of rotation.

3. Move the cursor over one of the rotation handles. The cursor changes to a pair of curved arrows. Notice the thin outline of the shape rotating as you drag the cursor. The status line reports the angle.

4. Click the **Pointer** tool button on the toolbar to exit the rotation mode.

Flipping the Shape

Use the following procedure to flip the shape:

1. Select the shape.

2. Select **Shape | Flip Horizontal** from the menu. Notice the shape has mirrored about its center point. The status line reports the new angle.

The Size & Position Window

Use the following procedure to precisely change the size and rotation angle of a shape by typing numbers:

1. Select the shape.
2. Make sure the Size & Position window is visible; if it isn't, select **View | Windows | Size & Position** from the menu bar.
3. To change the size of the shape, type new values in the Width and Height boxes.
4. To change the rotation, type a new angle in the Angle box.
5. To change the center of rotation, type new distances in the X and Y boxes.
6. Alternatively, change the center of rotation to one of nine locations by clicking on the Pin Pos box.

Bring to Front and Send to Back

Use the following procedure to change the visibility of overlapping shapes:

1. Select the shape.
2. Select **Shape | Bring to Front** from the menu bar. Notice that the shape moves on top of overlapping shapes.
3. Select **Shape | Send to Back**. Notice that the shape moves to the bottom of overlapping shapes.

Center Drawing

Use the following procedure to center the drawing:

1. Select **Tools | Center Drawing** from the menu; there is no need to select the shapes. Notice that Visio centers the drawing on the page.

Hands-On Activity

In this activity, you use the size functions to resize a shape. Ensure Visio is running with a new drawing and is displaying the Basic Shapes stencil.

1. Drag the **Triangle** shape onto the drawing page. If necessary, zoom in to make the triangle look larger. Notice the eight selection handles (green squares).

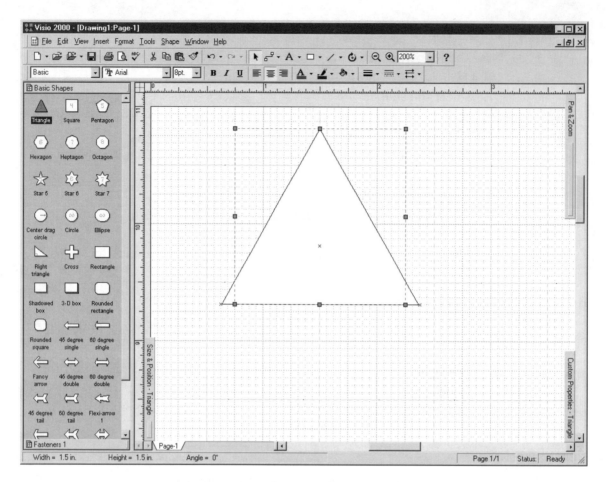

2. Ensure the Size & Position window is displayed. If necessary, select **View | Windows | Size & Position** from the menu bar.

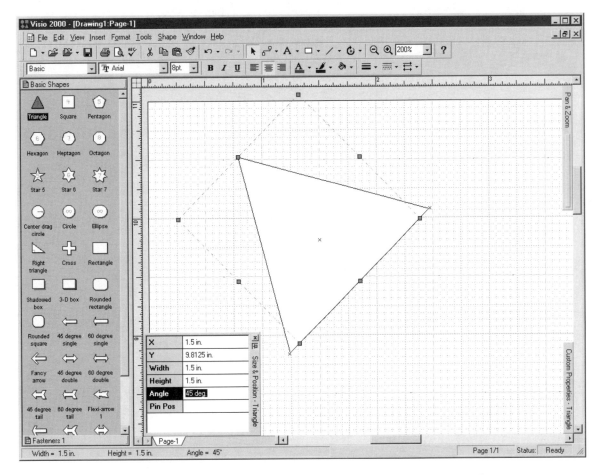

3. Type **45** in the Angle box. Notice the triangle is rotated.

4. Type **5** for both the X and Y position. Notice the triangle moves on the page.

5. Select **Bottom-Right** for Pin Pos. Notice the triangle moves again.

6. Exit Visio with **Alt+F4.**

This completes the hands-on activity for sizing and positioning shapes.

 *Placing Multiple Shapes*

Edit | Duplicate
Shape | Operations | Offset

Uses

Once a shape is placed in
the drawing, you may
want to make copies of
the shape. When you
change a shape, you
don't want to apply those

> **In this chapter you'll learn about:**
>
> ✓ **Making a copy**
>
> ✓ **Duplicating more than one copy**
>
> ✓ **Making an offset copy**

changes to every additional shape; instead, you would make copies (or
duplicates) of the modified shape.

Similarly, sometimes you want to create shapes parallel to existing shapes.
Visio allows you to *offset* simple lines and arcs.

Procedures

Before presenting the general procedures for placing multiple shapes, it is
helpful to know about the shortcut keys. These are:

Function	Keys	Menu
Duplicate (copy)	Ctrl+drag or Ctrl+D	Edit	Duplicate
Repeat last action	F4	Edit	Repeat
Offset	…	Shape	Operations	Offset

Making a Copy

Use the following procedure to copy a shape within the drawing:

1. Select a shape.
2. Hold down the **Ctrl** key. Notice that a small + (plus) sign appears next
   to the arrow cursor. Visio is reminding you that it will make a copy of
   the shape, rather than move it.

3. Drag the shape, and let go of the Ctrl key. Notice that an exact copy of the shape appears.

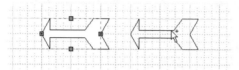

●◀ **Tip:** Holding down the **Ctrl** and **Shift** keys constrains the cursor. Thus, you can copy a shape and align it vertically or horizontally with the original shape.

Duplicating More Than One Copy

Use the following procedure to duplicate a shape several times at the same distance apart:

1. Select shape.
2. Hold down the **Ctrl** key, drag the shape, and let go. Notice that an exact copy of the shape appears.
3. Press **F4** to repeat the action.
4. Repeat pressing **F4** until you have enough copies.

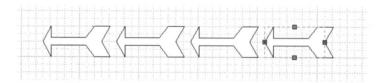

5. If you make too many copies, press **Ctrl+Z** to undo the copy action.

 Note: When it comes to making multiple copies, there is nothing specific about function key F4. It is, in fact, the short-cut for the Repeat operation (**Edit | Repeat**). Its purpose to do the last action again. You can probably find other uses for F4, such as using it to apply the same formatting to a number of shapes.

Making an Offset Copy

Use the following procedure to offset lines and arcs:

1. Draw a line or arc.
2. Select the line (or arc).
3. Select **Shape | Operations | Offset**. Notice the Offset dialog box.

4. Enter an offset distance in the Offset distance text box.
5. Click **OK**. Notice that Visio places a copy of the shape on both sides.

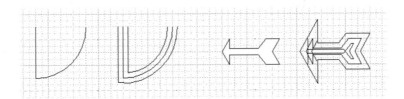

In some cases, Visio cannot accurately offset a shape, as illustrated.

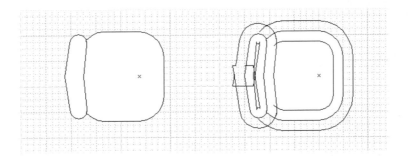

 Note: Visio 5.x would not offset complex shapes, such as a chair or plant shape. In that case, the **Offset** command would be grayed out. This restriction has been lifted in Visio 2000.

Hands-On Activity

In this activity, you use the Duplicate function. Ensure Visio is running and is displaying the Office Layout Shapes stencil.

1. Drag the **Bookshelf** shape into the drawing.

2. Hold down **Ctrl**, and start dragging the shape. Then hold down the **Shift** key while you're dragging the shape. (You cannot first hold down **Shift+Ctrl**, then drag, because Visio goes into Zoom window mode.)

3. Drag a copy of the **Bookshelf** shape to the right away from the first bookshelf.

4. Let go of the **Ctrl** and **Shift** keys.

5. Press **F4** again to place more bookshelves until you have four.

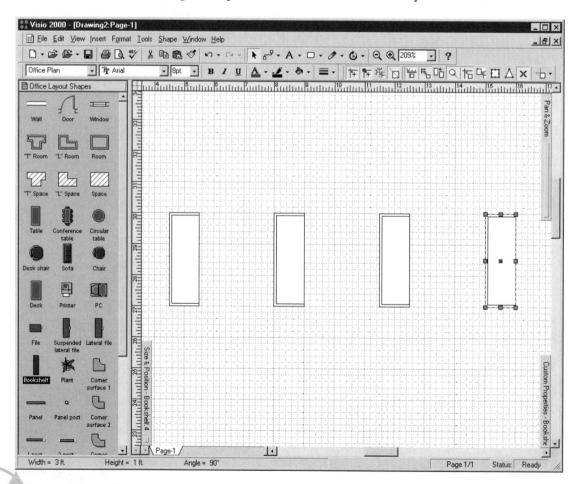

6. If necessary, use one of the **Zoom** commands to see all four bookcases.

7. Press **Alt+F4** to exit Visio.

This completes the hands-on activity for placing multiple shapes.

Connecting Shapes Together

Tools | Connect Shapes

Uses

Perhaps the most important concept in Visio is the connector. *Connectors* are the lines you see drawn between flowchart shapes, such as network shapes and organization shapes.

> **In this chapter you'll learn about:**
> ✓ **Connection points**
> ✓ **Glue**
> ✓ **Variations on connectors**
> ✓ **Creating connections**

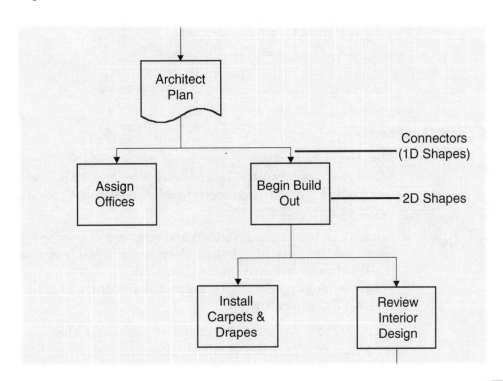

More accurately, a connector is a 1D (one-dimensional) shape that connects 2D (two-dimensional) shapes. The connector can be as simple as a line or an arc, or a more complex object. As we see later, <u>any</u> shape can be converted to 1D and, hence, become a connector.

 Note: In earlier versions of Visio, you could tell the difference between 1D and 2D shapes on a stencil. The 1D shapes had a yellow background, while 2D shapes had a green background. As of Visio 2000, this distinction has, unfortunately, been removed from stencils.

A connector has a start and an end. (This is important in determining which end of the connector, for example, should have an arrowhead.) The start is indicated by a tiny + (plus) sign, while the end is indicated by a small x. When a successful connection is made, the end turns red.

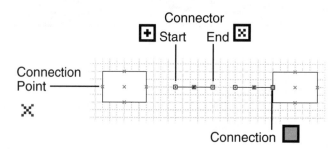

Connection Points

The connector attaches to specific points on a shape. These points are called *connection points*. The connection point is shown on shapes by a small blue x; when the connection is successful, the connection point becomes a red square.

Connection points can be added and removed from shapes; they do not need to lie on the shape, but can be anywhere inside and outside of it. Use the **Connection Point** tool to move, add, and remove connection points. From the toolbar, select the **Connection Point** tool (you find it hidden under the **Connector** tool):

▶ To move a connection, drag it to the new position.
▶ To add a connection to a shape, select the shape, hold down the **Ctrl** key, and click.
▶ To remove a connection, select it, and press the **Delete** key.

You can toggle (turn on and off) the display of connection points with **View | Connection Points**. While creating the diagram, you want connection points to be visible; when it comes time to give your presentation, you want the connection points turned off.

Connection points, like guidelines and the grid, do not print.

Glue

Connectors have a "stickiness" called *glue*. Glue is what forces the connector to stay connected to the shapes as they are moved.

Visio provides you with two types of glue: static and dynamic. *Static* glue causes the connector to stay connected to the connection point. *Dynamic* glue causes the connector to stay connected to the nearest connection point on the shape.

This means that static glue is best for connectors that you want to stay put, while dynamic glue is best when you want connectors to rearrange themselves automatically. A connector can have static glue at one end and dynamic glue at the other.

In the following illustration, a connector connects the rectangle and the triangle. At the rectangle end, the connector uses static glue; at the triangle end, the connector uses dynamic glue. As the triangle is moved, its dynamic connection jumps from connection point A (center of triangle) to B (left side) to C (top of the triangle). On the rectangle, however, the static connection stays fixed to a single connection point.

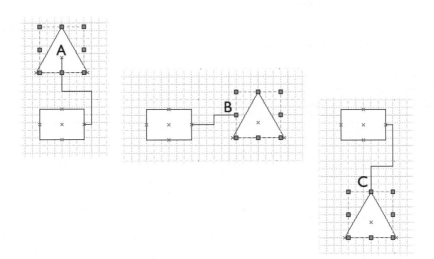

Here is how you tell whether a connection is made with static or dynamic glue:

▶ **Static** connections have a red box the same size as the connector's start and end boxes.

▶ **Dynamic** connections have a larger red box.

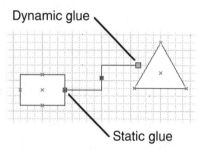

You can change the glue from static to dynamic and back, but in my opinion, this has got to be one of the most obscure parts of Visio:

▶ From the toolbar, select the **Pointer** tool.

▶ Drag the end of the connector away from its connection point.

▶ Drag the end of the connector into the shape (<u>not</u> to a particular connection point). Notice that the entire shape is outlined by a thick red rectangle.

▶ When you let go of the mouse button, the connector connects to the nearest connection point.

You can now drag the shape around and watch the connector jump from connection point to connection point.

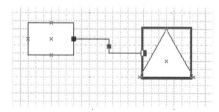

Tip: A connector can only have dynamic glue when it contains a "bend" and a control handle. The bend looks like a zigzag. A line used as a connector cannot have dynamic glue.

To convert dynamic glue back to static glue, follow the above procedure, but drag the end of the connector to a connection point. In this case, a heavy red square surrounds just the connection point, not the entire shape.

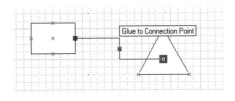

 Note: This procedure differs from earlier versions of Visio, where you held down the **Ctrl** key while dragging the end of the connector to a different connection point.

The printed documentation for Visio 2000 no longer refers to static and dynamic, calling them "point-to-point" and "shape-to-shape," respectively. Visio's online and programming documentation, however, continues to refer to static and dynamic.

Variations on Connectors

Visio comes with many dozens of connectors. Some are included with industry-specific stencils, such as network cabling. Others are general-purpose connectors. The Connectors stencil in the Visio Extras folder holds close to 80 different connectors.

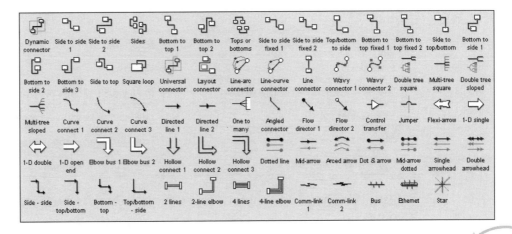

Earlier, I hinted that any shape in Visio could be a connector, provided it is a 1D shape. You turn a 2D shape into a 1D shape with the Behavior dialog box, and vice versa:

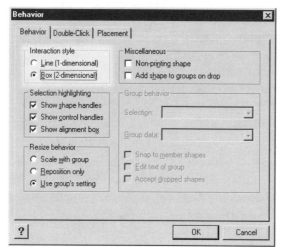

▶ Select the shape.

▶ From the File menu, select **Format | Behavior**.

▶ In the Interaction style section, click the radio button next to either **Line (1-dimensional)** or **Box (2-dimensional)**.

▶ Click **OK**.

Notice that the selection handles have changed. In summary:

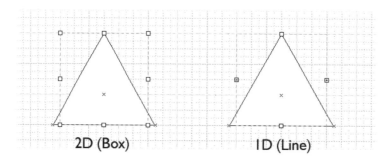

2D (Box)   ID (Line)

2D Shape	I D Shape
6 handles	4 handles
Top handle stretches relative to base	Top handle stretches relative to base
Side handles stretch	Side handles stretch and rotate
Side handles are not connectors	Side handles are connectors
Corner handles resize	Has no corner handles

Just like there are a couple of types of glue, there is more than one kind of connector:

Connector: A 1D shape with static glue.

Dynamic connector: A 1D shape with a bend and dynamic glue.

Routable connector: A dynamic connector that routes around *placeable* shapes (these are shapes that Visio will route connectors around).

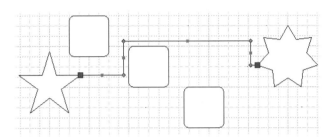

When the routable connector encounters a placeable shape between the two shapes it connects, it moves around the shape, rather than crossing through it. To make a 2D shape placeable:

▸ Select the shape.
▸ From the menu, select **Format | Behavior**.
▸ Select the **Placement** tab.
▸ In the Placement Behavior section, select **Layout And Route Around**.
▸ Click **OK**.

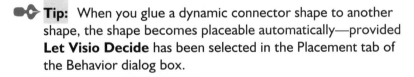

Tip: When you glue a dynamic connector shape to another shape, the shape becomes placeable automatically—provided **Let Visio Decide** has been selected in the Placement tab of the Behavior dialog box.

Creating Connections

There are three ways to connect shapes:

Method 1. Select the **Connector** tool button, then drag shapes from the stencil to the page. The shapes are automatically connected.

Method 2. Drag shapes to the page. Then use the **Connector** tool to manually connect the shapes.

Method 3. Select **Tools | Connect Shapes** to automatically place connections between selected shapes.

There is a fourth method that is not covered in this book. You can create a text file, a spreadsheet, or a database file that specifies the shapes and their connections. The file is imported into Visio, which creates the drawing, complete with connected shapes. See *Learn Visio 2000 for the Advanced User* for more information on this method.

Procedures

Before presenting the general procedures for using the Connector tool, it is helpful to know about the buttons and shortcut keys. These are:

Function	Keys	Menu	Toolbar Icon
Connector Tool	Ctrl+3	...	
Connect Shapes	Ctrl+K	Tools | Connect Shapes	...
Connection Point Tool	Ctrl+Shift+1	...	
Toggle display of connection points	Alt+VC	View | Connection Points	...

Connecting Shapes Automatically During Dragging

Use the following procedure to automatically connect shapes as you drag them onto the page:

1. Select the **Connector** tool. Notice that the cursor changes to a black arrow with a zigzag connector near it.
2. Drag a shape from the stencil to the page.
3. Drag another shape from the stencil to the page.
4. Notice that Visio draws a connector between the first and second shape.
5. As you drag additional shapes to the page, Visio connects them in sequential order: the shape dragged onto the drawing page connects to the currently selected shape.

Connecting Existing Shapes Automatically

Use the following procedure to automatically connect shapes that are already on the page:

1. Press **Ctrl+A** to select everything on the page.

2. Select **Tools | Connect Shapes**. Notice that Visio draws a connector between the shapes approximately in the order that you placed them in the drawing.

3. You may need to move some of the shapes to straighten out the connectors and make them look more pleasing. Notice how the connectors stick to the shapes as you move them around. This is one of Visio's most powerful features.

Tip: Visio connects shapes automatically in the order you placed the shapes. If you plan to use the automatic connection feature, think ahead about shape placement; otherwise you may end up with spaghetti-like connections.

Connecting Shapes Automatically

Use the following procedure to automatically connect shapes already on the page:

1. Hold down the **Shift** key and select the shapes you want to connect in the order you want to connect them.

2. Select **Tools | Connect Shapes**.

3. Notice that Visio draws a connector between the shapes.

Connecting Shapes Manually

Use the following procedure to connect shapes:

1. Select the **Connector** tool.

2. Click on a shape's connection point (the small blue x).

3. Drag the connector to another shape's connection point. Notice that the connector's endpoints are red squares; this tells you the endpoint successfully connected to a connection point. If the square is green, the endpoint is not connected to a connection point.

Adding a Connection Point

Use the following procedure to add a connection point to a shape:

1. Select the **Connection Point** tool from the **Standard** toolbar.

2. Select the shape, and then move the cursor to the location you want the connection point.

3. Hold down the **Ctrl** key, then click. Notice the magenta (pink) x; this is the new connection point.

Hands-On Activity

In this activity, you use the functions of the connection tools. Begin by starting Visio, then open a new document using the Network template supplied with Visio.

1. Select the **Connector** tool ⬚ button.

2. Drag the **Desktop PC** shape from the **Basic Network Shapes** stencil to the upper-left area of the page.

3. Drag the **Server/Tower** shape from the stencil to the center area of the page. Notice that Visio draws a connector between the first and second shape.

4. Drag the **Workstation** shape to the lower-right area of the page. Notice that Visio draws a second connector between the second and third shape.

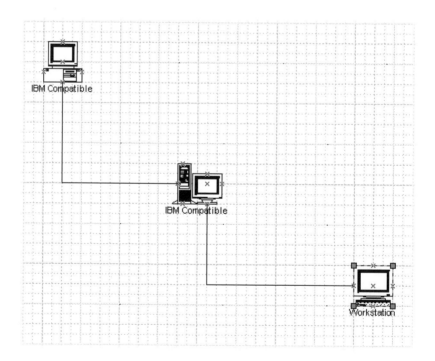

5. Select the **Pointer** tool ⬏ button on the toolbar.

6. Drag the **Macintosh** shape (aka **Mac II**) to the lower-left area of the page.

7. Drag the **Mac Classic** shape to the upper-right area of the page. Notice that Visio no longer connects the shapes.

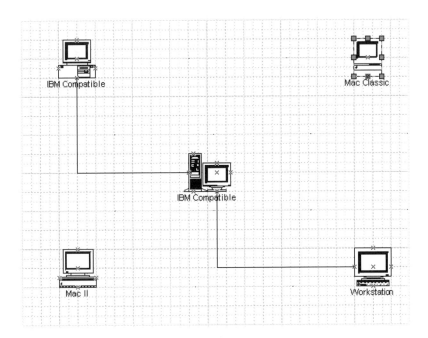

8. Press the **Connector** tool button on the toolbar.
9. Click a connection point (small blue **x**) on the **Mac II** shape.
10. Hold down the mouse button.
11. Drag the connector to a connection point on the **Server/Tower** shape.
12. Release the mouse button. Notice that Visio connects the two shapes and that a pair of red squares appear at the connection points.
13. Press the **Pointer** tool button.
14. Select the **Mac Classic** shape. Notice that Visio surrounds the selected shape with green squares, which acknowledge the selection.
15. Hold the **Shift** key and select the **Server/Tower** shape. Notice that Visio surrounds the selected shape with cyan (light blue) squares, which acknowledges the addition to the selection.
16. Select **Tools | Connect Shapes**.
17. Notice that Visio automatically connects the two shapes.

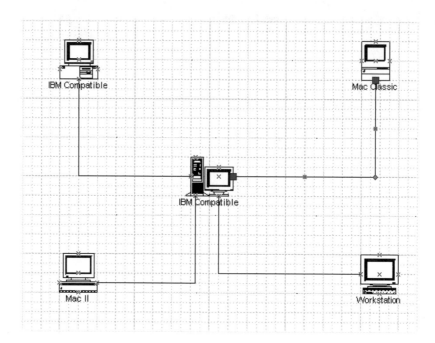

18. Press **Alt+F4** to exit Visio.

This completes the hands-on activity for connecting shapes.

Cutting, Copying, and Pasting

Edit | Cut
  Copy
  Paste
  Paste Special
  Paste Hyperlink

Uses

The **Cut**, **Copy**, and **Paste** selections of the **Edit** menu are used to move shapes and text from one location to another. As with all software running under Windows, nearly any object can be copied and pasted between applications. For example, an Excel spreadsheet can be pasted into a Visio drawing. A Visio drawing can be pasted into a Word document or into PowerPoint, as shown on the next page.

> **In this chapter you'll learn about:**
> ✓ **Cutting text and graphic objects**
> ✓ **Copying text and graphic objects**
> ✓ **Pasting text and graphic objects**
> ✓ **The Paste Special command**

Tip: A Visio 2000 drawing automatically picks up the color scheme of a PowerPoint slide. From within PowerPoint 95, 97, or 2000, select **New Slide** from the **Common Tasks** toolbar, then select the **Object** slide (you may need to scroll down to find this slide). Double-click the icon indicated by the slide; Visio appears in the slide.

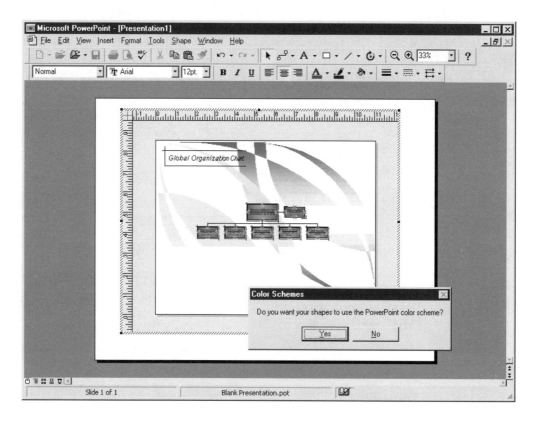

The terms *cut* and *paste* come from a time when a newspaper was put together by manually cutting strips of text and pasting them into columns to fit the pages. Today, with computers, it is more common to copy, rather than cut.

The **Cut** command removes the object from the document; this is like deleting the object. The **Copy** command makes a copy of the object; the original object remains in place. (Do not confuse the Copy command with the **Duplicate** command: while Copy can be used for duplication, Duplicate does not send a copy to the Clipboard.) When you use the Cut and Copy commands, Windows moves the object to the Clipboard, a temporary holding area. The next time you use the Cut or Copy command, the new object replaces the previous one being stored in the Clipboard.

The **Paste** command copies the object from the Clipboard and places it in the document. You can use the Paste command several times in a row to paste the same object several times into one or more documents. To control the format of the object that is pasted in your document, use the **Paste Special** command, which displays a dialog box that lets you select a format. In contrast, the Paste command pastes the first format listed in the Paste Special dialog box.

Paste Special sometimes lets you link the object back to its source. This makes it easier to update the object. See Module 28 "Inserting Objects" for more about linking.

 Tip: Use Paste Special's **ANSI Text** option when you want Visio's text formatting to override the source document's formatting.

The **Paste as Hyperlink** option only works when text is in the Clipboard. This command pastes the text as a hyperlink in the Visio document. See Module 36 "Creating a Web Document" for more about hyperlinks.

Procedures

Before presenting the general procedures for cutting, copying, and pasting text and graphic objects, it is helpful to know about the shortcut keys. These are:

Function	Keys	Menu	Toolbar Icon
Cut	Ctrl+X	Edit | Cut	✂
Copy	Ctrl+C	Edit | Copy	🗐
Paste	Ctrl+V	Edit | Paste	📋
Paste Special	Alt+ES	Edit | Paste Special	...
Paste as Hyperlink	Alt+EH	Edit | Paste as Hyperlink	...

Cutting Text and Graphic Objects

Use the following procedure to cut an object to the Clipboard:

1. Select a shape by clicking on it so that green square handles appear on a green, dotted frame.
2. Select **Edit | Cut** (or press **Ctrl+X**) to remove the selected shape from the page and place it in the Clipboard.

Copying Text and Graphic Objects

Use the following procedure to copy an object to the Clipboard:

1. Select a shape by clicking on it.
2. Select **Edit | Copy** (or press **Ctrl+C**) to copy the selected shape and place it in the Clipboard.

Pasting Text and Graphic Objects

Use the following procedure to paste an object onto the drawing page:

1. Select **Edit | Paste** (or press **Ctrl+V**) to paste whatever is in the Clipboard onto the page.
2. If an object is in the Clipboard (from a previous cut or copy operation), it is pasted in the center of the page.
3. Drag the object into place and resize, if necessary.

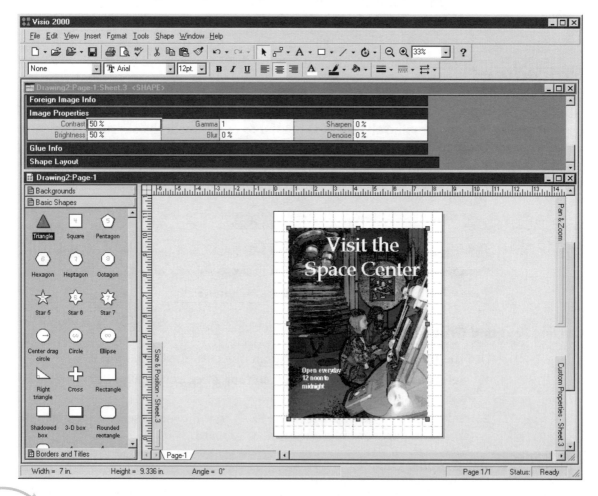

Tip: After pasting a raster image in the drawing, you can adjust the image (the image must be pasted as a bitmap, not a picture). Visio 2000, however, does not make this easy. Here are the steps:

1. Select the raster image.
2. From the menu, select **Window | Show ShapeSheet**. Notice that a new window opens.
3. Scroll down the window until you reach the section titled Image Properties. Notice the six image parameters that can be adjusted:

Image Properties					
Contrast	50 %	Gamma	1	Sharpen	0 %
Brightness	50 %	Blur	0 %	Denoise	0 %

Contrast increases the contrast—the difference between dark and light areas—when the value is above 50%, and decreases the contrast when below 50% (default = 50%).

Brightness darkens the image when the value is less than 50%, and brightens the image when above 50% (default = 50%).

Gamma makes the image brighter while leaving darks dark when the value is above 1 (default = 1).

Blur makes the image appear softer (default = 0%; maximum = 100%).

Sharpen makes the image appear sharper—less blurry. The effect is created by increasing the contrast of adjacent pixels (default = 0%; maximum = 100%).

Denoise removes "noise," which consists of pixels with randomly distributed color levels (default = 0%).

4. To change a value, click the value and type a new value. Notice the change to the raster image.
5. To close the ShapeSheet window, click the x (Close) button on the ShapeSheet's title bar.

Paste Special

Use the following procedure to control the paste format of an object:

1. Select **Edit | Paste Special**. Notice that Visio displays the Paste Special dialog box.

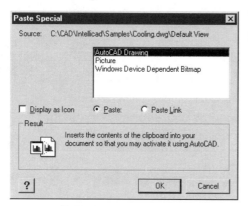

The Paste Special dialog box contains the following options:

▶ **Paste** pastes the object without linking.

▶ **Paste Link** pastes the object with a link back to the source application. If the source application does not allow linking, the **Paste Link** radio button is grayed out.

▶ The formats available in the Clipboard are displayed in the list box.

▶ **Display as Icon** pastes the object as an icon. Selecting this option displays a default icon, along with the **Change Icon** button to let you select another icon.

3. Select a format from the list box. When an object is available in several different formats, it may look different, depending on the format you select. When you paste a Visio object in a non-Visio format, the object loses all its intelligence, such as layers, connection points, and custom properties.

4. Click **OK**. Notice the object is pasted in the center of the page.

5. Drag the object into place and resize if necessary.

Hands-On Activity

In this activity, you use the cut, copy, and paste functions. Begin by starting Visio, then open the **Basic Network** template file found in the Network Diagram folder.

1. Click the title bar of the **Basic Network Shapes 3D** stencil to make it visible.

2. Drag the **Computer** shape into the drawing. If necessary, zoom in to get a better view.

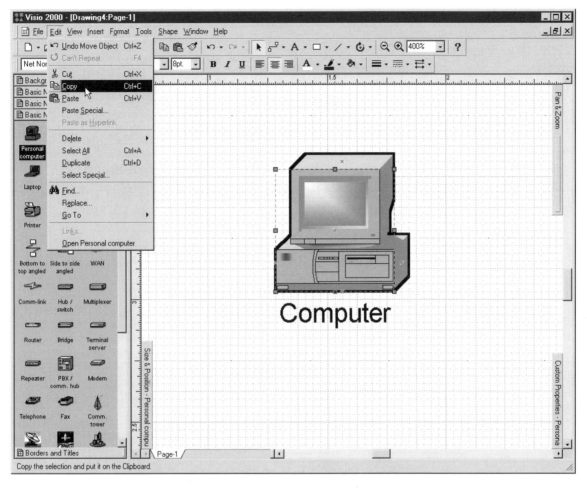

3. Ensure the shape is selected (green handle squares surround it), then press **Ctrl+C** to copy the shape to the Clipboard. Or, click the **Copy** icon from the toolbar. Or, right-click and select **Copy** from the shortcut menu.

4. Select **Insert | Page**, and click **OK** to create a new page.

5. Press **Ctrl+V** to paste the copied shape. Notice that Visio places the shape in the center of the page. Notice, also, that the shape retains its intelligence. For example, the connection points (small blue x's) are present.

6. Select **Edit | Paste Special**. Notice the Paste Special dialog box with several format options:

▶ **Visio 2000 Drawing**: The drawing in Visio 2000 format.

▶ **Visio Drawing Data**: The drawing in a format that can be read by earlier versions of Visio.

▶ **Picture**: A vector format known as Windows Metafile, or WMF for short.

▶ **Picture (Enhanced Metafile)**: A newer version of WMF found in Windows 95, 98, and 2000.

▶ **ANSI Text**: The text portion of the shape.

8. Select **Picture** and click **OK**. Notice that Visio places the graphic object in the center of the page. Notice, too, that the computer pasted as a picture lacks the connection points.

9. Select **Edit | Paste Special**.

10. This time select **ANSI Text** and click **OK**. Notice that Visio pastes the word "Computer" in the center of the drawing.

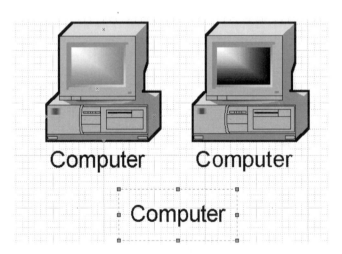

11. Press **Alt+F4** to exit Visio.

This completes the hands-on activity for cut, copy, and paste. These functions are identical in all Windows applications. Only the available formats in the Paste Special dialog box differ.

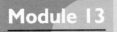
Formatting Shapes

Format | Line
          Corners
          Fill
          Shadow

Uses

In this chapter you'll learn about:

✓ **Formatting lines**

✓ **Formatting areas**

✓ **Shadow casting**

Most of Visio's shapes are plain black-and-white. But they don't need to be! Visio lets you change the look of a shape, such as its color and the thickness of its lines. Making these changes to a shape is called *formatting* the shape.

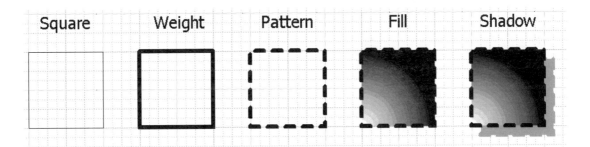

| Square | Weight | Pattern | Fill | Shadow |

Formatting Lines

You can change the look of the lines that make up all shapes. *Line* is a generic term applying not only to lines but also circles, arcs, curves, rectangles, and ellipses. The **Format | Line** command lets you select from:

▸ **Line pattern**: patterns of dashes and dots.

0 (none)	1	2
3	4	5
6	7	8
9	10	11
12	13	14
15	16	17
18	19	20
21	22	23

▶ **Line weight**: varying widths of line.

1

▶ **Color**: shades of gray ranging from black to white, plus the 16.7 million colors in the Windows palette.

3

5

▶ **End caps**: round or square ends to the line.

9

13

17

▶ **Line ends**: including arrowheads in seven sizes ranging from Very Small to Colossal.

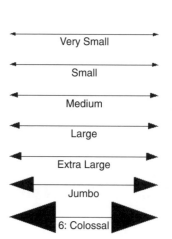

Very Small

Small

Medium

Large

Extra Large

Jumbo

6: Colossal

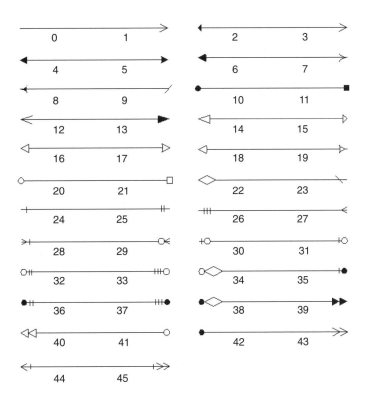

When two lines (or arcs or curves) meet, the **Format | Corners** command lets you select from seven different radii of rounded corners, as well as the default (no rounding—a sharp corner), and a custom radius.

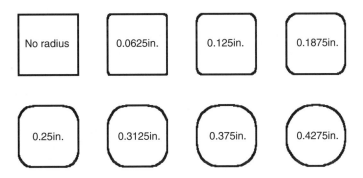

Formatting Areas

Areas are formed by lines, circles, arcs, curves, rectangles, and ellipses. Usually, these are empty or filled with white color. The **Format | Fill** command lets you select from patterns of lines and dots, and colors and shades of gray, as well as gradient fills for the foreground and background. *Foreground* refers to the lines and dots that make up the pattern, while *background* refers to the underlying area.

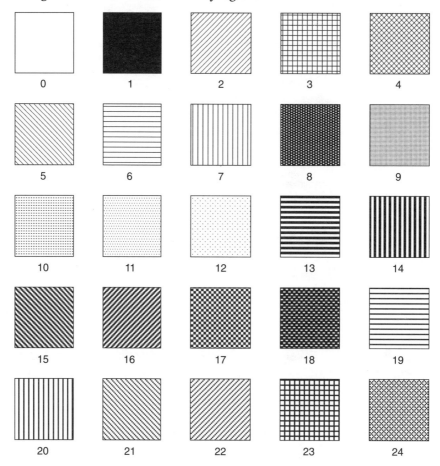

Tip: Visio 2000 includes preset color schemes, which apply colors to nearly all shapes in the entire drawing. This feature is called *single-click formatting*. It does not, however, change other formatting, such as line weights, line ends, line patterns, and end caps.

Specifically, the schemes apply to underlying styles; any shape formatted with styles based on these underlying styles will change. The scheme applies color changes to:

Line color: Changes the color of all lines in the drawing.

Text color: Changes the color of all text in the drawing.

Foreground color: Changes the color used by solid fills and the foreground color of pattern fills.

Background color: Changes the background color of pattern fills.

Shadow color: Changes the color of shadows in the drawing.

From the menu, select **Tools | Macros | Visio Extras | Color Schemes**. From the Color Schemes dialog box, select a named scheme. Click the **Apply** button to see the effect on your drawing. To create your own color scheme, click **New**. This brings up the Color Scheme Details dialog, in which you can make your changes.

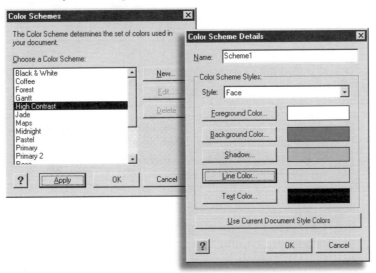

Shadow Casting

Every object—whether a shape, a block of text, or a pasted object—can cast a shadow in a Visio drawing. By default, no shadow is cast; adding the shadow helps make the object stand out on the page from other objects. The **Format | Shadow** command lets you select a pattern and color for the shadow. Be careful, though; some printers print the shadow as black, no matter how you format it.

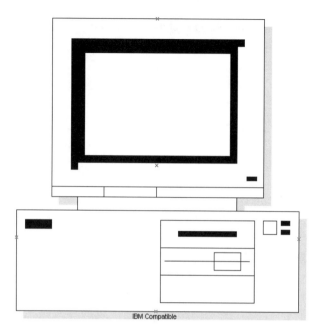

IBM Compatible

Tip: You can create a more interesting shadow effect by using a graduated fill pattern, such as #34, along with foreground color black and background color light gray.

The size and direction of the shadow is specified, strangely enough, in the Page Properties tab of the Page Setup dialog box (and not the Shadow dialog box). From the menu, select **File | Page Setup**. In the Page Properties tab, change the values in the Shape shadow offset fields. To make the shadow cast up and to the left, use negative values, such as –0.25 in. The same shadow offset values apply to all shapes on the page.

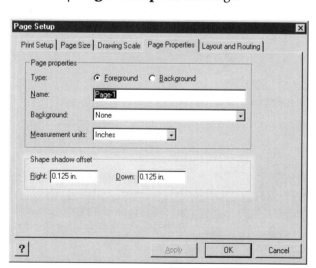

Procedures

Before presenting the general procedures for formatting, it is helpful to know about the shortcut keys. These are:

Function	Keys	Menu	Toolbar Icon
Line Color	Alt+FL	Format | Line	
Line Ends	Alt+FL	Format | Line	
Line Pattern	Alt+FL	Format | Line	
Line Weight	Alt+FL	Format | Line	
Format Corners	Alt+FC	Format | Corners	
Fill Pattern	F3	Format | Fill	
Fill Color	Alt+FF	Format | Fill	
Format Shadow	Alt+FW	Format | Shadow	

Notice that the **Format | Line** menu selection also displays **Corner** options. In the same way, the **Format | Fill** selection displays **Shadow** options.

Formatting Lines

Use the following procedure to format the look of lines, arcs, curves, rectangles, and ellipses:

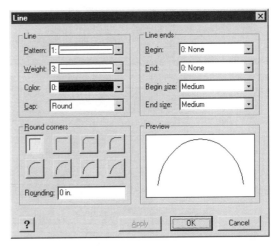

1. Select the shape.

2. Select **Format | Line**. Notice that Visio displays the Line dialog box.

3. To change the line pattern, click on the **Pattern** list box and select one of the patterns (also known as linetypes in CAD software). When you select pattern **None**, the line becomes invisible. Notice that as you make selections from this dialog box, the Preview window displays the effect of the change on an arc.

4. To see the effect of the changes without exiting the dialog box, click **Apply**. You may need to move the dialog box aside to see the affected shapes.

5. To change the width of the lines, click the **Weight** list box and select one of the widths ranging from 1 to 17:

Weight	Points	Inches	Millimeters
1	0.24pt	0.0033"	0.085mm
3	0.72pt	0.0100"	0.254mm
13	3.12pt	0.4333"	1.10mm
17	4.08pt	0.5667"	1.44mm

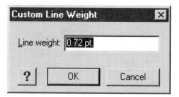

6. To choose a line weight other than the pre-programmed weights, select **Custom** from the Weight list box. Notice that Visio displays the Custom Line Weight dialog box.

7. Type a number and follow it with a unit, such as 10 in. Visio allows the following units:

Unit	Meaning
"	inch
in	inch
'	foot
ft	foot
mi	mile
mm	millimeter; 25.4mm = 1"
cm	centimeter
m	meter
pt	point; 72.72 points = 1"
p	pica; 6 picas = 1"

8. To change the color of the shape's lines, click the **Color** list box and select one of the colors.

9. If you prefer a color that is not shown, select **Custom**. Notice that Visio displays the standard Windows Edit Color dialog box.

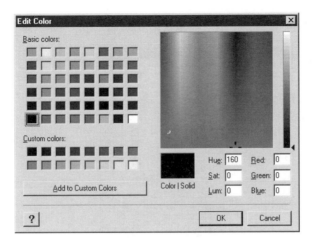

10. Select one of the Basic colors or one of the 16.7 million custom colors. Click **OK** to dismiss the Edit Color dialog box.

11. To change the end cap, click the **Cap** list box and select **Round** or **Square**. Notice the difference between round and square end caps. In most cases, the difference between rounded and square corners is unnoticeable, unless applied to very wide lines or seen at a very high zoom level.

12. To change the line ends (also known as arrowheads), click the **Begin** list box to select the beginning of the line.

13. Visio allows you to have a different line end and a different size for each end of the line. Click the **End** list box to select the ending of the line.

14. Click the **Begin size** and **End size** list boxes to select the size of the line end.

15. To round the corners of rectangles, or two or more lines, arcs, and curves, select a corner radius in the Round corners area.

16. As an alternative, you can specify the radius by typing a value in the **Rounding** field.

17. Click **Apply** to make the change without dismissing the dialog box.

18. Click **OK** to make the changes and dismiss the dialog box.

Applying a Fill Color and Pattern

Use the following procedure to change the fill of rectangles, circles, and ellipses, or the area created by lines, arcs, and curves:

1. Select the shape.

2. Select **Format | Fill**. Notice that Visio displays the Fill dialog box.

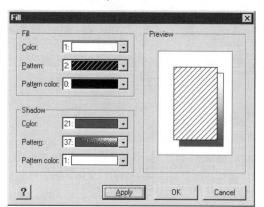

3. To change the pattern, click on the **Pattern** list box and select one of the patterns. Notice that pattern #0 is None, which means the object is transparent.

4. To change the color of the pattern lines and dots, click the **Color** (called Foreground in earlier versions of Visio) list box and select one of the colors. Or, select Custom to choose a color from the 16.7 million available in Windows.

5. To change the color underneath the pattern of lines and dots, click the **Pattern color** (called Background in earlier versions of Visio) list box and select a color. Notice that Visio displays the changes you make in the Preview box.

Tip: There is a difference between *no* fill and *white* solid fill: the grid lines show through the no-fill rectangle.

---

6. To give the shape a shadow, select a pattern from the **Pattern** list box.

7. To change the color of the shadow's pattern, click the **Color** list box and select one of the colors. Or, select Custom to choose a color from the colors available in Windows.

8. To change the color underneath the shadow pattern, click the **Pattern color** list box and select one of the colors.

9. Click **Apply** to make the change without dismissing the dialog box.

10. Click **OK** to make the changes and dismiss the dialog box.

Tip: If a shape is not filled, the shadow "shows through." You cannot select a shape by clicking on its shadow.

Quick Formatting

To quickly format a shape, Visio provides a number of buttons that cycle though the most common formats. You find these on two toolbars: Format and Format Shape.

1. Select one or more shapes.

2. On the Format toolbar, click the arrow next to the Line Color button. Notice that Visio displays a small palette of colors.

3. Select a color. Notice that the color becomes the default for the Line Color button. If you want other shapes to be the same color, you need only to select the shape, then click the **Line Color** button; Visio applies the color to the shape.

4. Alternatively, select **No Line** to make the object invisible or select **More Line Colors** to display the Line dialog box.

5. A similar procedure works for changing other properties. Specifically:

   ▶ The Format toolbar changes line color, fill color, line weight, line patterns, line ends, and text.

   ▶ The Format Shape toolbar changes corner rounding, fill pattern, and shadow color, and applies styles.

135

Hands-On Activity

In this activity, you use the shape formatting functions. Begin by starting Visio. Then open the **Charts and Graphs** solution found in the **Forms and Charts** folder. Click the title bar of the **Borders and Titles** stencil to make it current.

1. Drag the **Title block notepad** shape into the drawing from the Borders and Titles stencil.

2. Adjust the zoom level to clearly see the shape.

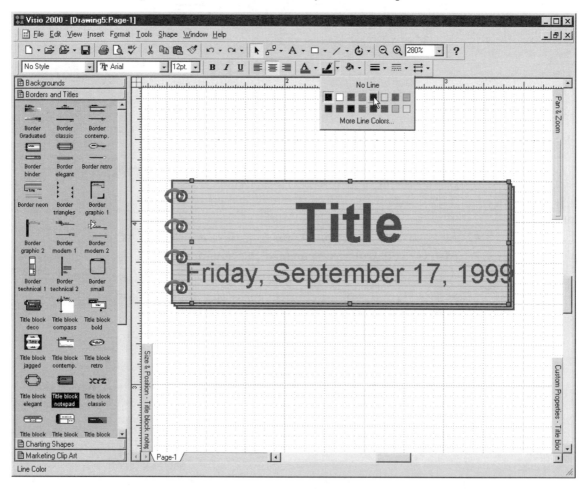

3. Click the arrow next to the Line Color button. Notice the color palette.

4. Select the blue color square. Notice that the shape's lines turn blue.

5. Click the arrow next to the Line Weight button. Notice the palette of line weights.

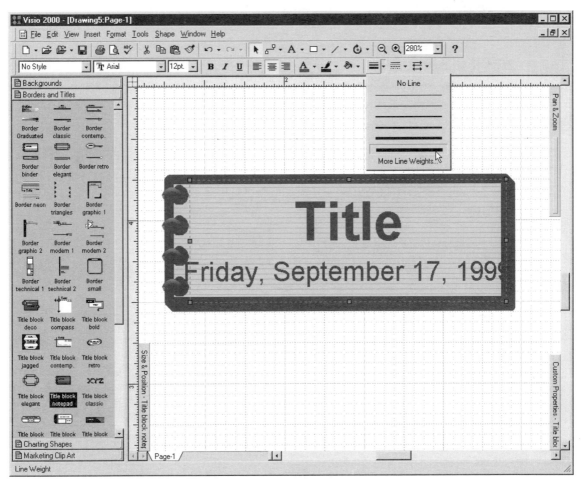

6. Select the widest line weight. Notice the shape's line becomes thicker.

7. Press **Alt+F4** to exit Visio. Click **No** in response to the Save Changes dialog box.

This completes the hands-on activity for formatting shapes in the drawing.

Formatting Text

Format | Text
Shape | Rotate Text

Uses

The **Text** formatting function, found on the **Format** menu, changes the look of text in a Visio drawing. The command displays a tabbed dialog box that lets you change the font, size, case, position, language, style, horizontal and vertical alignment, margins, text and background color, tab spacing, and bullet style. As you can see from that list, there are many ways to format text!

In this chapter you'll learn about:

- ✓ *Text blocks*
- ✓ *The text formatting bar*
- ✓ *Selecting all text in a shape*
- ✓ *Selecting a portion of the text*
- ✓ *Changing the font*
- ✓ *Changing the justification of a paragraph*
- ✓ *Changing the vertical alignment*
- ✓ *Setting tabs*
- ✓ *Adding bullets to text*

 Note: Unlike a word processor, text in a Visio drawing does not flow onto the next page. Instead, the text spills off the page and onto the pasteboard (the light blue area surrounding the page).

Text Blocks

In Visio, text is never "on its own"; instead, Visio works with text blocks, which can contain a single word or many paragraphs. A *text block* is all the text within a single alignment box. An *alignment box* is the rectangle that outlines all shapes when you click the shape. The following illustration shows two text blocks:

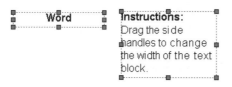

You can specify the size of the text block before entering the text. Use the **Text Block** tool (press **Ctrl+Shift+4**) to create a text block of a specific size.

Because text is in a block, you can position the text within the block. This is called *alignment*. Visio provides three types of alignment: top, middle, and bottom. The middle alignment is the default, which means the text is centered vertically in the text block.

 Tip: To format all text in a block, you do not need to highlight it. When you select only a portion of a block of text, the changes apply to the selected portion. This allows you to apply a different look to different parts of the text.

To quickly switch between selection mode and text editing mode, press function key **F2**.

You can format:

▶ All text on the page by selecting everything with **Ctrl+A**.

▶ All text in a block by selecting the block or the shape containing the block.

▶ Some of the text in the block by highlighting text within the block.

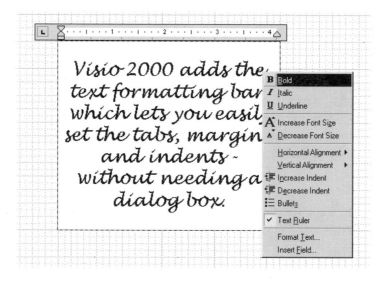

Text Format Bar

Visio 2000 adds the Text Ruler, which lets you easily set the tabs and indents—without needing a dialog box. Right-click a shape when you're in the text mode, and then choose Text Ruler.

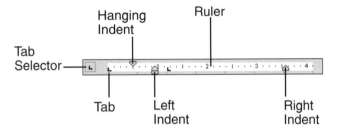

Click the **Tab Selector** button to select the type of tab: left, right, center, or decimal. To place a tab, simply click the cursor on the ruler; to move a tab, drag the tab marker to the new location. Changing indents is similar: drag the indent marker to the required position.

Procedures

Before presenting the general procedures for formatting text, it is helpful to know about the shortcut keys. (The default values are shown in parentheses.) Note that Visio 2000 distributes the text formatting functions among two toolbars: **Format** and **Format Text**.

Function	Keys	Menu	Toolbar Icon
Selection-Text edit toggle	F2	...	...
Format Font:	F11	Format | Text | Font	...
Select Font Name (Arial)	...	...	T̄ Arial
Font Size (8 pt)	...	...	12pt.
Increase Font Size	...	...	A˙
Decrease Font Size	...	...	A˅
Bold	Ctrl+Shift+B	...	**B**
Italic	Ctrl+Shift+I	...	*I*
<u>Underline</u>	Ctrl+Shift+U	...	U̲
SMALL CAPS	Ctrl+Shift+Y	...	ABC

Function	Keys	Menu	Toolbar Icon
Sub$_{script}$	Ctrl+Shift+X	...	x₂
Super^{script}	Ctrl+Shift+Z	...	x²
Font Color	...	...	A ▾
Format Paragraph:	Shift+F11	Format | Text | Paragraph	...
Left Justify	...	...	≣
Center Justify (default)	...	...	≣
Right Justify	...	...	≣
Full Justification	...	...	...
Increase Indentation	...	...	🔧
Decrease Indentation	...	...	🔧
Increase Paragraph Spacing	...	...	🔧
Decrease Paragraph Spacing	...	...	🔧
Format Text Block	Alt+FT	Format | Text | Text Block	...
Top Alignment	...	...	≣
Middle Alignment (default)	...	...	≣
Bottom Alignment	...	...	≣
Set Tabs	Ctrl+F11	Format | Text | Tabs	...
Select Bullet	Alt+FT	Format | Text | Bullet	≔
Rotate Text	Shift+Ctrl+4	Shape | Rotate Text	Text Block Tool (Shift+Ctrl+4)

▲ **Note:** You may have noticed that Visio does not use **Ctrl+B** to apply boldfacing to text, as is specified by the Microsoft Office standard. Visio uses **Ctrl+B** to move a selected shape to the background. Using **Ctrl+Shift+B** to boldface text comes from the Macintosh environment. Other non-conforming shortcuts include **Ctrl+I** (100% view) and **Ctrl+U** (ungroup).

Selecting All Text in a Shape

Use the following procedure to select text:

1. Click the shape containing text.

2. Press function key **F2**. Notice that Visio highlights the text by displaying it in reversed color. As an alternative, you can double-click the shape to select the text; however, double-click behavior can be changed, as described in Module 32 "Double-clicking the Mouse Button," and so double-clicking might not select the text.

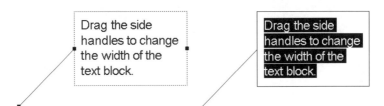

Selecting a Portion of the Text

To format part of a text block (such as a single word), use the following procedure:

1. Select the shape.
2. Press **F2**. Notice that Visio highlights all of the text.
3. Drag the cursor over the characters you want to select.

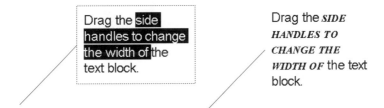

Changing the Font

Use the following procedure to change the look of the text font:

1. Select the text.
2. Select **Format | Text**. Select the **Font** tab.
3. Click the **Font** list box to change the font (default = Arial). Notice that the list displays the names of fonts installed on your computer. A "TT" next to a font name indicates it is a TrueType font. A printer symbol means the font is installed on the printer.
4. Select a font name. If necessary, scroll down the list.
5. Click **Apply** to see the font change without leaving the dialog box.

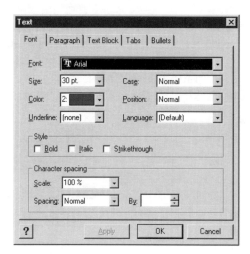

6. To change the size of the text, click the **Size** list box. The default is 8 pt. The size is measured in *pt* (short for "point"), where one point equals 1/72" or 72 points = 1 inch.

7. Select a font size. For half-inch tall text, select 36 pt.

8. To change the color of the text, click the **Color** list box. The default is black. To change the background color of the text, go to the **Text Block** tab of this dialog box.

9. Select a color under **Text Background**. You select from 12 colors and 12 shades of gray. Alternatively, select **Custom** to display the Windows standard Edit Color dialog box.

10. Click the **Font** tab. You can select <u>single</u> or <u>double</u> underlining for the text. Make your selection from the **Underline** list box.

11. *Case* refers to whether text is all UPPERCASE or Initial Capitals (the first letter of every word is capitalized), which is excellent for titles. To change the case of the text, click the **Case** list box.

12. Select **Normal**, **All Caps**, **Initial Caps**, or **Small Caps**.

13. *Position* moves the selected text higher (superscript) or lower (subscript), which is often used for footnotes and formulae. To change the position of the text, click the **Position** list box.

> Normal text.
> ALL UPPERCASE.
> Initial Caps.

14. Select **Normal**, **Super-script**, or **Subscript**.

15. To select the language, click the **Language** list box.

16. Select a language name. This selection has no effect on the text until you use Visio's dictionary to check the spelling.

17. To change the look of the text, select the **Style** check boxes. You may select any combination of the following: **bold**, *italic*, and ~~strikethrough~~.

18. To change the spacing between characters, make your selections from the **Scale** and **Spacing** list boxes. Selecting a value larger than 100% spreads letters apart, while a smaller value squeezes the characters together.

19. Click **Apply** to see the format changes without leaving the dialog box.

20. Click **OK** to dismiss the dialog box.

Normal text

Text with ^{superscript} $x^2+y^2=z^2$

Text with $_{subscript}$ H_2O

Normal text.

Boldface text.

Italicized text.

Underlined text.

SMALL CAPS TEXT.

Combination text.

Changing the Justification of a Paragraph

Use the following procedure to change the paragraph formatting of the text block:

1. Select the text.

2. Select **Format | Text**.

3. Select the **Paragraph** tab, which controls the formatting of paragraphs of text.

4. Click the **Horizontal alignment** list box to change the justification, which is sometimes called "paragraph alignment" in other software.

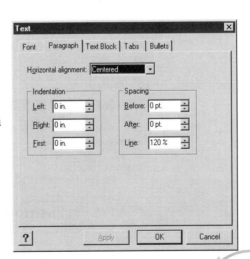

5. Select left, center (the default), right, justify, and force justified. *Force justified* means that the last line of text in the paragraph is forced to fit the width of the paragraph.

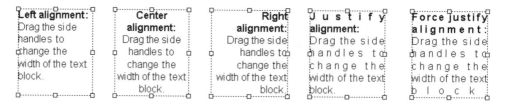

6. To change the left, right, and first line indentation of a paragraph, notice the Indentation section has three text entry boxes.

Indentation specifies how far in the text starts (left) and ends (right) from the margin:

▶ **Left** indentation "pushes" all text rightward from the left margin.

▶ **Right** indentation pushes all text leftward from the right margin.

▶ **First Line** indentation indents the first line. In most cases, you would use the First Line indentation if you want to create the look of a traditional paragraph with the indented first line. To create a *hanging indent*, type a negative number for the First Line indentation.

To set the spacing between paragraphs, or change the spacing between text lines, notice the Spacing section has three text entry boxes. *Spacing* specifies the distance between lines of text.

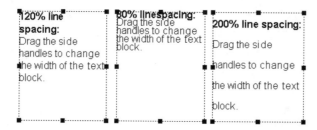

▶ The **Above** spacing increases the distance between the top of the paragraph and the preceding paragraph.

▶ The **Below** spacing increases the distance between the bottom of the paragraph and the following paragraph.

▶ The **Line** spacing sets the distance between lines of text within a paragraph, measured as a percentage of the font size; default = 120%. For example, if the font size is 8 pt, the line spacing is 8 pt * 120% = 9.6 pt, measured from the baseline of one line of text to the baseline of the following line of text.

7. Click **Apply** to see the format changes without leaving the dialog box.

8. Click **OK** to dismiss the dialog box.

Changing the Vertical Alignment

Use the following procedure to change the vertical alignment of a text block (text within its alignment box):

1. Select the text.

2. Select **Format | Text** from the menu bar.

3. Click the **Text Block** tab, which controls the formatting of a text block:

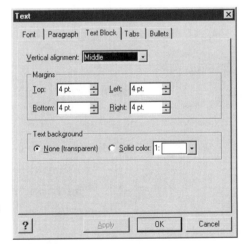

▶ The **Top** alignment pushes the text block to the top of its alignment box.

▶ The **Middle** alignment centers the text block in its alignment box.

▶ The **Bottom** alignment pushes the text block to the bottom of its alignment box.

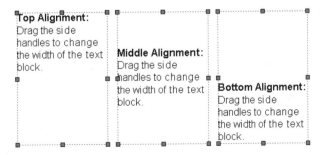

Top Alignment:
Drag the side handles to change the width of the text block.

Middle Alignment:
Drag the side handles to change the width of the text block.

Bottom Alignment:
Drag the side handles to change the width of the text block.

4. The *margin* is the distance between a text block and its alignment box:

   ▶ The **Top** and **Bottom** margins specify the distance between the top (or bottom) of the text block to the alignment box. Type a number to increase the margin distance.

   ▶ The **Left** and **Right** margins specify the distance between the left (or right) of the text block to the alignment box. Type a number to increase the margin distance.

5. To change the color of the alignment box, which appears behind the text:

   ▶ Click **None (transparent)** to eliminate color from the alignment box; this is the default.

   ▶ Alternatively, click **Solid color**, then select a color. The adjacent illustration shows the difference between the two options:

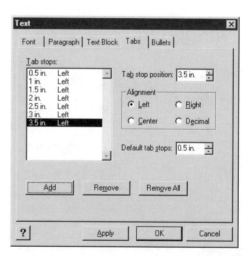

6. Click **Apply** to see the format changes without leaving the dialog box.

7. Click **OK** to dismiss the dialog box.

Setting Tabs

Tabs make it easier to line up columns of text. Press the **Tab** key to move the cursor to the next tab setting. Use the following procedure to set the tab spacing:

1. Select the text.

2. Select **Format | Text**.

3. Click the **Tabs** tab, which controls the tab spacing. Notice that no tabs are initially set.

4. Type a number in the **Tab stop position** text box.

5. Select an alignment from the **Alignment** box: Left (default), Center, Right, or Decimal. The *decimal* tab right-aligns numbers according to the position of their decimal number; it left-aligns text.

6. Click **Add** to set a tab.

7. Click **OK**. Notice the new tab setting in the dialog box.

8. Click **Remove** to erase the tab.

9. Click **Apply** to see the tab changes without leaving the dialog box.

10. Click **OK** to dismiss the dialog box.

Adding Bullets to Text

A *bullet* is a small dot that starts off a paragraph of text. Using bullets can aid the readability of a list of instructions. A bullet can be any symbol, but most commonly is a dot or square.

1. Select the text.

2. Select **Format | Text**.

3. Click the **Bullets** tab. Notice that the dialog box displays seven bullet styles, as well as space for a custom bullet.

4. Click on the button with the bullet style of your liking.

5. Click **Apply** to see the tab changes without leaving the dialog box. Notice that a bullet is added to the start of every paragraph.

6. Click **OK** to dismiss the dialog box.

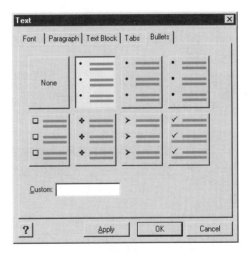

Hands-On Activity

In this activity, you use the text formatting functions. Begin by starting Visio. Then open a new drawing.

1. Right-click the toolbar. From the shortcut menu, select **Format Text**. Notice that Visio displays the Format Text toolbar.

2. Select the **Text** tool from the Standard toolbar.

3. Click anywhere in the page. Notice that Visio zooms in (to 100%) so that you can more easily read the text. Notice, too, the text ruler.

4. Type a sentence, such as **Text in Visio**.

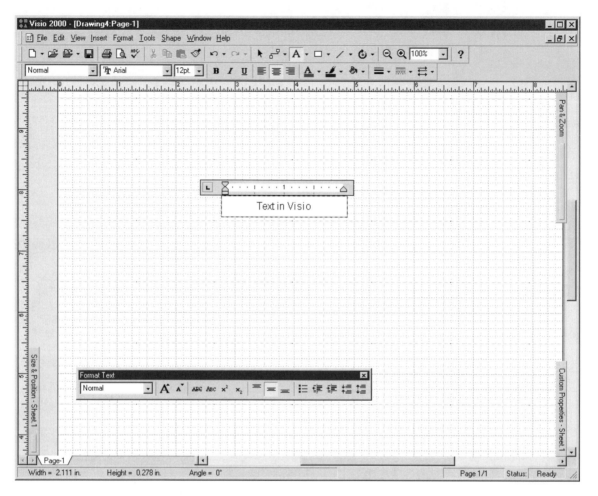

5. On the Format Text toolbar, click the **Increase Font Size** button three times. Notice the font size of all the text increases with each click.

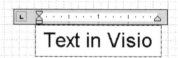

6. Click the **Font Color** button on the Format toolbar. Select the red color square. Notice that all the text turns red.

7. Click the **Bullets** button on the Format Text toolbar. Notice a bullet that prefixes the words.

8. Click the **Bold** button on the Format toolbar. Notice all the text becomes bolder.

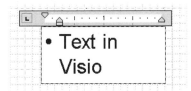

9. Click the **Italic** button. Notice all the text becomes italicized.

10. Click the **Underline** button. Notice all the text becomes underlined.

11. Press **Alt+F4** to exit Visio. Click **No** in response to the Save Changes dialog box.

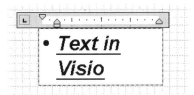

This completes the hands-on activity for formatting text in the drawing.

Creating and Applying Styles

Format | Define Styles
Styles
Format Painter

Uses

The **Style** selection of the **Format** menu lets you apply a uniform format to shapes, called a style. A *style* is a collection of properties saved by name. In Visio, properties are based on text, line, and fill formats. A style is based on the

In this chapter you'll learn about:

✓ *Format Painter*

✓ *Defining a style*

✓ *Applying a style*

✓ *Text style list*

✓ *Line style list*

✓ *Fill style list*

properties defined by the **Define Styles** selection of the **Format** menu.

In Modules 13 "Formatting Shapes" and 14 "Formatting Text," you saw how to apply one style at a time. In this module, you learn how to apply a number of styles at once. The advantages to using a defined style include:

▶ **Faster formatting**: Since the defined style applies all properties at once, it is faster to apply a single style than to apply each property individually. As Modules 13 and 14 illustrate, shapes and text can have as many as 40 different properties.

▶ **Consistent look**: When your company defines its corporate look, using styles ensures all illustrators employ the same text, line, and fill formats.

▶ **Flexibility**: While applying a style can make everything look similar, Visio gives you the option to override the style with local formatting. *Local* is formatting applied directly.

Style definitions are saved with the drawing. Visio includes a number of predefined styles with every template. In addition, you can create your own styles. You apply a style by selecting it from the **Text**, **Line**, and **Fill** style lists or with the Style dialog box. Visio has two aids that help you apply styles quickly:

▸ The **Format Painter** button of the toolbar lets you copy the formatting of one shape to another.

▸ The **Format**, **Format Shape**, and **Format Text** toolbars have lists with the names of styles in the drawing.

The **Format** toolbar lists all styles stored in the drawing; "all" has a drawback, since you can't tell if the style applies to text, lines, fill, or all three. For this reason, the other two formatting toolbars are more useful. The **Format Shape** toolbar has separate lists for line and fill styles; the **Format Text** toolbar has a list for text formats.

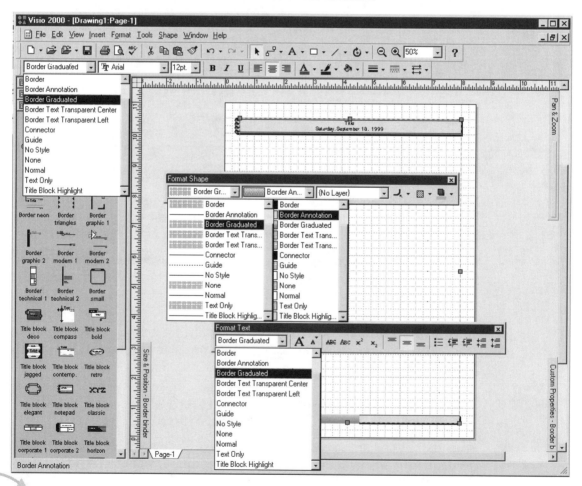

Procedures

Before presenting the general procedures for defining and using styles, it is helpful to know about the shortcut keys and icons. These are:

Function	Keys	Menu	Toolbar Icon
Format Painter	...	...	✐
Define Style	Alt+FD	Format | Define Styles	...
Apply Style	Alt+FS	Format | Style	...

Format Painter

Use the following procedure to copy properties from one shape to another:

1. Select the shape with the style you want copied.

2. Click the **Format Painter** button on the toolbar. Notice that the cursor turns into a paintbrush.

3. Select another shape to apply the style.

> ●← **Tip:** To copy the style to more than one object, double-click the **Format Painter** button.

Defining a Style

Use the following procedure to create a style:

1. (*Optional*) To create a named style based on an existing shape, first select the shape.

2. Select **Format | Define Styles** from the menu bar. Notice that Visio displays the Define Styles dialog box.

3. Every style must have a name, which is how Visio identifies the style. Type a descriptive name in the Style text box. After creating the style, it will appear in the style list boxes on the toolbars.

4. If you want to modify an existing style, first select the style name from the Style list box. The list box shows the names of all styles already defined in the drawing.

5. Decide whether the style will affect text, lines, and/or fills by selecting the **Text**, **Line**, and **Fill** check boxes:

▸ Click **Text** to set the text properties of this style. Notice that Visio displays the Text dialog box. Refer to Module 14 "Formatting Text" for the details of changing text properties.

▸ Click **Line** to set the line properties of this style. Notice that Visio displays the Line dialog box. Refer to Module 13 "Formatting Shapes" for the details of changing line properties.

▸ Click **Fill** to set the fill properties of this style. Notice that Visio displays the Fill dialog box. Refer to Module 13 "Formatting Shapes" for the details of changing fill properties.

6. Decide whether you want this style to preserve or override local formatting. To override local formatting, keep **Preserve local formatting on apply** turned off.

Tip: *Local* formatting is a change that you make manually. For example, you place some text at the default height of 8 points. Then you change the height to 12 points. The change is a *local* format. Whether you preserve or override local formatting depends on the situation: sometimes, you want to keep local formatting; other times you want to override all those changes.

---

7. Click **OK** to exit the dialog box.

Applying a Style

Use the following procedure to apply a style:

1. Select one or more shapes. To select more than one shape, hold down the **Shift** key. To select all shapes on the page, press **Ctrl+A**.

2. Select **Format | Style** from the menu bar. Notice the Style dialog box.

3. Select one or more styles from the three available: **Text style**, **Line style**, and/or **Fill style**. For example, you could select a line and fill style together.

 Note: In earlier versions of Visio, the color of the titles Text style, Line style, and Fill style would change. When you first opened the dialog box, the style titles were black (at their default value) or blue (meaning they been changed at some point); when you changed a style, the title text would turn green. As of Visio 2000, these useful color codes no longer exist.

4. To override local formatting, keep **Preserve local formatting** turned off.

5. Click **Apply** to view the style changes without exiting the dialog box.

6. Click **OK** to exit the dialog box. Notice that the style list boxes on the toolbar update to reflect the selections you made in the Style dialog box.

Text Style List

Use the following procedure to apply a predefined style to text:

1. Select a text block or paragraph in the drawing.

2. Click the **Text Style** list box in the Format Text toolbar.

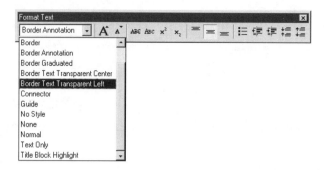

3. Select one of the defined style names.
4. Notice that the text changes to match the style.

Line Style List

Use the following procedure to apply a predefined line style to a shape:

1. Select a shape in the drawing.
2. Click the **Line Style** list box in the Format Shape toolbar.

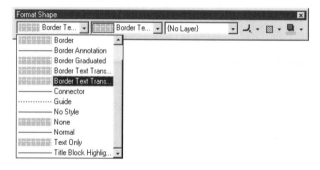

3. Select one of the defined style names.
4. Notice that the shape changes to match the style.

Fill Style List

Use the following procedure to apply a predefined fill style to an area:

1. Select a shape in the drawing.
2. Click the **Fill Style** list box in the Format Shape toolbar.

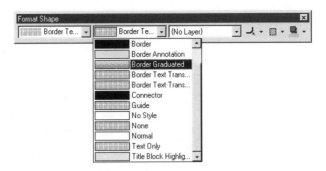

3. Select one of the defined style names.

4. Notice that the fill changes to match the style.

Hands-On Activity

In this activity, you use the text formatting functions. Begin by starting Visio.

1. Open the **Basic Diagram** solution found in the Block Diagram folder.

2. Right-click any toolbar. From the shortcut menu, select **Format Text** and **Format Shape**. Notice that Visio shows the toolbars.

3. Select the **Borders and Titles** stencil (click its title bar to make the stencil visible).

4. Drag the **Border binder** shape onto the page. Notice that Visio automatically fits the shape to the page.

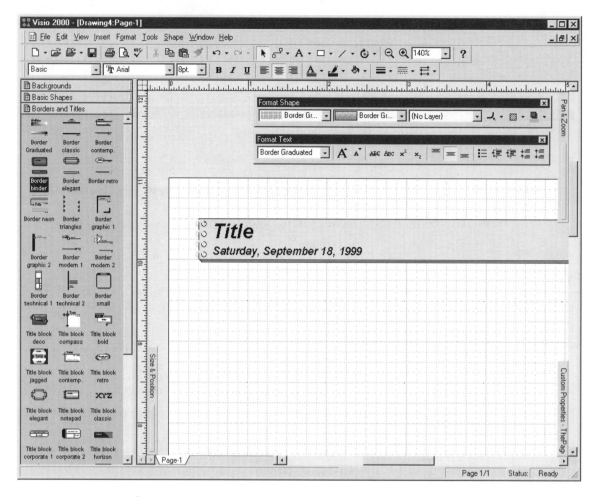

5. If necessary to see it better, zoom in to the top portion of the shape.

6. Select the shape. Notice the style list boxes on the toolbar. All of them read "Border Graduated." This is the name of a predefined style for the text, line, and fill.

7. Click the **Text Style** list box. Notice the long list of style names.

8. Select style **Basic** from the Text Style list box. Notice the warning dialog box Visio displays: "Text style 'Basic' also includes line and fill formatting. Do you want to apply all of the included formatting?"

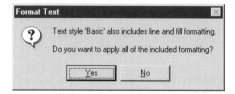

Visio is warning you that the text style also includes style elements for lines and fills. If you click **Yes**, the existing line and fill styles present in the shape will be overridden.

9. Click **Yes**. Notice that the border shape changes its text, lines, and fill.

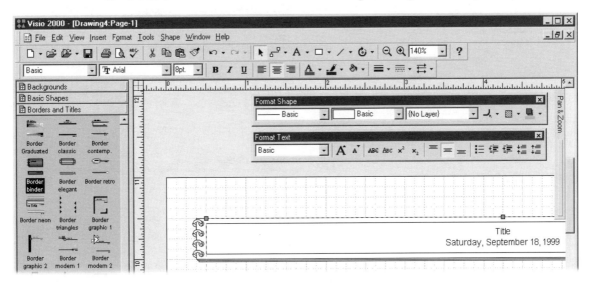

10. Press **Alt+F4** to exit Visio. Click **No** in response to the Save Changes dialog box.

This completes the hands-on activity for using styles in the drawing.

Module 16

Aligning Shapes

Tools | *Align Shapes*
Distribute Shapes
Lay Out Shapes

Uses

The **Align Shapes**, **Distribute Shapes**, and **Lay Out Shapes** selections of the **Tools** menu automatically rearrange shapes in the drawing:

> *In this chapter you'll learn about:*
>
> ✓ *Aligning shapes*
>
> ✓ *Distributing shapes*
>
> ✓ *Laying out shapes*

▶ **Align Shapes** lines up shapes along a horizontal or vertical axis; the tool works with two or more shapes, which are aligned to the first shape selected.

▶ **Distribute Shapes** repositions shapes to create an equal distance between them; the tool works with three or more shapes.

▶ **Lay Out Shapes** places shapes in a predetermined pattern, such as the pattern common to an organization chart or a flowchart.

Procedures

Before presenting the general procedures for rearranging shapes, it is helpful to know about the shortcut keys and icons. These are:

Function	Keys	Menu	Toolbar Icon
Align	F8	Tools | Align Shapes	
Distribute	Alt+TD	Tools | Distribute Shapes	
Lay Out	Alt+TL	Tools | Lay Out Shapes	...

Align Shapes

When you align shapes, Visio moves the shapes so that they line up vertically or horizontally. Use the following procedure to align several shapes
along a baseline:

1. Select at least two shapes. This tool does not work when one or no
    shapes are selected.

    Tip: Notice the color of the selection handles. This is very
    important to obtaining the correct alignment result:

Color	Meaning
Green	First selected shape.
Cyan	Other selected shapes.

    The first shape you select has green handles; the ensuing
    shapes have cyan (light blue) handles. The Align tool aligns the
    ensuing shapes to the first shape.

    Which is the "first selected" shape when you use Ctrl+A to
    select all shapes? Surprisingly, it is the *last* shape added to the
    page. Similarly, when you click and drag or use Select Special,
    the shape with the green handles will be the shape added last
    to the page.

    ---

2. Select **Tools | Align Shapes**. Notice that
    each of the buttons of the Align Shapes dia-
    log box has one green (the first selected) and
    two cyan (subsequent selected) rectangles.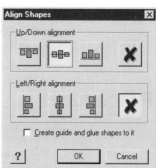

3. Select the type of alignment (you can select
    either, neither, or both types of alignment):

    ▸ **Up/Down alignment**: Align the top,
      center, or bottom of the shapes to the first
      shape selected.

    ▸ **Left/Right alignment**: Align the left,
      center, or right of the shapes to the first shape selected.

    ▸ **X (no alignment)**: No alignment takes place.

4. (*Optional*) Click **Create guide and glue shapes to it** when you
    want Visio to create a guideline along the alignment axis; the selected
    shapes will be glued to the guideline.

5. Click **OK**. Notice that Visio moves the shapes into alignment.

Tip: It is possible for some shapes to "disappear." This happens when a larger shape covers up a smaller shape.

The illustration shows unaligned shapes (left) and center-aligned shapes (right). The circle was the first shape selected, so the other shapes aligned to the center of its alignment box. The triangle disappeared since it is covered up by the square.

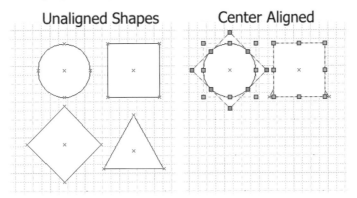

Distribute Shapes

When you distribute shapes, Visio moves the shapes so that they are evenly spaced from each other. For this reason, you must select three or more shapes before Visio lets you use this tool. The two outer shapes remain stationary, while the center shape moves to create the even spacing. Use the following procedure to distribute shapes:

1. Select at least three shapes. The order in which you select the shapes does not matter.

2. Select **Tools | Distribute Shapes**. Notice the Distribute Shapes dialog box.

3. Select one type of distribution.

4. (*Optional*) Click **Create guides and glue shapes to them** when you want Visio to create guidelines along the alignment axis; the selected shapes will be glued to the guideline.

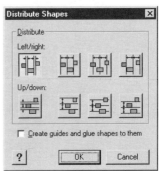

5. Click **OK**. Notice that the middle shape moves so that the spacing is equal between the shapes. The outer shapes (on the left and right side) remain in place. In the illustration, three shapes were distributed horizontally.

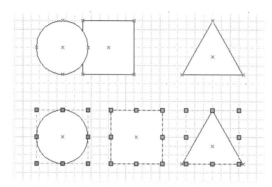

Lay Out Shapes

When you lay out shapes, Visio rearranges the connected shapes into a pattern. This tool works only with connected shapes; unconnected shapes are ignored. In most cases, you will select all shapes on the page. Use the following procedure to lay out shapes:

1. Press **Ctrl+A** to select all shapes.

2. Select **Tools | Lay Out Shapes** from the menu bar. Notice the Lay Out Shapes dialog box.

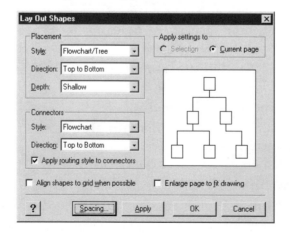

3. The **Placement** section of the dialog box determines how the shapes are placed:

Style: Determines how the shapes will be laid out. **Radial**, for example, is meant for network diagrams. Watch the preview image to see what the style looks like.

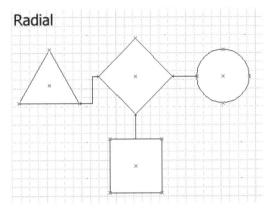

Direction: Specifies the direction that shapes are placed for diagrams that have a "flow," such as flowcharts, tree diagrams, and organization charts (i.e., all non-radial styles).

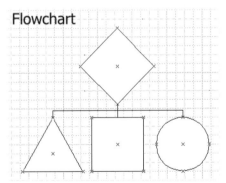

Depth: Determines the amount of space to leave between shapes:

- ▶ **Shallow** creates more of a horizontal layout.
- ▶ **Medium** is a combination of the Shallow and Deep options.
- ▶ **Deep** creates more of a vertical layout.

4. The **Connectors** section determines how the connectors are placed:
    Style: Determines the route used to connect shapes.

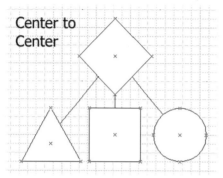

Direction: Specifies the direction of the routing, such as top to bottom, or left to right.

 Tip: The **Direction** you select in the **Placement** and **Connectors** sections should match.

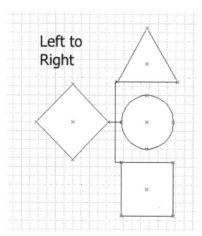

Apply routing style to connectors: Means the routing style is applied to all connectors.

5. The **Align shapes to grid when possible** option is self-explanatory.

6. The **Enlarge page to fit drawing** option enlarges the page to accommodate the shapes.

7. Click the **Spacing** button. Notice the Layout and Routing Spacing dialog box.

   Layout and Routing Spacing

   Space between shapes
   Horizontal: 0.375 in.
   Vertical: 0.375 in.

   Average shape size
   Horizontal: 0.25 in.
   Vertical: 0.25 in.

   Connector to connector
   Horizontal: 0.125 in.
   Vertical: 0.125 in.

   Connector to shape
   Horizontal: 0.125 in.
   Vertical: 0.125 in.

   ?   Defaults   OK   Cancel

   Space between shapes: Specifies the space between placeable shapes.

   Average shape size: Specifies the average size of the shapes in your drawing.

   Connector to connector: Specifies the minimum space between connectors.

   Connector to shape: Specifies the minimum space between connectors and shapes.

8. Click **Apply** to see the effect of the layout on the shapes and connectors in your drawing.

9. Click **OK** to apply the layout.

Hands-On Activity

In this activity, you align, distribute, and lay out shapes. Begin by starting Visio.

1. Open a new drawing with the **Basic Diagram** template found in the **Block Diagram** folder.

2. Drag the **Triangle**, **Square**, and **Circle** shapes from the **Basic Shapes** stencil anywhere onto the page. Make no attempt to line them up.

3. Press **Ctrl+A** to select them all.

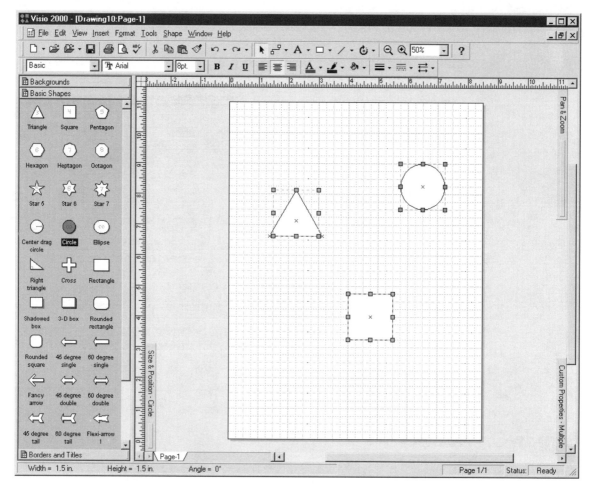

4. Let's line up the shapes. From the menu bar, select **Tools | Align Shapes**. When the Align Shapes dialog box appears, click the middle **Up/Down** alignment button.

5. Click **OK**. Notice that the three shapes are aligned by the center of their alignment boxes.

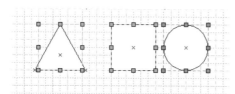

6. Let's distribute the shapes evenly. Select **Tools | Distribute Shapes**. When the Distribute Shapes dialog box appears, click the first **Left/Right alignment** button.

7. Click **OK**. Notice that the three shapes are equally spaced.

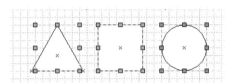

8. Let's connect the shapes. First, though, drag the **Cross** shape into the drawing.

9. From the **Standard** toolbar, select the **Connector** tool (or press **Ctrl+3**).

10. Use shape-to-shape (or dynamic) glue to connect the three shapes to the cross shape. (Recall that shape-to-shape glue means you place the cursor inside the shape so that the shape is surrounded by a heavy red rectangle.)

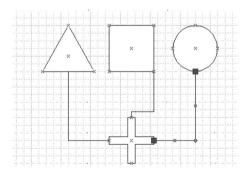

11. Let's lay out the shapes in a couple of patterns. From the menu, select **Tools | Lay Out Shapes**. When the Lay Out Shapes dialog box appears, select **Radial**.

12. Click **Apply**. Notice that the three shapes move to surround the cross shape.

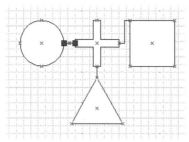

13. In the Lay Out Shapes dialog box, select **Flowchart/Tree** in the Placement section of the Style list box.

14. Click **Apply**. Notice that the cross shape moves to the head of the three other shapes.

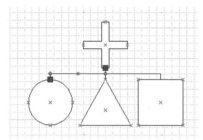

15. Click **Cancel** to exit the dialog box.

16. Press **Alt+F4** to exit Visio. Click **No** in response to the Save Changes dialog box.

This completes the hands-on activity for aligning, distributing, and laying out shapes in the drawing.

Creating Groups

Shape | Grouping

Uses

The **Grouping** function, found on the **Shape** menu, is used to group shapes together into a single unit. A group contains shapes and can contain other groups.

In this chapter you'll learn about:

✓ **Creating a group from shapes**

✓ **Adding to a group**

✓ **Removing from a group**

✓ **Disbanding a group**

Once in a group, editing commands apply equally to all members of the group (unless you select a single member of a group). For example, when you apply the color red to lines, all shapes in the group get red lines.

You can **Add** and **Remove** shapes from a group. You can **Convert** some non-Visio objects to a group, such as an image placed from another program.

To edit individual lines of a group, you can open the group window or select the member you want to edit.

To break up a group, you **Ungroup** the grouped shapes.

Caution: Many shapes that you drag into the drawing from a stencil are groups. If you ungroup them, they lose their link to the stencil. Proceed with care when ungrouping.

 Tip: When you select a group, a single alignment box surrounds the group:

Grip Color	Meaning
Black box, green fill	First selected group.
Black box, cyan fill	Subsequent selected groups

When you select a member of the group, the grips have a gray box:

Grip Color	Meaning
Gray box, green fill	First selected member of a group.
Gray box, cyan fill	Subsequent selected member

Procedures

Before presenting the general procedures for grouping, it is helpful to know about the shortcut keys and icons. These are:

Function	Keys	Menu	Toolbar Icon
Group	Ctrl+G	Shape | Grouping | Group	🔲
Add	Alt+SGA	Shape | Grouping | Add to Group	...
Remove	Alt+SGR	Shape | Grouping | Remove from Group	...
Convert	Alt+SGC	Shape | Grouping | Convert to Group	...
Ungroup	Ctrl+U	Shape | Grouping | Ungroup	🔲

Create a Group from Shapes

Use the following procedure to make a group:

1. Select one or more shapes.
2. Select **Shape | Grouping | Group**.
3. Notice that Visio indicates the group status by placing a single set of handles around all shapes.

Add to a Group

Use the following procedure to add shapes to a group:

1. Select a group and one or more shapes.
2. Select **Shape | Grouping | Add to Group**.
3. Notice that Visio indicates the group status by placing a single set of handles around all shapes.

Remove from a Group

Use the following procedure to remove a shape from a group:

1. Select one or more shapes within a group (click the shape(s) twice).
2. Select **Shape | Grouping | Remove from Group**.
3. Notice that Visio indicates the group status by placing handles around the removed shapes.

Disband a Group

Use the following procedure to ungroup shapes:

1. Select a group.
2. Select **Shape | Grouping | Ungroup**.
3. Notice that Visio indicates the removal of group status by placing handles around all shapes within the group.
4. If the group contains nested groups, you may need to apply the **Ungroup** command a second time.

 **Tip:** The Remove From Group and Ungroup tools have different effects:

Remove From Group: A shape is removed from the group; the other shapes remain a group.

Ungroup: All shapes are removed from the group; the group no longer exists.

Hands-On Activity

 In this activity, you use the grouping functions. Begin by starting Visio.

1. Open a new drawing, along with the **Directional Map** template found in the **Map** folder.
2. Select the **Metro Shapes** stencil.
3. Have fun making a subway map similar to the one shown in the illustration on the following page. Make two lines. *Hint*: Place the **Station** shapes last, or use **Ctrl+F** to bring them to the foreground (on top of the metro track shapes).
4. Select all the metro (track) shapes of the Blue Line.
5. Select **Shape | Grouping | Group** from the menu bar. Notice that one set of handles surrounds all the selected shapes.

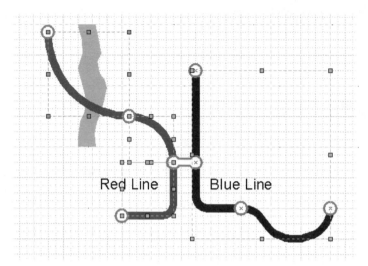

6. Select the group.

7. Change the color of the group (the blue line) from red to blue. Notice that the change applies to all members of the group.

8. Change the size of the group by dragging one of the handles. Notice that all shapes in the group change.

9. To select a member of the group, click it twice. The first click selects the group; the second click selects the member.

10. Select **Shape | Grouping | Ungroup**. Notice that each shape has its own set of handles again.

11. Press **Alt+F4** to exit Visio. Click **No** in response to the Save Changes dialog box.

This completes the hands-on activity for working with groups in the drawing.

 **Boolean Operations**

Shape | Operations
Tools | Macro | Maps | Build Region

Uses

The **Operations** selection of the **Shape** menu performs Boolean operations on shapes. You use Boolean operations to create new shapes. Very often, the order in which you select shapes is important to the outcome, as noted below.

In this chapter you'll learn about:

✓ **The Union operation**

✓ **The Combine operation**

✓ **The Fragment operation**

✓ **The Intersect operation**

✓ **The Subtract operation**

✓ **Building a region**

For operations to work, the shapes must be overlapping. (The stacking order of overlapping shapes is not important.) In all cases, the first shape you select dictates the properties of the "booleaned" shapes. In some cases, the order in which you select shapes is very important.

▶ **Union** joins all selected shapes into a single shape. The new shape takes on the attributes of the shape selected first.

▶ **Combine** is like the Union operation but removes the portions in common. The new shape takes on the attributes of the shape selected first.

▶ **Fragment** creates three new shapes from two overlapping shapes; the overlapping portion becomes an independent shape. All three shapes take on the attributes of the first selected shape.

▶ **Intersect** removes everything except the overlapping areas of the two shapes. Intersect is the opposite of the Combine operation.

▶ **Subtract** removes the overlapping portion of the second shape from the first shape. Another way of looking at it is that the overlapping portion is removed from the first shape. Selection order is crucial for the correct result.

▶ **The Build Region macro** repositions shapes that have been enabled for arranging. Specifically, the macro joins map shapes, such as countries and states.

Procedures

Before presenting the general procedures for Boolean operations, it is helpful to know about the shortcut keys. These are:

Function	Shortcut Keystroke	Menu
Union	Alt+SOU	Shape | Operations | Union
Combine	Alt+SOC	Shape | Operations | Combine
Fragment	Alt+SOF	Shape | Operations | Fragment
Intersect	Alt+SOI	Shape | Operations | Intersect
Subtract	Alt+SOS	Shape | Operations | Subtract
Build Region	...	Tools | Macro | Maps | Build Region

Union Operation

Use the following procedure to join two or more shapes together:

1. Select one shape. This is the shape whose properties the new shape takes on.

2. Hold down the **Shift** key and select one or more additional shapes.

3. Select **Shape | Operations | Union**. Notice that Visio creates one new shape with the outline of all selected shapes and the attributes of the first shape.

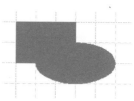

Combine Operation

Use the following procedure to join two or more shapes together, then subtract the areas in common:

1. Select one shape. This is the shape whose properties the new shape takes on.

2. Hold down the **Shift** key and select one or more additional shapes.

3. Select **Shape | Operations | Combine**. Notice that Visio creates one new shape with the outline of all selected shapes and the attributes of the first shape. Overlapping areas are removed.

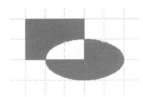

Fragment Operation

Use the following procedure to create three or more shapes from two or more shapes, where overlapping portions become independent shapes:

1. Select one shape. This is the shape whose properties the new shape takes on.

2. Hold down the **Shift** key and select one or more additional shapes.

3. Select **Shape | Operations | Fragment**. Notice that Visio creates a new fragmented shape from the overlapping portions of the original shapes. All shapes take on the attributes of the first shape. The illustration shows the three shapes moved apart.

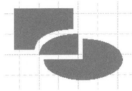

Intersect Operation

Use the following procedure to create one shape from the overlapping portion of two or more shapes:

1. Select one shape. This is the shape whose properties the new shape takes on.

2. Hold down the **Shift** key and select one or more additional shapes.

3. Select **Shape | Operations | Intersect**. Notice that Visio creates one new shape from the overlapping portions of the original shapes; the new shape takes on the attributes of the first shape.

Subtract Operation

Use the following procedure to subtract one shape from another shape:

1. Select one shape. This is the shape whose properties the new shape takes on.

2. Hold down the **Shift** key and select one or more additional shapes.

3. Select **Shape | Operations | Subtract**.
   Notice that Visio creates one new shape by
   removing the second shape and the overlapping
   portions of the second shape from the first shape.

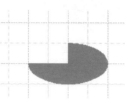

Building a Region

Use the following procedure to build a region from map shapes:

1. Select two or more map shapes.

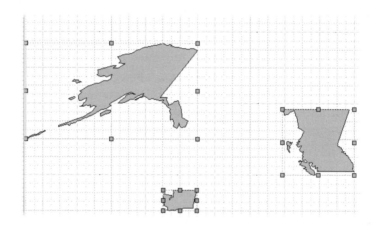

2. Select **Tools | Macro | Maps | Build Region**
   from the menu bar. Wait while the macro runs and
   Visio moves the regions together.

3. Notice that Visio moves the map shapes together so
   that they match up logically
   along borders. In the illustration, the American states of
   Alaska and Washington and
   the Canadian province of
   British Columbia have been
   brought together by the
   Build Region macro.

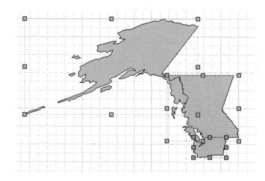

Hands-On Activity

In this activity, you use the Boolean operations. Begin by starting Visio.

1. Open a new drawing using the **Basic Shapes** solution found in the **Block Diagram** folder.

2. Drag the **Triangle** shape into the drawing.

3. Drag the **Circle** shape into the drawing, half overlapping the triangle.

4. Apply the diagonal line fill pattern to the circle. This will help you see how the properties of one shape are applied to another, as a result of Boolean operations.

5. Select both shapes.

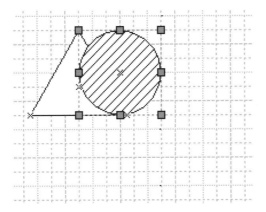

6. With both shapes selected, hold down the **Ctrl** key to make five copies of the originals. Remember to use the **Shift** key to force the movement to horizontal and vertical. Use the **F4** key to repeat an action. You now have a total of six pairs of shapes, on which we will perform Boolean operations.

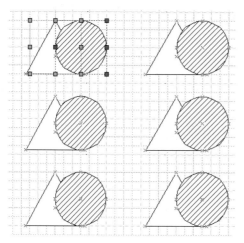

7. Select the first circle, then the triangle. Remember to hold down the **Shift** key when selecting the triangle.

8. Select **Tools | Operations | Union**. Notice that the two shapes become a single shape, which takes on the fill pattern of the circle.

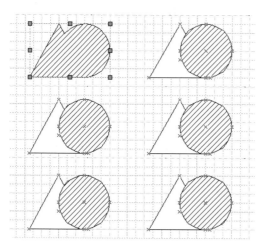

9. Select the second circle, then the triangle.

10. Select **Tools | Operations | Combine**. Notice that the two shapes become a single shape, which takes on the fill pattern of the circle—except for the area in common.

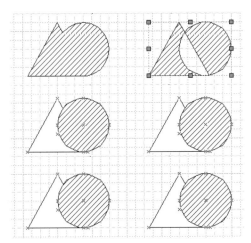

11. Select the third circle, then the triangle.

12. Select **Tools | Operations | Fragment**. Notice that the two shapes become three shapes, which take on the fill pattern of the circle. (For clarity, the illustration shows the three shapes moved apart.)

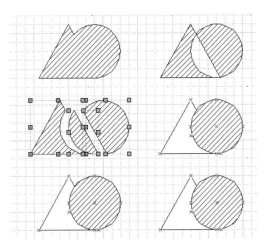

13. Select the fourth circle, then the triangle.

14. Select **Tools | Operations | Intersect**. Notice that the two shapes become a single shape—consisting of the area in common—which takes on the fill pattern of the circle.

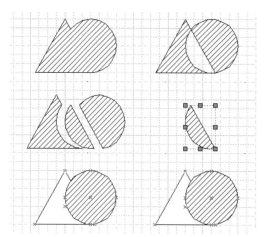

15. Select the fifth circle, then the triangle.

16. Select **Tools | Operations | Subtract**. Notice that the triangle is removed from the circle.

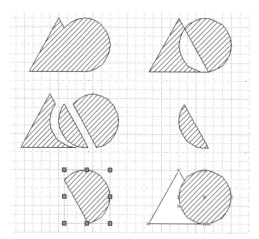

17. To show the importance of selection order, this time select the sixth triangle, then the circle.

18. Select **Tools | Operations | Subtract**. Notice that the circle is removed from the triangle. Since the triangle was selected first, the resulting Boolean shape takes on the attributes of the triangle.

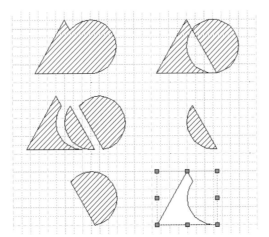

19. Press **Alt+F4** to exit Visio. Click **No** in response to the Save Changes dialog box.

This completes the hands-on activity for Boolean operations. Being familiar with these five operations makes it easier to create many interesting (and sometimes unique) new shapes.

Module 19   *Previewing Before Printing*

File | Print Preview

Uses

In this chapter you'll learn about:

✓ **Print Preview**

Before you print your drawing, you should always do a print preview. *Print preview* means that Visio displays your drawing on a white rectangle that represents the paper. By previewing the drawing, you see how it will print, and then you can make the appropriate changes to orientation, paper size, and so on. This action takes only a few seconds, and saves you a lot of wasted paper.

The **Print Preview** selection of the **File** menu lets you see how the drawing will appear on the paper, before committing to printing.

Procedures

Before presenting the general procedure for print preview, it is helpful to know the following shortcuts:

Function	Keys	Menu	Toolbar Icon
Print Preview	...	File | Print Preview	🔍
Once in print preview mode, the following shortcut keys are available:			
Print dialog box	Ctrl+P	File | Print	Print...
Page Setup dialog box	...	File | Print Setup	Setup...
Whole Page	Ctrl+W	View | Whole Page	🔲
Zoom Out	Shift+F6	View | Zoom Out	🔍⊖
Zoom In	...	View | Zoom In	🔍⊕
Close	Ctrl+F4	...	Close
Help	F1	Help | Visio Help	?

Print Preview

Use the following procedure to preview the drawing before printing:

1. Select **File | Print Preview**.

2. Notice that Visio displays the drawing on a white background, representing the sheet of paper. The light gray edging represents the printer margins. If any portion of the drawing extends into the margin, that part will not be printed.

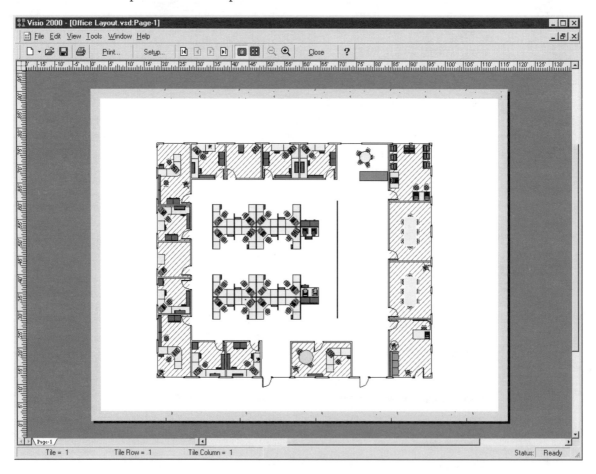

3. Notice that the Print Preview window has its own toolbar:

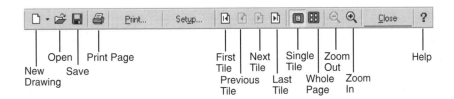

New Drawing, **Open**, and **Save** icons: You can open new and existing Visio drawings from print preview mode; the drawings, however, are opened in the Visio drawing window, not in print preview.

Print Page: Prints the drawing.

 Caution: The **Print Page** button is a shortcut that immediately prints the drawing to the current printer. Do not click this button unless you know all settings are correct. In fact, I never click this icon, which I consider dangerous.

Usually, you use print preview to see how your drawing is going to print; you make adjustments and you preview the drawing again. When you preview a drawing for the last time, and don't need to make any more adjustments, you simply click the **Print Page** button.

Print: Displays the Print dialog box; see Module 20 "Printing Drawings."

Setup: Displays the Page Setup dialog box; see Module 4 "Setting Up Pages and Layers."

First Tile, **Previous Tile**, **Next Tile**, **Last Tile**: These buttons perform double-duty; they work for multipage drawings and tiled drawings:

▶ When the drawing contains more than one page, these buttons display the first, previous, next, and last pages of a multipage drawing.

▶ When the drawing is tiled, these buttons take you from tile to tile. The **Previous Tile** and **Next Tile** buttons move left to right, then top to bottom. The status line reports which tile you are looking at. For example:

Tile = 2   Tile Row = 1   Tile Column = 2

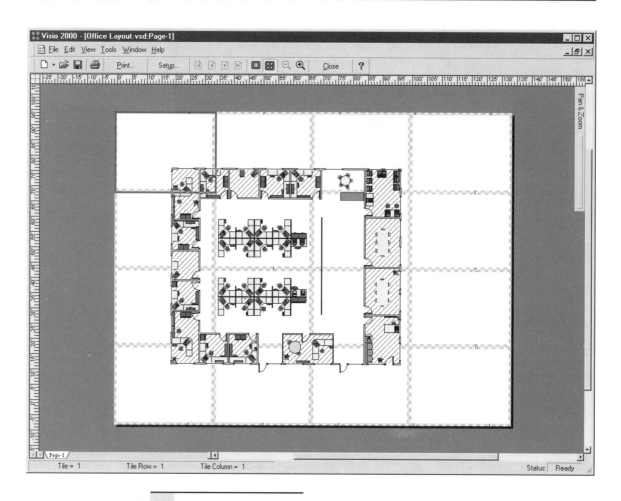

Tip: Most office printers and fax machines are limited to printing on letter-size paper (8.5" x 11", also known as "A-size" paper), as well as legal-size paper (8.5" x 14"). Tiling allows you, if somewhat awkwardly, to use the printer or fax to create an engineering-size printout, such as D-size (22" x 34"). Hey, why not use Visio and tiling to create Happy Birthday and Bon Voyage banners?

Happy 43rd Birthday, Heather!

Single Tile and **Whole Page**: When the drawing is larger than one sheet of paper, Visio tiles the drawing. *Tiling* means that the drawing will be printed on enough sheets of paper to print the full drawing, which you can tape together. Visio can tile to a maximum of 2,500 sheets of paper, limited to 50 sheets horizontally and 50 vertically—not that you would probably ever want to tape together that many sheets! Click the **Single Tile** button to see one sheet of a multi-tile printout; click the **Whole Page** button to show all sheets.

Zoom Out and **Zoom In**: The **Zoom Out** button displays the whole page; the **Zoom In** button displays the drawing in full size.

Tip: You never need to use the zoom buttons. That's because the cursor becomes the zoom tool in print preview mode. Click the drawing to examine it full size; click the drawing again to return back to the full-page view.

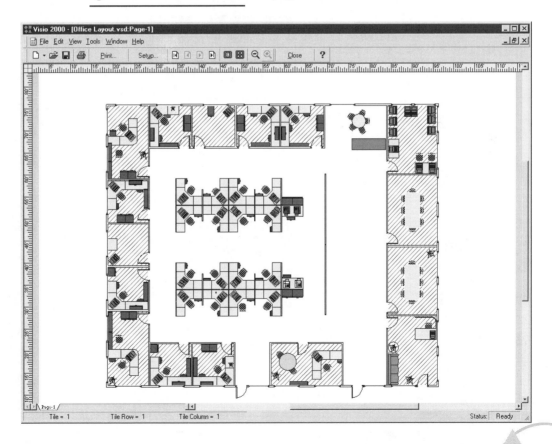

191

Close and **Help**: **Close** takes you back to the Visio drawing screen, which it calls "normal view." If you have more than one print preview window open, all are closed. The **Help** button brings up the help window.

4. Select **File | Print** to print the drawing.

5. Or, click the **Close** button on the toolbar to return to the drawing without printing.

Hands-On Activity

In this activity, you use the print preview function. Begin by starting Visio.

1. Select **File | New | Browse Sample Drawings**.

2. From the Browse Sample Drawings dialog box, go to the **Organization Chart** folder and double-click **Global Organization Chart.Vsd**. Wait while Visio loads the three-page drawing.

3. Select **File | Print Preview**. Notice that Visio displays the drawing in a window with a gray background.

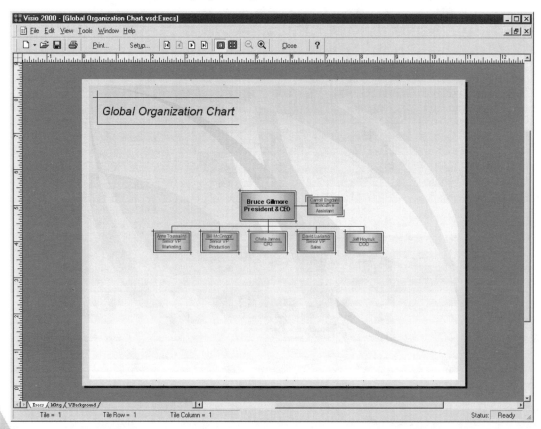

4. Move the cursor over the drawing. Notice the cursor is a magnifying glass with a plus sign (+). This indicates Visio is in zoom mode.

5. Click the drawing. Notice that Visio enlarges the view.

6. Notice that the cursor's plus sign (+) has changed to a minus sign (–). This indicates Visio is ready to zoom out to the full-page view.

7. Click the drawing.

8. Notice Visio reduces the view.

9. Click **Close** on the toolbar to return to the drawing.

10. Press **Alt+F4** to exit Visio.

This completes the hands-on activity for print preview.

Printing Drawings

File | Print

Uses

The purpose of creating a drawing with Visio is to print it out, paste it into other programs, and save it as a Web page. While you can gain satisfaction from creating the drawing, there is a certain amount of pleasure to be

In this chapter you'll learn about:

✓ *Printing the drawing*

✓ *Tiling drawings*

✓ *Transmitting faxed drawings*

✓ *E-mailing drawing attachments*

✓ *Printing to file*

gained from showing off your work to co-workers, friends, and family—in serious black-and-white, or in brilliant color! Visio provides several ways to output your drawing, which can be done on paper or electronically.

Printing on paper:

▶ **Office printer**: The **Print** selection of the **File** menu prints the drawing. In most cases, you will want Visio to print the drawing to fit the standard letter-size paper on a laser or inkjet printer.

▶ **Engineering plotter**: In some cases, you may want to produce accurate scale drawings on engineering-size paper, such as 22" x 34" or larger. Visio can print to large printers and plotters that handle this size of media, or it can tile a print so that a large drawing is printed on two or more letter-size sheets.

Outputting electronically:

▶ **Fax transmission**: Windows does not limit you to printing to one particular printer. If your computer is connected to a fax modem, you can send the Visio drawing as a fax.

▶ **E-mail attachment**: If your computer is hooked up to an e-mail system, you can attach the drawing to an e-mail message with the **File | Send To** command.

▶ **Web display**: For displaying the Visio drawing on a Web site, it can be published as a static, raster GIF image, or as an interactive, vector VML file; see Module 36 "Creating a Web Document."

▶ **Printing to file**: In some cases, it may make sense to print the drawing to a file on disk. This is an alternative method of exporting the drawing; see Module 29 "Exporting Drawings."

Tip: Before you print the drawing, always select **File | Print Preview** to ensure that the drawing will be printed to your satisfaction. See Module 19 "Previewing Before Printing."

Procedures

Before presenting the general procedures for printing, it is helpful to know about the shortcut keys. These are:

Function	Keys	Menu	Toolbar Icon
Print	Ctrl+P	File | Print	🖨
Page Setup	Shift+F5	File | Page Setup	...
E-mail	...	File | Send To	...

Tip: Clicking the **Print** button reacts differently from selecting **File | Print** from the menu bar. Here's the difference between the two:

- Clicking the **Print** button on the toolbar causes Visio to immediately print the drawing, without displaying a dialog box. This may result in wasted paper, since you don't get a chance to check things like the printer model and the number of copies. Only click this button if you are sure the print will be completed correctly.

- Selecting **File | Print** from the menu displays the Print dialog box, which gives you a chance to check the printer's parameters before committing to placing the drawing on paper.

Printing the Drawing

Use the following procedure to print the drawing to your office printer:

1. Select **File | Print**. Notice the Print dialog box.

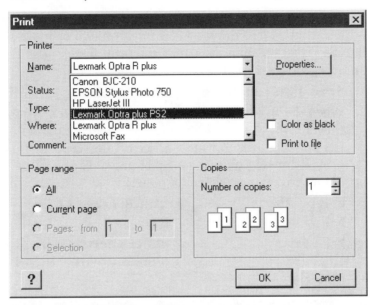

2. Select the name of the printer from the Name list box.

3. Click the **Properties** button to change the characteristics of the printer, such as resolution and paper orientation. Click **OK** to return to the Print dialog box.

4. Click **Color as black** to ensure all shapes are printed on a mono-chrome printer (one that is incapable of printing color or shades of gray).

5. If the drawing consists of more than one page, select which pages you want printed in the **Page range** area:

    All: Prints all pages in the drawing (the default).

    Current page: Prints the currently displayed page.

    Pages: When the drawing consists of more than one page, specifies the range of pages to print.

    Selection: Prints the selected objects of the current page.

6. Type the number of copies in the **Number of copies** box.

7. Click **OK** to begin printing; as an alternative, you can click **Cancel** to dismiss the dialog box without printing the drawing.

Tiling Drawings

When your drawing is larger than a single sheet of paper, Visio can tile the print so that a large drawing is printed on two or more sheets. Since the drawing is larger than the paper, the print is *tiled*. Use the following procedure to print the drawing on several sheets of paper:

1. Select **File | Page Setup** from the menu.
2. When the Page Setup dialog box appears, click the **Print Setup** tab. In this tab, you specify the number of sheets of paper Visio should spread the drawing over. For most office printers, set the following options to print a drawing on two sheets of paper. For example, to print the drawing on two (1 x 2) sheets of paper:

    ▶ Paper size: **Letter 8 1/2 x 11 in**
    ▶ Paper orientation: **Portrait**
    ▶ Fit to: **2 sheets across**
                                   1 sheets down

    Click **OK**.

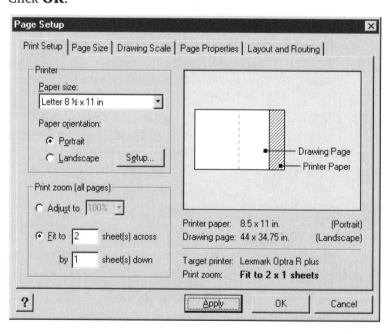

3. Go to print preview mode to see the drawing span two pages by selecting **File | Print Preview**.

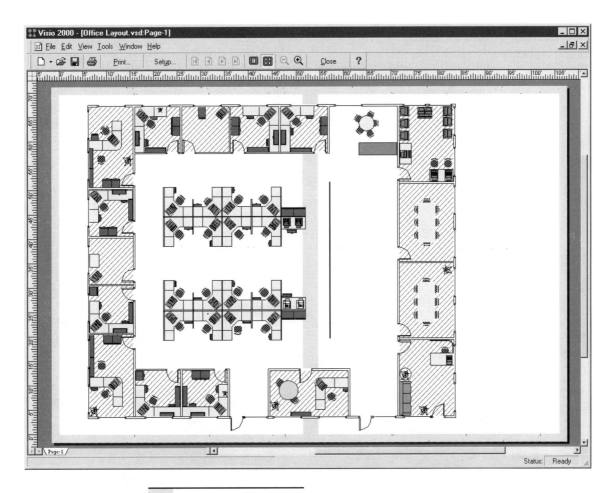

Tip: Only use the method outlined above if the accurate scale is not important. When you have a large scaled drawing and you don't specify the number of sheets you want your drawing to fit on, Visio still tiles the drawing. If the drawing must be plotted at a specific scale, use the following method via the Page Setup dialog box:

Step 1: Select the size of paper used by the printer (**Print Setup** tab).

Step 2: Select the size of the drawing page (**Page Size** tab).

Step 3: Specify the drawing scale, so that the drawing covers the page (**Drawing Scale** tab).

Transmitting Faxed Drawings

Use the following procedure to fax the drawing:

Windows does not limit you to printing to one particular printer. If your computer is connected to a fax modem, you can send the Visio drawing as a fax. Just like with any other printer, you can fax a drawing tiled over several pages.

> **Note:** Unlike other printers, faxed drawings cannot be faxed in color—keep in mind that colors will be converted to shades of gray. For this reason, it is probably a good idea to avoid using backgrounds with drawings you intend to fax.

1. Select **File | Print**. Notice the Print dialog box.

2. To fax the drawing, click the **Name** list box and select **Microsoft Fax** or another fax "printer" from this list.

3. To be more economical, faxes are usually sent at 200 dpi (dots per inch resolution) and in monochrome (just black and white). A Visio drawing, however, contains much detail. To improve the quality of the faxed drawing, click the **Properties** button.

4. When the Fax Properties dialog box appears, click the **Graphics** tab. Select the following options.

    ▶ Dots per inch (dpi):
       300 dpi

    ▶ Grayscale—Halftoning:
       Patterned Grays

    Click **OK**.

5. Back in Visio's Print dialog box, select the pages you want printed, then click **OK**. Notice that Visio spends a few moments converting the drawing to fax format.

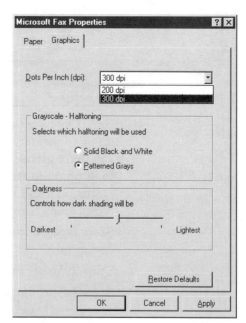

6. Notice that your fax software's dialog box appears. The look of the dialog box will vary, depending on the brand of fax software installed on your computer. Fill in the required information, then send the fax on its way.

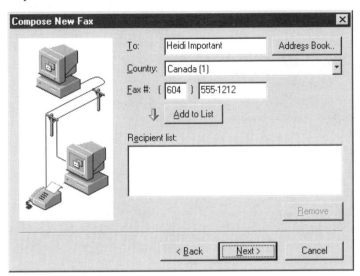

E-mailing Drawing Attachments

Use the following procedure to e-mail the drawing:

If your computer is hooked up to an e-mail system, you can attach the drawing to an e-mail message.

1. Select **File | Send To** from the menu bar. Notice that you may have several options:

   ▸ **Mail Recipient**: A message appears with your drawing attached.

   ▸ **Routing Recipient**: Displays the Routing Slip dialog box. Select a recipient by clicking the **Address** button, then clicking **OK**. This option is useful when you want to send the drawing via the addresses stored in the Address Book provided with Windows.

   ▸ **Exchange Folder**: Displays the Send to Exchange Folder dialog box; select a folder. The drawing is saved in the folder so that you can later open the drawing from within Microsoft Exchange.

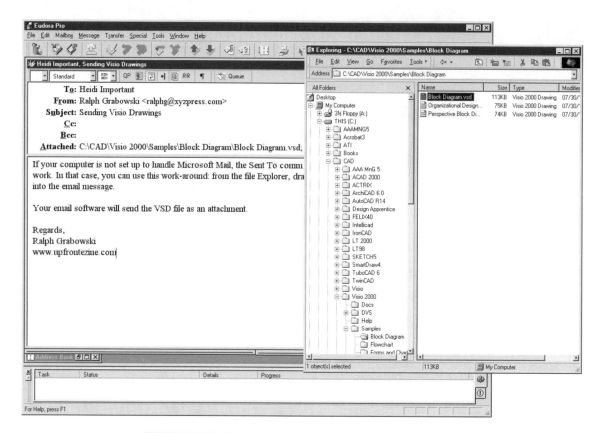

 Caution: If your computer is not set up to handle Microsoft Mail, the **Send To** command may not work. In that case, you can use this workaround: from the file Explorer, drag the VSD file into the e-mail message.

To display the Visio drawing on a Web site, it can be published as a GIF image or as a vector VML file. See Module 36 "Creating a Web Document."

Printing to File

There are some cases where it makes sense to print the drawing to a file on disk:

▶ One case is when you need to translate the drawing to a file format not found in Visio's Save As dialog box. One common example is converting the file to HPGL (short for Hewlett-Packard graphics language), which can be imported into another drawing or CAD program. Printing to disk is an alternative method of exporting the drawing; see Module 29 "Exporting Drawings."

▶ Another case is when you want to print the drawing, but you have no access to the printer. Print the file to diskette or ZIP disk, then carry the disk to the computer with the printer. To print the file you can use the following DOS command:

C:\> **copy /b d:\filename.prn port**

where

copy	The DOS command that copies the print file to the printer.
/b	Ensures the Copy command does not stop sending the print file before the end of the file.
d:	Name of the drive containing the print file.
filename.prn	Name of the print file.
port	Name of the port to which the printer is attached; you may use **ltp1** for the first parallel port or **lpt2** for the second parallel port.

Use the following procedure to print the drawing to a file on disk:

1. Ensure that the required Windows printer driver is installed on your computer. To add a printer, such as an HP plotter (for creating HPGL files), from the **Start** menu, select **Settings | Printers**, then click the **Add Printer** icon. Follow the instructions of the **Add Printer Wizard**; it is not necessary for the printer to be attached to your computer.

2. In Visio, select **File | Print** from the menu bar.

3. Click the **Name** list, and select the appropriate printer.

4. Click **Print to file** to save the drawing in a file.

5. Click **OK**. Notice that Visio displays the Print to File dialog box.

6. Enter the filename and select the folder for the file. Notice that you must provide the extension to the filename; use the following standards:

HP Plotter:	**HPG** or **PLT**
PostScript:	**PS** or **EPS**
Others:	**PRN**

7. Click **OK**. Visio saves the drawing as a print file on disk.

Hands-On Activity

In this activity, you use the print function. Ensure Visio is running.

1. Select **File | New | Browse Sample Drawings**. Notice the Browse Sample Drawings dialog box.

2. From the **Flowchart** folder, double-click the **Hoshin Flowchart.Vsd** drawing file.

3. Select **File | Print**. Notice the Print dialog box.

4. Click **OK**. Notice the Printing dialog box, which tells you of Visio's progress in sending the drawing to the printer. Wait for the printer to print the drawing.

5. Press **Alt+F4** to exit Visio.

This completes the hands-on activity for printing.

Undoing and Redoing

Edit | Undo
Redo

Uses

When you make a mistake, such as deleting a shape, **Undo** returns the deleted shape. Visio remembers the actions you performed, so that

> *In this chapter you'll learn about:*
> ✓ *Undoing an action*
> ✓ *Redoing an undo*
> ✓ *Multiple undo levels*

repeating the Undo command reverses each action, one at a time. To help you remember what the next undo action will be, the **Edit** menu follows Undo with the action, such as **Undo Drop On Page**.

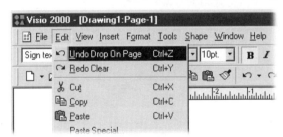

If you change your mind, the **Redo** command undoes the Undo. Like Undo, Visio remembers as many Redo actions as undoes. Naturally, you can undo a redo.

Visio 2000 allows you to undo and redo more than one action at a time. To view the list of all actions stored in the undo list, click the small arrow to the right of the Undo button on the toolbar.

Some actions cannot be undone, such as saving, printing, and certain shape operations.

When the action cannot be undone, the **Edit** menu shows **Can't Undo** instead of Undo.

Procedures

Before presenting the general procedures for undoing and redoing, it is helpful to know about the shortcut keys. These are:

Function	Keys	Menu	Toolbar Icon
Undo	Ctrl+Z	Edit | Undo	↰
Redo	Ctrl+Y	Edit | Redo	↱

Tip: When first installed on your computer, Visio is set up for ten levels of undo and redo. That means Visio remembers the last ten actions you performed. You can change the number of levels via the **Tools | Options** command. In the Options dialog box, look for **Undo levels**. The default value of **10** can be reduced to **0**, or increased to **99**. The higher the number of levels, the more memory Visio uses to store the actions to be undone.

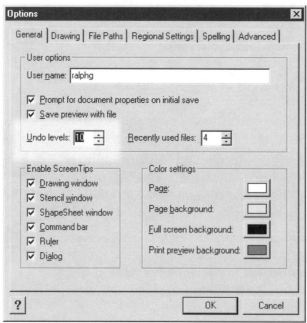

Undoing an Action

Use the following procedure to undo the most recent action:

1. Select **Edit | Undo** or press **Ctrl+Z**.
2. If necessary, select **Edit | Undo** again.

Redoing an Undo

Use the following procedure to redo the undo:

1. Select **Edit | Redo** or press **Ctrl+Y**.

Multiple Undo Levels

Use the following procedure to undo more than one action:

1. Click the arrow button to the right of the **Undo** button. Notice that Visio displays a list of actions in the list.
2. Holding down the mouse button, slide the cursor down the list. Notice that Visio highlights the actions, and reports the number of undo actions, such as **Undo 4 Actions**.
3. Release the mouse button. Notice that Visio instantly changes the drawing back to its previous state.

 Note: You cannot pick and choose the actions to undo; undo and redo work in sequential order only.

Hands-On Activity

 In this activity, you use the undo and redo functions. Begin by starting Visio. Then start a new document with the **Basic Diagram** template:

1. Drag the five-point **Star 5** shape from the **Basic Shapes** stencil to the center of the page.
2. Drag the **Square** shape from the stencil to a location above the star.

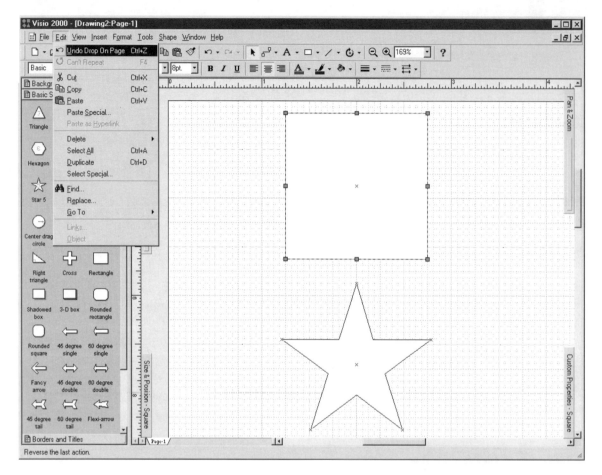

3. Select **Edit | Undo Drop On Page**. Notice that the square disappears from the page.

4. Drag the **Circle** shape from the stencil to on top of the **Star**.

5. Select gray fill from the Fill Color list box to turn the circle gray.

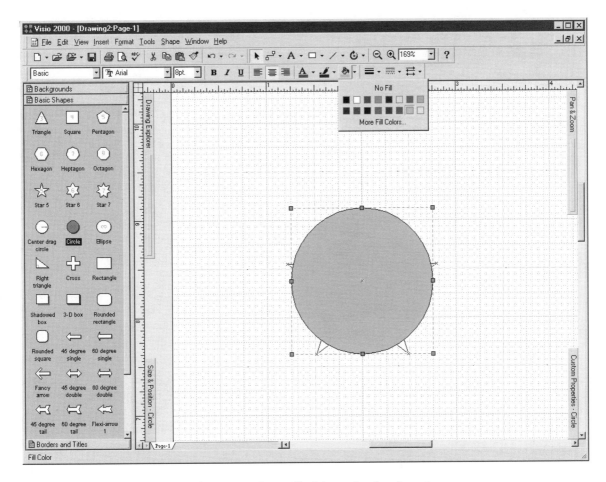

6. Press **Ctrl+A** to select all objects in the drawing.
7. Select **Shape | Operations | Combine**. Notice that the star shape is "punched" out of the gray circle.

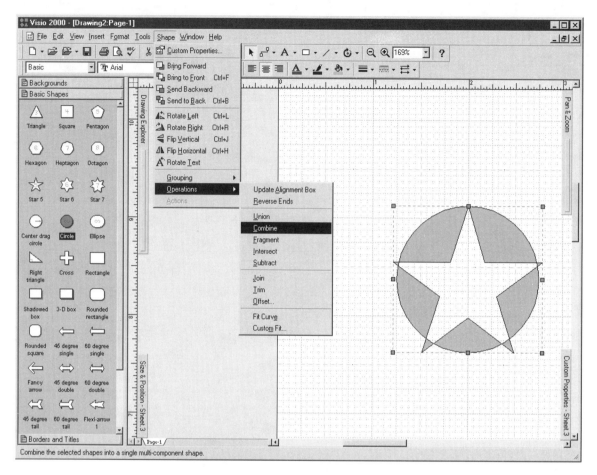

8. Click the arrow to the right of the **Undo** button on the toolbar. Notice that Visio displays a list in reverse order of the four actions you performed since the last **Undo**:

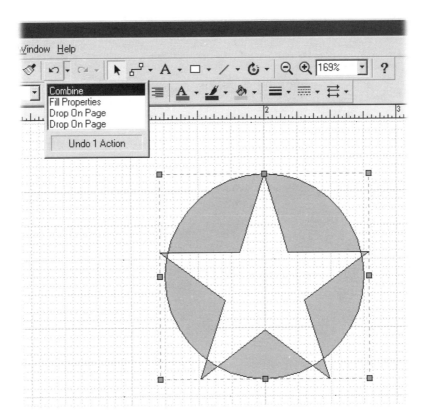

Combine: Combining the star with the circle (**Shape | Operations | Combine** of step 7, above).

Fill Properties: Filling the circle with the gray color (step 5).

Drop On Page: Dragging the circle shape onto the page (step 4).

Drop On Page: Dragging the star shape onto the page (step 1).

Other actions are not recorded, such as selecting all objects (the **Ctrl+A** of step 6, above), adding and removing the square shape (steps 2 and 3), nor any pan and zoom operations you may have performed.

9. Select three undo actions, so that you see **Undo 3 Actions**. Notice that the circle disappears and the star returns to its original self.

10. Click the arrow to the right of the **Redo** button on the toolbar. Notice that Visio displays a list in reverse order of the three actions you undid.

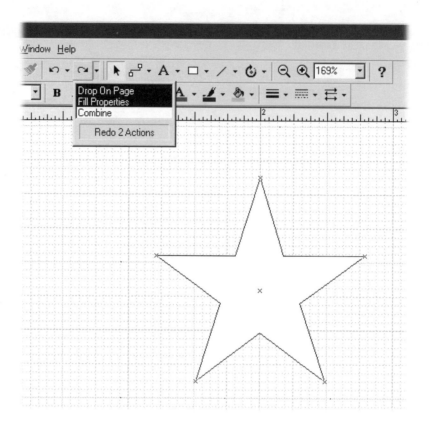

11. Select two redo actions, so that you see **Redo 2 Actions**. Notice that the circle reappears, shaded in gray.

12. Press **Alt+F4** to exit Visio. Click **No** in response to the Save Changes dialog box.

This completes the hands-on activity for undo and redo operations.

Help

Help | Visio Help

Uses

The **Help** menu displays an expanded version of the printed documentation provided with the Visio 2000 package. Via

> **In this chapter you'll learn about:**
>
> ✓ **Visio Help**

the Help menu item, you access information helpful to you in these areas:

▶ **Visio Help**: Assistance in using Visio menus, toolbars, and other program features.

▶ **Shape Basics**: Aids in connecting shapes, selecting shapes, and adding text to shapes.

▶ **Developer Reference**: Information for programming Visio's shapesheet and VBA (Visual Basic for Applications).

The online help gives specific details, whereas the printed documentation gives a general overview. I find it is faster to locate online help on a specific topic than search the printed index and flip through pages.

As an alternative, you can visit Visio on the Web. Selecting **Help | Visio on the Web** from the menu bar opens your Web browser with the http://www.visio.com/visioontheweb address. The Knowledge Base section of the Support area is quite helpful when you have a specific problem.

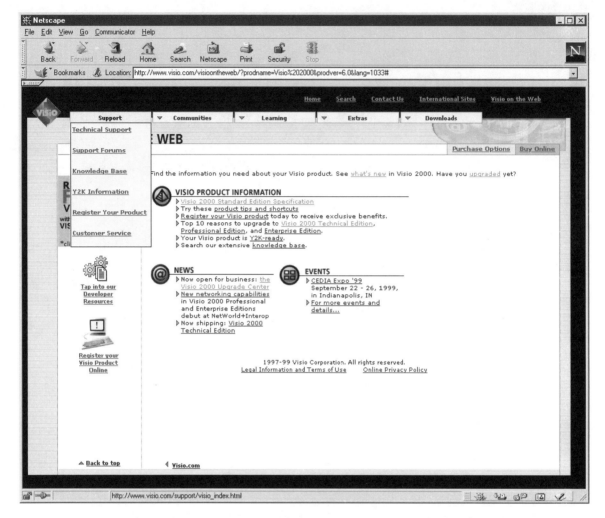

When you select **Help | Visio Help**, you can search for documentation via the **Contents**, **Index**, and **Search** functions. The **Contents** lists help topics in logical order; the **Index** lists topics in alphabetical order; and the **Search** function searches for specific keywords.

Note: Visio 2000 uses a different method of displaying help. Previous versions of Visio used the Microsoft Help system, which you are probably familiar with from other software programs. Visio 2000 uses an HTML-based help system. The advantage of the new help system is that it lets you create a list of help topics in the **Favorites** tab. The drawbacks are that the useful **What's This?** help command is no longer available, and that useful options (such as font size and don't keep on top) are missing.

As an alternative to using the **Help** menu, you can call up help directly within Visio itself. Here are some examples:

Almost all dialog boxes include a **Help** button, which displays help for the options of that dialog box. That means you don't need to search the online help for how to use that dialog box.

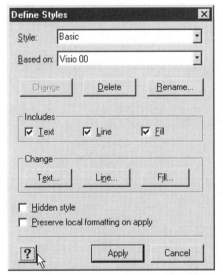

Right-click a shape at any time—whether in a stencil or on the drawing page—to display help for that shape. More specifically, right-click the shape, then select **Help** from the shortcut menu.

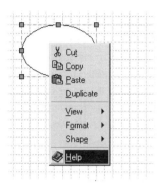

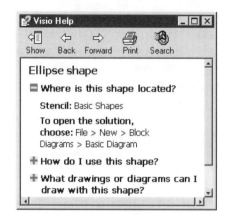

The help for toolbar buttons and menu items is less comprehensive. Pausing the cursor over a toolbar button displays the yellow tooltip (a one- or two-word description). Pause the cursor over a menu item, and a one-sentence description is provided on the status line. When you press **F1** while holding down a toolbar button or menu item, the Visio Help window unhelpfully displays the general Visio Help item.

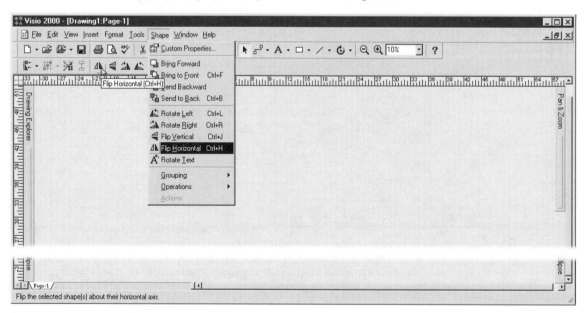

Procedures

Before presenting the general procedures for help, it is helpful to know about the shortcut key:

Function	Keys	Menu	Toolbar Icon
Help	F1	Help | Visio Help	**?**

Hands-On Activity

Begin by starting Visio with no document open.

Finding a Help Topic Using the Contents Tab

1. Select **Help | Visio Help**. Notice that Visio displays the Visio Help.

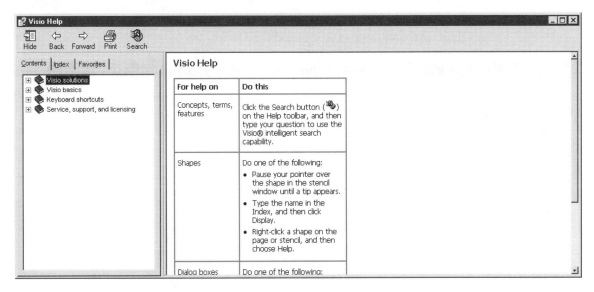

2. Click the **Contents** tab. Click the + (plus) sign next to the Visio solutions book icon. Notice the list of topics that appears, such as Audit flowcharts and Basic diagrams.

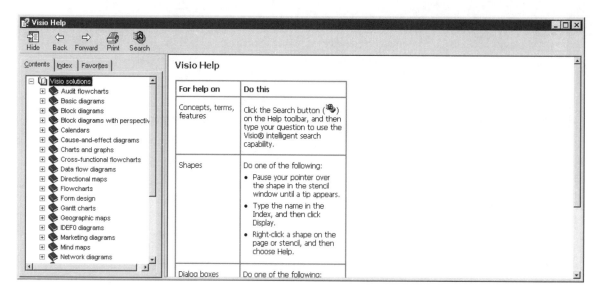

3. Click the plus sign (+) next to Audit flowcharts, then click the **About audit flowcharts** topic. Notice that Visio Help displays in the right pane the documentation associated with the help topic.

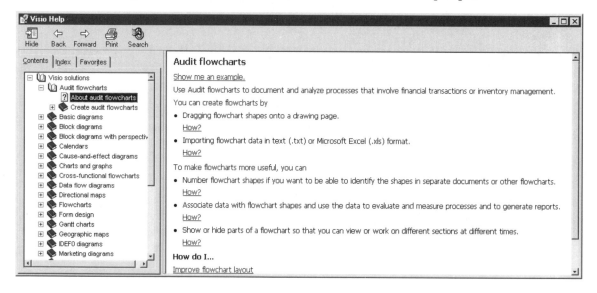

4. Notice the blue underlined text: this text is linked to other help topics. Click the blue underlined word **How?** under Dragging flowchart shapes onto a drawing page. Notice that the help text changes.

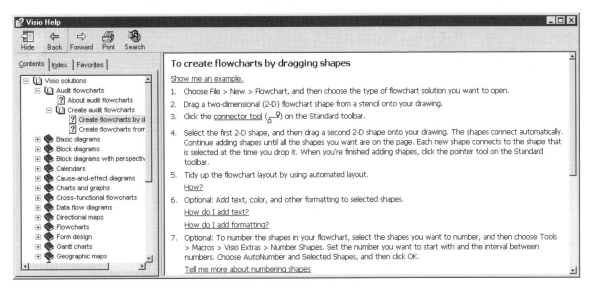

5. Click **Back** on the toolbar to return to the previous topic.

Finding a Help Topic Using the Index Tab

1. Click the **Index** tab in the Visio Help window. Notice that it displays an alphabetical list of topics in the left pane.

2. Type the word **flowchart** in the Type in the keyword to find field. Notice that the left pane displays many topics starting with the word "Flowchart."

3. Select the **Flowchart Shapes shape** phrase, then click the **Display** button. (As a faster alternative, double-click the phrase.) Notice that the Visio Help window displays related help in the right pane.

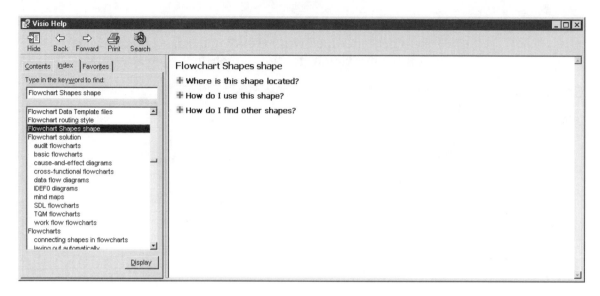

4. Sometimes, there are two or more help topics related to a topic. In that case, Visio Help displays an additional dialog box. To see this, double-click the **Flowchart solution** phrase. Notice the Topics Found dialog box lists several related topics.

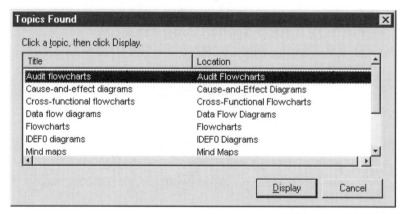

5. Double-click any topic, such as **Audit flowcharts**. Notice the help information in the right pane.

Finding a Help Topic Using the Search Function

1. Click the **Search** button. Notice that the right pane takes on a new look. The What would you like to know? prompt allows you to enter questions in natural English.

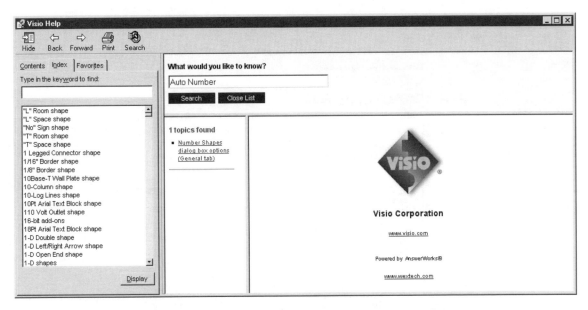

2. Type **Where do I find a flowchart shape?** and click **Search**. Notice that Visio Help displays a list of topics.

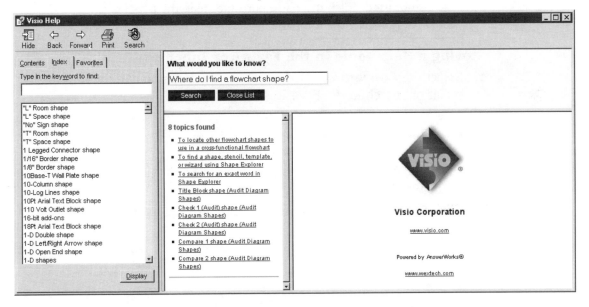

3. Narrow your search by selecting one of the phrases under Topics found. Click the first item in the list. Notice that Visio Help displays helpful information in the rightmost pane.

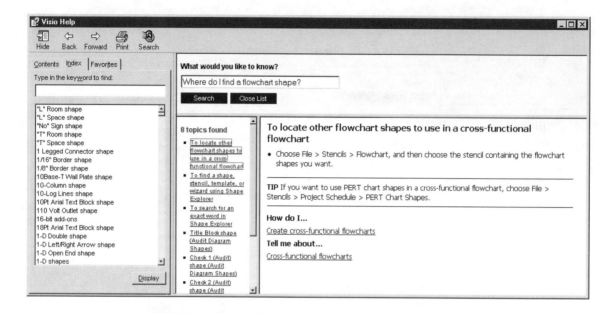

Tip: In Search mode, the left pane (Contents, Index, Favorites) is not used. Click the **Hide** button to hide the pane; click **Show** to redisplay the left pane.

Storing a Help Topic in the Favorites Tab

1. Select the **Contents** or **Index** tab. (Note that you cannot store the result of Search in the Favorites list.)

2. Select any item listed in the left pane.

3. Click the **Favorites** tab. Notice the topic you selected is listed in the Current topic field. You may edit the text to make it say anything you want; the help system remembers the link to the help topic, regardless of the wording.

4. Click **Add**. Notice that the topic is added to the list under Topics.

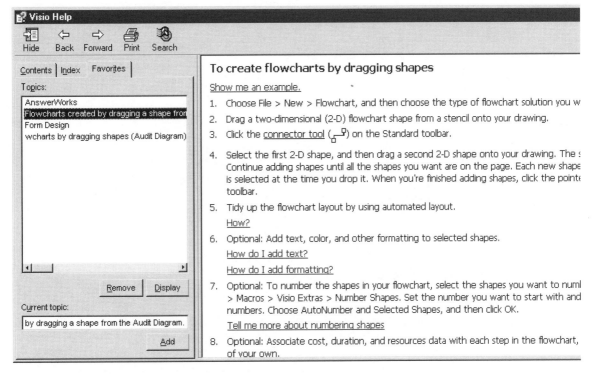

5. To display a help topic, select the topic wording and click **Display**.
6. To remove a help topic from the list, select the topic and click **Remove**.
7. Click the icon next to Visio Help on the title bar, and select **Close** to close the help window.

This completes the procedures for using help.

Drawing Tools

Pencil, Line, Arc, Freeform, Rectangle, Ellipse

Uses

Most of the time when you create a drawing with Visio, you work with shapes. You drag shapes into the drawing, position them, resize them, copy them, and so on. Sometimes, however, the thousands of shapes provided with Visio 2000 Standard Edition are not enough. You may want to draw your own shape, or need to draw one-of-a-kind objects, like a squiggly line.

In this chapter you'll learn about:

✓ *Drawing with the Pencil tool*

✓ *Drawing with the Line tool*

✓ *Drawing with the Arc tool*

✓ *Drawing with the Rectangle tool*

✓ *Drawing with the Ellipse tool*

✓ *Drawing closed objects*

✓ *Adding segments to an object*

✓ *Moving the vertex*

For these reasons, Visio includes a basic set of six drawing tools. These tools are found on the **Standard** toolbar—not on any menu. The tools draw straight and curved lines, circles and arcs, rectangles, and ellipses. Many of Visio's drawing tools are dual-purpose: a different object is created depending on how you move the mouse or hold down a key:

Tool	*Draws*	*Special Action*
Pencil	Straight line	Move mouse in a straight line.
	Circular arc	Move mouse in a curve.
	Line at 45-degree increments	Hold down Shift key.
Line	Straight line	
	Line at 45-degree increments	Hold down Shift key.
Arc	Elliptical arc	

Tool	Draws	Special Action
	Line	Move mouse in horizontal or vertical direction.
Rectangle	Rectangle	
	Square	Hold down Shift key.
Ellipse	Ellipse	
	Circle	Hold down Shift key.
Freeform	NUBS curve	

The only tool that isn't dual-purpose is the **Freeform** tool (also called the **Spline** tool), which draws NUBS curves. *NUBS* is short for non-uniform Bezier spline and should not be confused with the more common NURBS curve (non-uniform *rational* Bezier spline) found in computer-aided design software.

Another way of looking at the drawing tools is to list them by the objects they draw:

To draw a...	Use this tool...
Line	Line tool.
	Pencil tool, and move mouse in a straight line.
Constrained line	Line tool, and hold down Shift key.
	Pencil tool, and hold down Shift key.
	Arc tool, and move mouse in a horizontal or vertical direction.
Circular arc	Pencil tool, and move mouse in a curve.
Curve	Freeform tool.
Circle	Ellipse tool, and hold down Shift key.
Elliptical arc	Arc tool.
Ellipse	Ellipse tool.
Rectangle	Rectangle tool.
Square	Rectangle tool, and hold down Shift key.
Spline	Freeform tool.

The **Pencil** tool also creates new vertices and allows you to move the vertices, as described later in this module.

Tip: So that you know where an open object, such as a line or arc, starts and ends, Visio uses these symbols:

Symbol	Meaning
x	Starting point of a line or arc
□	Midpoint (control point)
+	Ending point

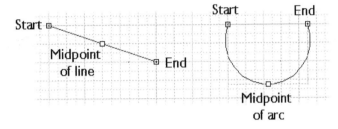

After you draw a line or arc, notice that there is a small x where you began drawing and a small + where you stopped drawing. To connect one line or arc to another, start drawing from the endpoint. Visio automatically connects the two. The control point is used to change the radius of arcs and splines.

Procedures

Before presenting the general procedures for drawing, it is helpful to know the shortcut keys. These are:

Function	Keys	Toolbar Icon
Arc Tool	Ctrl+7	⌐
Ellipse Tool	Ctrl+9	◯
Line Tool	Ctrl+6	╱
Pencil Tool	Ctrl+4	✎
Rectangle Tool	Ctrl+8	▢
Spline Tool	Ctrl+5	∿

Visio 2000 has combined the six drawing tools into two flyout toolbars. One flyout contain the drawing tools for closed objects (Rectangle and Ellipse); the other flyout contains the drawing tools for open objects (Line, Arc, Spline, and Pencil).

Accessing a tool is now a two-step process:

1. Click the small arrow next to the **Rectangle** or **Line** tool.

2. Move the cursor down to the tool you want.

3. Click the tool's button.

Drawing with the Pencil Tool

Use the following procedure to draw a line or a circular arc with the Pencil tool:

1. Click the **Pencil** tool.

2. Drag (hold down the button and move the mouse) to draw with the Pencil tool.

3. Move the mouse in a straight line to draw a straight line at any angle.

4. Hold down the **Shift** key to draw a line in 45-degree increments.

5. Or, slowly move the mouse in the shape of an arc and the **Pencil** tool draws a circular arc. You cannot draw a circle with this tool.

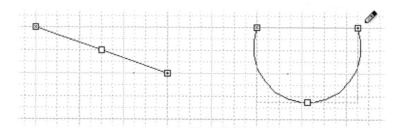

Tip: To draw a line in *45-degree increments* means that Visio draws the line at one of the 45-degree angles—0, 45, 90, 135, 180, 225, 270, and 315 degrees—nearest to the angle your mouse is moving. The illustration shows lines drawn at 45-degree increments.

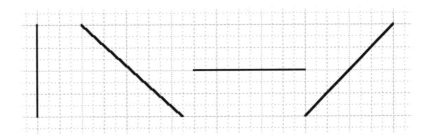

Drawing with the Line Tool

Use the following procedure to draw a line with the Line tool:

1. Click the **Line** tool.
2. Drag to draw a line at any angle with the Line tool.
3. Hold down the **Shift** key to draw a line in 45-degree increments.

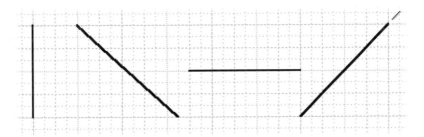

Drawing with the Arc Tool

Use the following procedure to draw an elliptical arc or a line with the Arc tool:

1. Click the **Arc** tool.
2. Drag to draw an elliptical arc with the Arc tool.

3. Or, move the mouse in a horizontal or vertical direction to draw a horizontal or vertical line.

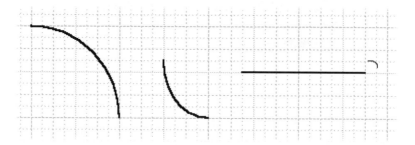

 Note: The arcs drawn by the **Arc** and **Pencil** tools may seem the same, but they have a couple of differences. The **Arc** tool draws a quarter elliptical arc, while the **Pencil** tool draws a circular arc that isn't necessarily a quarter of a circle.

Drawing with the Rectangle Tool

Use the following procedure to draw a rectangle or a square with the Rectangle tool:

1. Click the **Rectangle** tool.
2. Drag diagonally to draw a rectangle with the Rectangle tool. By default, the rectangle is filled with a white fill.
3. Or, hold down the **Shift** key to draw a square.

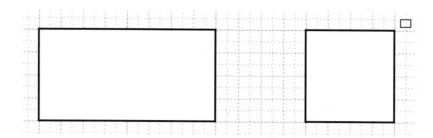

Drawing with the Ellipse Tool

Use the following procedure to draw an ellipse or a circle with the Ellipse tool:

1. Click the **Ellipse** tool.

2. Drag diagonally to draw an ellipse with the Ellipse tool. By default, the ellipse is filled with a white fill.

3. Or, hold down the **Shift** key to draw a circle.

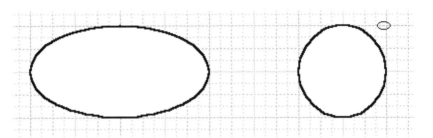

●◆ **Tip:** As you draw with the **Rectangle** or **Ellipse** tools, keep an eye on the status line. Visio reports the rectangular size of the object, such as:

Width = 1.25 in   Height = 4.5678 in

For the other drawing tools, the status line reports the current x,y-coordinates, such as:

X = 2.345 in   Y = 10 in

Drawing Closed Objects

The types of objects drawn with the tools discussed in this chapter fall into two categories: open and closed. An *open object* is like a line, arc, or open spline. A *closed object* is like a circle, rectangle, or square.

Visio lets you create closed objects using the Line, Arc, and other open object tools. For example, you would use these tools to create shapes that look like a triangle, the letter D, and so on. You cannot, however, easily convert a closed object (drawn with the Rectangle and Ellipse tools) into an open object—without getting into the ShapeSheet, which is beyond the scope of this book (see *Learn Visio 2000 for the Advanced User*, also from Wordware Publishing).

Use the following procedure to draw a closed object in the shape of a triangle:

1. Click the **Line** tool.

2. Hold down the **Shift** key, then click and drag to create a line at a 45-degree angle.

3. Ensure the cursor is over the endpoint of the line. When the cursor is over the endpoint, it changes to look like a small + sign.

4. Click and drag to create the horizontal base of the triangle. Notice that the endpoints of the two line segments have changed, from small squares to small diamonds, called a *vertex*.

5. Hold down the **Shift** key, then click and drag to create the last 45-degree segment of the triangle.

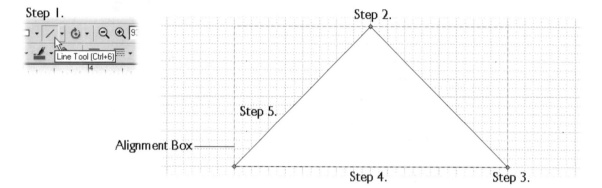

Step 1.

Step 2.

Step 5.

Alignment Box

Step 4.

Step 3.

> ▲ **Note:** As soon as you release the mouse button, notice that the triangle is filled with white, and is surrounded by a green, dashed rectangle called the *alignment box*. These two indicators tell you that you have successfully created a closed object.

Adding Segments to an Object

Once you have drawn an object, you can add additional segments along the existing lines and arcs making up the object. This works with any open or closed object drawn with any of the drawing tools. You add a segment by inserting a vertex. Here's how:

1. Select one of the open drawing tools (Pencil, Line, Arc, or Freeform).

2. Click anywhere on the object to select it.

3. Between two existing vertices, hold down the **Ctrl** key and click on the line at the point at which you want to add the vertex. It is not important that you click at a precise location, since the new vertex can be later moved to the correct location. Notice the new vertex at your click point, resulting in two segments where previously there was just one.

4. You may now use the **Pointer** tool to adjust the location of the vertex.

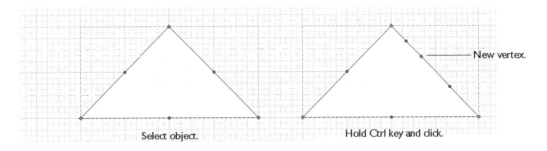

Select object.   Hold Ctrl key and click.   New vertex.

●◖ **Tip:** You will find it easier to draw a closed object when snap is turned on (which it normally is). If you find it difficult to connect to the ends, select **Tools | Snap & Glue** from the menu bar. In the Snap & Glue dialog box, ensure the following options are set:

Currently active: **Snap**

Snap to: **Shape geometry**

Click **OK**.

Moving the Vertex

With the vertex added, you can now drag it to a different location.

1. Select the **Pencil** tool and select the shape. Notice that the vertex and control points are displayed.
2. Move the pencil cursor over a control point.
3. When the cursor changes to a four-headed arrow, drag the control point.

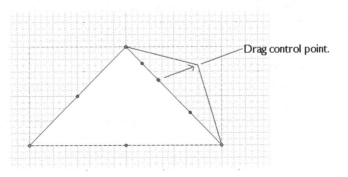

Drag control point.

Hands-On Activity

In this activity, you use the drawing tools. Begin by starting Visio. Then open a new document with no template.

1. Click the **Pencil** tool. Notice that the cursor looks like a tiny pencil with a small crosshair at the "pencil" tip.

2. Drag across the page (hold down the button, move the mouse, let go of the button). Notice that Visio has drawn a line (or an arc, depending on your mouse movement).

Tip: While holding down the mouse button for the Pencil tool, carefully examine the cursor. It has changed to a + marker, along with either a short straight line or a small arc. The straight line means Visio has sensed your mouse movement to be in a straight line; Visio accordingly draws a straight line.

The small arc means Visio has sensed your mouse movement to be curved; Visio accordingly draws an arc. If the arc looks to you like a straight line—even though Visio shows the arc indicator—it probably is a straight line.

---

3. Using the Pencil tool is tricky. Practice drawing lines with the Pencil tool by moving the mouse straight.

4. Practice drawing arcs with the Pencil tool by moving the mouse in a curve. I find it easier to move the mouse slowly and in an exaggerated curving motion.

5. Hold down the **Shift** key while drawing with the Pencil tool. Notice how Visio constrains the line to 45 or 90 degrees; if you are drawing an arc, holding the **Shift** key constrains the curvature of the arc.

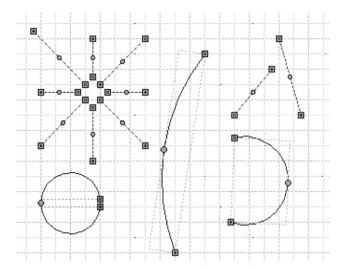

6. Select one of the arcs you have drawn.

 Note: Notice that the lines and arcs have three green shapes, called *handles*. At one end, the green square has a small x in it. That handle is Visio's reminder of where you began drawing the line or arc.

At the other end, the green square has a small + in it. That is where you ended drawing the line or arc.

At the center, the green circle is empty. This handle shows you the center of the line or arc. It also functions as a *control point*. When you grab it and move it toward the midpoint of the other two handles, an arc straightens out into a line. Moving the midpoint of a line moves the line.

7. Drag the center handle back and forth. Notice how the arc changes its curve.
8. Press **Ctrl+A** to select all objects in the drawing.
9. Press **Delete** to erase all objects.
10. Select the **Rectangle** tool.

11. Drag to draw a rectangle. Notice the rectangle is filled with white.

12. Select **gray** from the Fill list box.

13. Hold the **Shift** key while dragging with the **Rectangle** tool to draw a square.

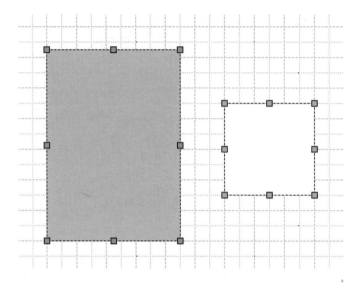

14. Press **Alt+F4** to exit Visio. Click **No** in response to the Save Changes dialog box.

This completes the hands-on activity for using the drawing tools. While just using stencil shapes and connector tools can create many Visio drawings, it is useful to know about the drawing tools.

Module 24 *Placing Text and Fields*

Text Tool
Insert | Field

Uses

> **In this chapter you'll learn about:**
> ✓ **Placing text**
> ✓ **Inserting a text field**

You can add text to the drawing in two ways: to an existing shape by double-clicking on it, or anywhere in the drawing via the **Text** tool. Once the text is placed, you change the size, font, color, etc., as described in Module 14 "Formatting Text."

A *field* is a piece of text attached to a shape that automatically updates itself. For example, the Date/Time field displays the current date and time, making it a time stamp. Some fields update themselves each time the drawing is opened; other fields update when the attached shape changes.

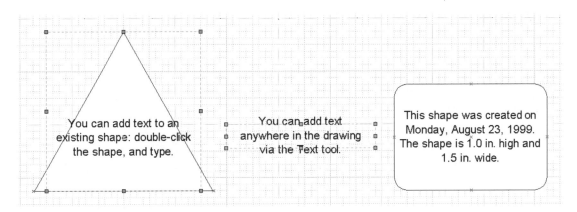

You can add text to an existing shape: double-click the shape, and type.

You can add text anywhere in the drawing via the Text tool.

This shape was created on Monday, August 23, 1999. The shape is 1.0 in. high and 1.5 in. wide.

Caution: There are some shortcomings you should be aware of in how Visio 2000 handles text. Visio does not automatically resize the alignment box to fit the text (see the center figure on the previous page). To partially overcome this limitation, Visio 2000 now displays the text as you adjust the alignment box.

Text can only be flowed into a rectangular frame; you cannot, for example, flow text in a triangular or circular frame. The problem is illustrated by the text in the triangle shape, shown at left in the figure.

Procedures

Before presenting the general procedures for placing text and fields, it is helpful to know about the shortcut keys. These are:

Function	Keys	Menu	Toolbar Icon
Add text to shape	F2 (*)	…	…
Text Tool	Ctrl+2	…	**A**
Field	Ctrl+F9	Insert | Field	…

(*) As an alternative, you can double-click shapes (not groups) to add text, provided the double-click behavior has been set to edit text.

Placing Text

Use the following procedure to add text to a page:

1. Select the **Text** tool from the toolbar.
2. Click on the page at the location you want the text. As an alternative, you can click and drag a rectangle that defines a *text box* to hold the text.

 Note: When you use the **Text** tool to click the position for the text, Visio creates an invisible rectangle shape to hold the text. What appears to be the alignment box for the text is actually the alignment box of the rectangle.

3. Begin typing.

4. Select the **Pointer** tool when finished typing.

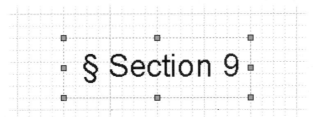

5. Resize and position the text block by dragging on the handles.

6. By default, the text is 8 pt Arial font, and is centered horizontally and vertically relative to the alignment box. Format the text, as described in Module 14.

Note: Visio lets you include special characters in the text. These characters are ones that you cannot normally type at the keyboard:

Special Character	Keystroke
' Beginning single quote	Ctrl+[
' Ending single quote	Ctrl+]
" Beginning double quote	Ctrl+Shift+[
" Ending double quote	Ctrl+Shift+]
● Bullet	Ctrl+Shift+8
– (en dash)	Ctrl+=
— (em dash)	Ctrl+Shift+=
- (discretionary hyphen)	Ctrl+hyphen
- (nonbreaking hyphen)	Ctrl+Shift+hyphen
/ (nonbreaking slash)	Ctrl+Shift+/
\ (nonbreaking backslash)	Ctrl+Shift+\
§ (section)	Ctrl+Shift+6
¶ (paragraph)	Ctrl+Shift+7
© (copyright)	Ctrl+Shift+C
® (registered trademark)	Ctrl+Shift+R

A *discretionary* hyphen shows Visio where to hyphenate a word if necessary, such as *dis-cretionary*; the hyphen is normally invisible. A *nonbreaking* hyphen tells Visio not to hyphenate the word at the hyphen, such as "on-line." The nonbreaking slash is useful for fractions, such as "11/32." See Appendix A for a list of all keyboard shortcuts, including command shortcuts.

239

Tip: You can place text in the drawing from any other Windows application. Copy the text to the Clipboard (using **Ctrl+C**), then switch to Visio. Press **Ctrl+V** (you don't need to select the Text tool first) and Visio places the text in the center of the drawing.

If the text was formatted in the other application, Visio faithfully mimics the formatting, including font, size, bolding, and so on. If you don't want the text formatting copied, follow these steps:

- Select **Edit | Paste Special** from the menu.
- Select **ANSI Text** from the Paste Special dialog box.
- Click **OK**.

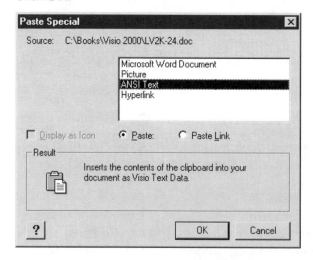

For more information on using the Clipboard with Visio, see Module 12 "Cutting, Copying, and Pasting."

Inserting a Text Field

Use the following procedure to insert a text field:

1. Select a shape.
2. Select **Insert | Field**. Notice the Field dialog box.

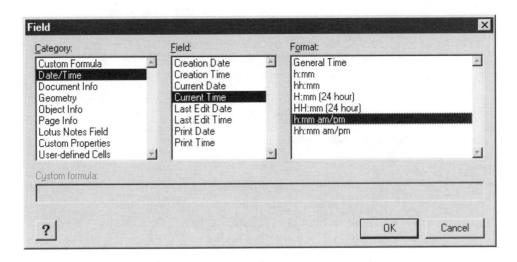

3. Select a **Category**:

Custom Formula: Allows you to enter a formula that would be valid in a ShapeSheet cell.

Date/Time: Displays the current date and time, or the date and time the drawing was created, last edited, or most recently printed. The date and time are based on your computer's clock.

Document Info: Displays the data stored in the Properties dialog box (File | Properties), such as title, author, and keywords.

Geometry: Displays the height, width, and rotation angle of the shape.

Object Info: Displays the data recorded by the Special dialog box (Format | Special) and stored in the ShapeSheet.

Page Info: Displays the page number, number of pages, and name of the background shape.

Lotus Notes Field: Displays the data stored in the Lotus Notes Field dialog box (Insert | Lotus Notes Field).

Custom Properties: Displays the shape's custom property data as defined by the Custom Properties dialog box (Shape | Custom Properties).

User-defined Cells: Displays the data stored in the shape's Value cell of the User-defined Cells section of the ShapeSheet.

4. Select an item in the **Field** column. The variety of fields available differs, depending on the category selected. In some cases, such as Custom Properties and User-defined Cells, the Field column is blank until you define those items.

5. Select an item in the **Format** column. The formats available vary, depending on the field selected.

6. Click **OK**. Notice that Visio adds the field to the shape.

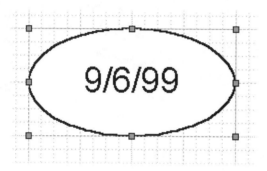

 Note: Visio allows you to insert some text fields without needing to access the Field dialog box. Use the following keystrokes to insert these fields as you type:

Text Field Functions	Keystroke
Rotation angle of text	Ctrl+Shift+A
Height of text	Ctrl+Shift+H
Width of text	Ctrl+Shift+W

Hands-On Activity

In this activity, you use the text and field functions together. Begin by starting Visio. Then open any template.

1. Select the **Text** tool.

2. Click anywhere on the page.

3. Type **This drawing was created on:**.

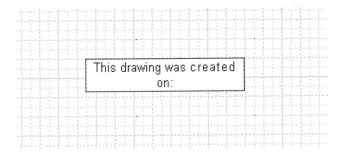

4. Select **Insert | Field**. Notice the Field dialog box.
5. Select **Date/Time** from the Category list.
6. Select **Creation Date** from the Field list.
7. Select **Long Date** from the Format list.

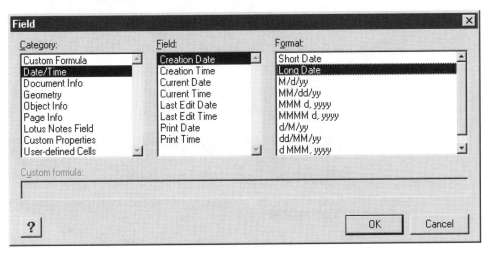

8. Click **OK**. Notice the date text placed in the drawing. (The date displayed in your drawing depends on the date you perform this task.)

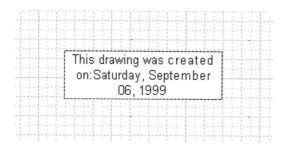

Creating a Dimension Line

One useful application of text and fields is geometry that mimics the dimension lines used in CAD (computer-aided design) drawings. You can have the dimension display the length or the angle of the line.

1. Click the **Line** tool.
2. Draw a line at any angle on the lower half of the page.
3. Select **Insert | Field**, ensuring that the line is still selected.
4. Select **Geometry** from the Category list.
5. Select **Angle** from the Field list.
6. Select **Degrees** from the Format list.

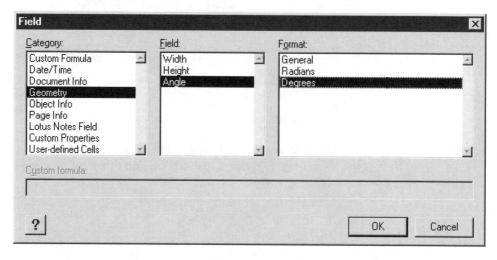

7. Click **OK** to close the Field dialog box.

8. If necessary, zoom in to better read the text. Notice the text "27.65 deg." (The text displayed in your drawing may differ from the illustration below, depending on the angle that you drew the line.)

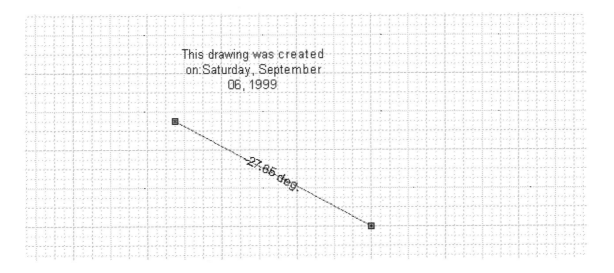

9. Click the **Pointer** tool.

10. Move an endpoint of the line to change its angle. Notice that the text automatically updates itself (to "6.84 deg." in my drawing).

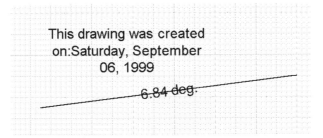

11. Press **Alt+F4** to exit Visio. Click **No** in response to the Save Changes dialog box.

This completes the hands-on activity for placing text and inserting fields. While text is important for annotating the drawing, the field feature is a very powerful way to display information that automatically updates itself.

 *Spelling*

Tools | Spelling

Uses

The **Spelling** function, found on the **Tools** menu, is used to check the spelling of words in

In this chapter you'll learn about:

✓ **Spell checking**

the current drawing. You can have Visio check the spelling of words in the entire drawing, on a specific page, or of selected text. You may add words to the Visio dictionary, such as trademarked names, personal names, and words particular to your discipline.

 Caution: The spell checker does not check correct word usage. Instead, it looks for words it does not recognize (i.e., words it does not find in its lengthy word list). The speller has no way of knowing whether a correctly spelled word is used incorrectly, such as using "weather" instead of "whether."

Procedures

Before presenting the general procedures for spelling, it is helpful to know about the shortcut key. It is:

Function	Keys	Menu	Toolbar Icon
Spell Check	F7	Tools	Spelling	ABC✓

Check Spelling

Use the following procedure to check the spelling of all words in the current page:

1. Select **Tools | Spelling**.

2. When Visio finds a word it does not recognize, it displays the Spelling dialog box.

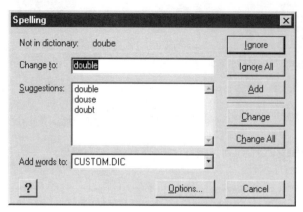

3. Click **Ignore** to have the Speller skip checking the word.
4. Click **Change** to select the word the Speller guesses might be correct.
5. Click **Add** to add the word to the Speller's word list.
6. Click **Options** to display the Spelling Options dialog box.

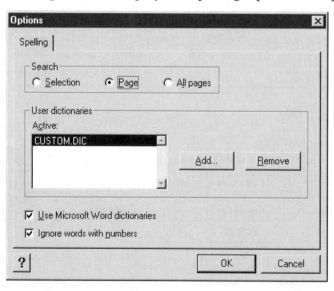

7. In the **Search** section, select if you want selected text, all text on the current page, or all text on all pages checked.
8. The **User dictionaries** section lets you maintain different custom dictionaries for different disciplines.

9. The **Use Microsoft Word dictionaries** option lets you use the dictionary provided with Microsoft Word; if the dictionary is not installed, this option is grayed out.

10. The **Ignore words with numbers** option does not spell check words containing a number, which are often dimensions and angles.

11. Click **OK**.

12. Click **OK** in the Visio dialog box when the spell check is complete.

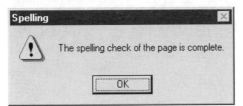

Hands-On Activity

In this activity, you use the spelling function. Begin by starting Visio. Then open any template.

1. Select the **Text** tool.

2. Type the following sentences:

   How to save Visio dramings.

   A tutorial by R. H. Grabowski.

Notice the spelling error "dramings" and the uncommon surname "Grabowski."

> How to save Visio dramings.
> A tutorial by R. H. Grabowski.

3. Select **Tools | Spelling** or press function key **F7**. Notice the Spelling dialog box shows "dramings" is not in its dictionary.

4. Click **Change**.

5. Notice that the Spelling dialog box now shows that "Grabowski" is not in its dictionary. Click **Add** to add the word to the **Custom.Dic** dictionary file. Visio gives no indication it has done so.

6. Visio displays a dialog box to indicate the spelling check is complete. Click **OK**. Notice that the spelling is correct in the drawing.

> # How to save Visio drawings.
> # A tutorial by R. H. Grabowski.

7. Exit Visio.

This completes the hands-on activity for spell checking text.

 **Module 26** **_Finding and Replacing Text_**

Edit | Find
Edit | Replace

Uses

> **In this chapter you'll learn about:**
> ✓ **Finding text**
> ✓ **Replacing text**

The **Find** and **Replace** selections of the **Edit** menu are used to find and replace text in the current drawing. You can have Visio search:

▶ The selected text block.
▶ The entire page.
▶ All pages of the current drawing.

Being computer software, Visio's find function finds <u>all</u> instances of a word or phrase, which the human eye can easily miss. This is particularly useful when your drawing contains several pages.

Another example is when another company buys out yours, and you have to change the name in all your drawings. Or, perhaps you have a standard set of drawings that you provide to a variety of clients; the replace function lets you change all instances of the client name. (It would be embarrassing to have the wrong client's name.)

You cannot use Visio's find and replace functions on text stored in custom properties, the Special data fields, or the Properties data fields.

Procedures

Before presenting the general procedures for finding and replacing text, it is helpful to know about the shortcut keys. These are:

Function	Keys	Menu	Toolbar Icon
Find	...	Edit | Find	...
Replace	...	Edit | Replace	...
Repeat	F4	Edit | Repeat	...

Finding Text

Use the following procedure to find text:

1. Select **Edit | Find** to display the Find dialog.

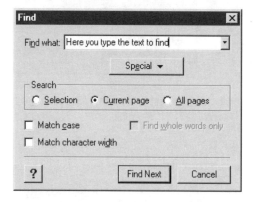

2. Type the word or phrase to find in the Find what text box.
3. Click **Special** to insert a special character.

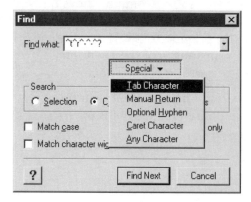

Note: Visio lets you search for some special characters that cannot be typed at the keyboard. For example, you cannot press the **Tab** key to search for tabs in text (pressing **Tab** takes you to the next field in the dialog box). For this reason, Visio provides a list box to insert non-typeable characters. Or, you can type these special characters:

Special Character	Meaning
^t	Tab
^r	Return (end of paragraph)
^-	Discretionary hyphen
^^	Caret (^) symbol
^?	Any character

A *discretionary* hyphen shows Visio where to hyphenate a word if necessary, such as *hy-phenate*; the hyphen is normally invisible.

4. The **Search** section indicates where to look for the phrase:

   Selection: The currently selected text.

   Current page: The currently visible page (the default).

   All pages: All pages of the drawing.

5. Click **Match case** to find a phrase that matches the same pattern of upper- and lowercase characters. When turned off (the default), the case is not matched. Searching for "visio" finds "Visio," "VISIO," and "visio." When on, the case is matched; searching for "visio" finds "visio" but not "VISIO" or "Visio."

6. Click **Find whole words only** to find a phrase that matches the same set of words. Searching for "visio" finds "Visio" but not "vision." When turned off (the default), the exact wording is not matched. Searching for "visio" finds "Visio" and "vision."

7. The **Match character width** option is meant for the Japanese Kanji version of Visio.

8. Click **Find Next** to find the next occurrence of the word or phrase.

9. When you are done finding words, click the **Cancel** button. When **Find** or **Replace** can't find or replace more text, the **Cancel** button becomes the **Close** button.

Tip: If you are not sure of the spelling, or want to search for variants of a word (such as Tool and Tools), use the ^? *wild-card* character. The ^? searches for any single character. In this example, you would ask Visio to search for **tool^?**.

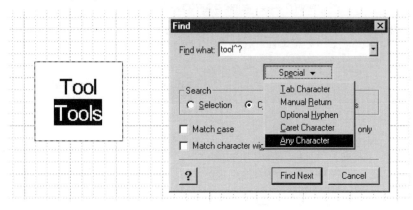

Replacing Text

The procedure for replacing text is similar to that of finding text:

1. Select **Edit | Replace**.

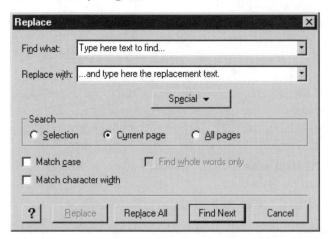

2. Type the word or phrase to find in the Find what text box.
3. Type the replacement word or phrase in the Replace with text box.

4. Click **Special** to insert a special character, as described earlier.

5. Click **Replace** to replace the next occurrence of the word or phrase.

6. Or, click **Replace All** to replace all occurrences of the word.

7. When you are done replacing words, click the **Cancel** or **Close** button.

Hands-On Activity

In this activity, you use the find function. Begin by starting Visio.

1. In the Welcome to Visio 2000 dialog box, select **Browse existing files**.

2. From the **Organization Chart** folder, double-click on the **Global Organization Chart.Vsd** drawing. Notice that this is a two-page drawing showing an organization chart. You want to find "Rob Nickerson" but are not sure where he is in the company structure.

3. Select **Edit | Find**. Notice the Find dialog box.

4. In the Find what text box, type **Rob Nickerson**.

5. Click the **All pages** button in the Search area to search both pages of this drawing.

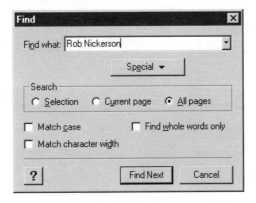

6. Click **Find Next**. Notice that Visio takes you directly to the page with Rob Nickerson's name and highlights the text block.

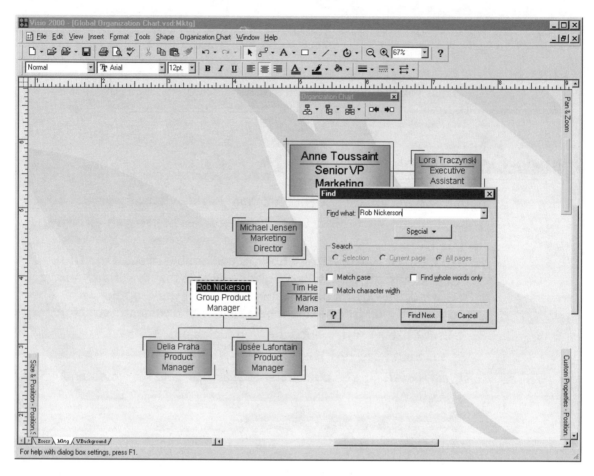

7. Click **Cancel** to close the Find dialog box.

This completes the hands-on activity for finding text in a drawing.

Dimensioning

Uses

Architects and engineers use dimensions to indicate the exact measurements of distances and angles. Specifying the distance is much more accurate than measuring off the paper with a ruler. Dimensions are usually used in office layout drawings, where you might need to indicate distances, such as the length of a wall or the clearance between a wall and a desk.

In this chapter you'll learn about:

✓ *Automatically dimensioning a wall shape*

✓ *Manually dimensioning any shape*

✓ *Changing the dimension line*

✓ *Changing the extension line*

✓ *Changing the dimension text*

Visio 2000 Standard Edition supports a single dimension, which can be used for indicating horizontal, vertical, and angled distances.

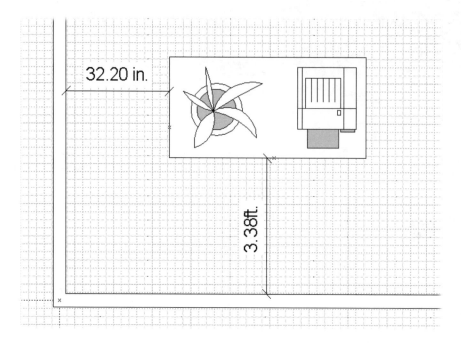

A *horizontal* dimension measures the horizontal distance between two points, while a *vertical* dimension measures the vertical distance between two points. The dimension is made up of five parts:

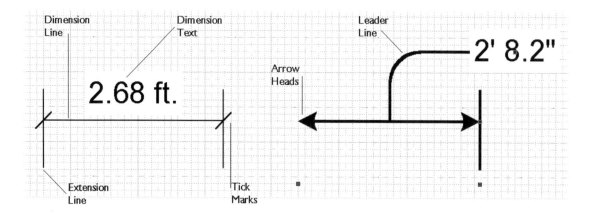

Dimension line shows the distance being measured. You may change the color and line weight of the dimension line; changing it to another line pattern is not usually done in dimensioning.

Dimension text explicitly states the distance. You can choose from Visio's many different dimension formats, such as imperial and metric units, and different numbers of decimal places. The text can be placed anywhere relative to the dimension line.

Leader line matches the dimension text to the dimension in cases where the text is not right next to the line.

Arrowheads (which look like tick marks and are called *line ends* by Visio) indicate the ends of the dimension line. Visio has dozens of line ends available, plus you can define your own line end.

Extension lines extend from the dimension line down to the points being measured. These lines can be any length you desire, including zero length. In some cases, it is not uncommon to have just one extension line. As with dimension lines, you may change the color and line weight of the extension line; changing it to another line pattern is not usually done in dimensioning.

The dimension has five control points that affect the look of the dimension. The control handles change the length of the extension lines, the length and angle of the dimension line, and the position of the text. You learn more about using these control points later in this module.

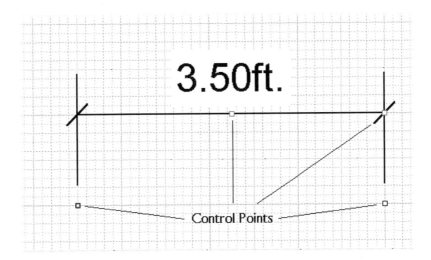

259

Procedures

The dimensioning "function" is not found on any menu or toolbar, nor are there are any shortcut keys for dimensioning in Visio. For best results, start with the **Office Layout** template (choose the **Office Layout** folder, and then the **Office Layout** drawing type; then click **OK**). Note that Visio Technical includes a broader range of dimension types, which are not covered in this book. You create dimensions by two methods:

Automatic dimensioning: Right-click a wall object, and select **Add a Dimension** from the shortcut menu.

Manual dimensioning: Drag the **Dimension line** shape into the drawing, and attach it to the shape(s) being dimensioned.

Automatically Dimensioning a Wall Shape

1. With Visio already running, from the menu bar select **File | New | Office Layout | Office Layout**. Notice that Visio opens a new drawing and the Office Layout Shapes stencil.

2. Drag the **Wall** shape into the drawing. Notice that the shape looks like a long, narrow rectangle.

3. Right-click the wall shape. Notice the shortcut menu.

4. From the shortcut menu, select **Add a Dimension**. Notice that Visio immediately adds a horizontal dimension.

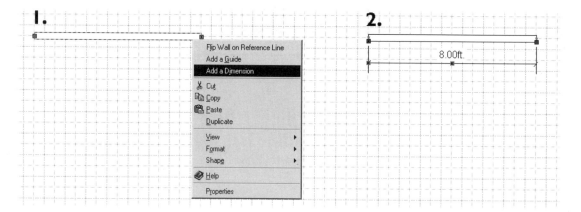

●◆ **Tip:** When a drawing contains many wall shapes, you can dimension them all at one time. Select all walls (hold down the Shift key while selecting them). Right-click one of the walls, and select **Add a Dimension**. Visio places a dimension on all walls you selected.

Manually Dimensioning Any Shape

1. With Visio already running, from the menu bar select **File | New | Office Layout | Office Layout**. Notice that Visio opens a new drawing and the Office Layout Shapes stencil.

2. Drag the **Panel** shape into the drawing.

3. Drag the **Dimension line** shape into the drawing. As you drag it, notice that it looks like a diagonal line.

4. Attach an end of the dimension line to one end of the Panel shape. When you let go of the mouse button, notice that you see the dimension line at an angle.

5. Drag the free end of the dimension line to the remaining end of the panel. Notice that the dimension text updates itself to reflect the length of the dimension line.

I.

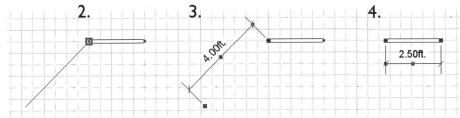

●◆ **Tip:** You can create your own dimension lines. Recall from Module 24 "Placing Text and Fields" that you can insert a field in a shape that automatically updates as the shape changes. Here's how to create a custom dimension shape:

1. Draw a line with the **Line** tool.

2. Use **Format | Line** to add arrowheads at both ends.

3. Use **Insert | Field** to attach a **Geometry | Width | General Units** field to the line. (Substitute **Height** for vertical dimensions and **Angle** for angular dimensions.)

4. Use **Format | Text** to make the font a legible size.

5. Once the dimension line looks good to you, use **Format | Define Styles** to create text and line styles for the named dimension.

As an alternative, you can take the Dimension shape provided with Visio and format it. See Module 13 "Formatting Shapes."

Changing the Dimension Line

To change the angle and length of the dimension line, move either of two control handles located at the base of the extension lines.

1. Drag a control handle back and forth, horizontally, to lengthen and shorten the dimension. Notice that the dimension text updates itself. When the dimension becomes too small, first the dimension lines move outside the extension lines; then the dimension text moves outside the extension lines.

2. Rotate to make the dimension vertical or at an angle. Notice that the text rights itself when the dimension goes upside down.

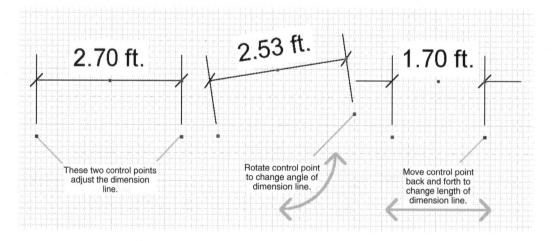

Changing the Extension Line

To change the length of both extension lines, move the single control handle located at the end of the dimension line. An option on the shortcut menu allows you to select additional options for extension lines.

1. Drag the control handle up and down to change the length of the extension lines.

2. When you drag the control handle to the other side of the shape, the dimension relocates to that side.

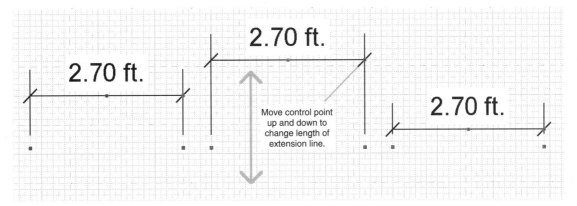

3. Right-click the dimension, and select **Extension Lines** from the shortcut menu. Notice that Visio displays the Custom Properties dialog box.

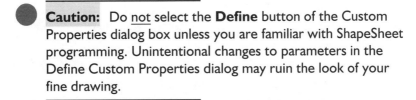

Caution: Do <u>not</u> select the **Define** button of the Custom Properties dialog box unless you are familiar with ShapeSheet programming. Unintentional changes to parameters in the Define Custom Properties dialog may ruin the look of your fine drawing.

4. From the dialog box, you can select whether you want both, neither, or either extension line displayed.

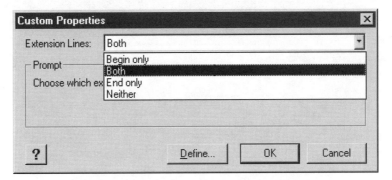

5. Make a selection and click **OK**. Notice that the visibility of the extension lines disappears.

Changing the Dimension Text

To change the position of the dimension text, move the control handle located in the center of the text. Options on the shortcut menu allow you to set additional options for dimension text.

1. Drag the control handle around to move the location of the dimension text.

2. If you drag the text away far enough, notice the leader line, which shows which dimension the text belongs to.

3. Right-click the dimension, and select **Reset Text Position** from the shortcut menu. Notice that Visio moves the dimension text to its original position over the dimension line.

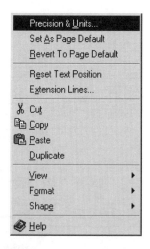

4. To rotate the dimension text, use the **Text Block** tool. (The **Reset Text Position** option does not apply to the angle of the text.)

5. To change the display format of the text, right-click the dimension, and select **Precision & Units** from the shortcut menu. (The *display format* is the format that Visio displays the text in; it does not affect the measured accuracy of the dimension.) Notice that Visio displays a Custom Properties dialog box.

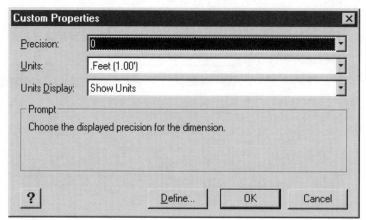

▶ **Precision**: Determines the number of decimal places displayed by the dimension text. Select from **0** through **4** decimal places. For example, selecting **0** precision means that a dimension **2.85** long is displayed as **3**.

▶ **Units**: Determines the units by which the dimension text is displayed. You can select from **Use Drawing Page's Units** or one of nine other imperial and metric units. Selecting a metric unit automatically converts the dimension's value. For example, selecting **cm** units means that a dimension **1** inch long is displayed as **2.54 cm**.

▶ **Units Display**: Toggles between turning the display of dimension text on and off.

6. Once you have made changes to the dimension's display format, you can make that the style for all dimensions on the page. Right-click the dimension, and select **Set As Page Default** from the shortcut menu. Notice that the text of all other dimensions changes to match the one you modified. In addition, when you now drag dimension shapes into the page, their text resembles the one that you modified.

7. If you accidentally "over modify" some dimension text, you can quickly return it to the default settings of the page. Right-click the dimension, and select **Revert To Page Default** from the shortcut menu.

Hands-On Activity

In this activity, you use the dimensioning functions. Begin by starting Visio.

1. Start Visio. The Welcome to Visio 2000 dialog opens.

2. Select **Choose drawing type**, then select **Office Layout** and **Office Layout**.

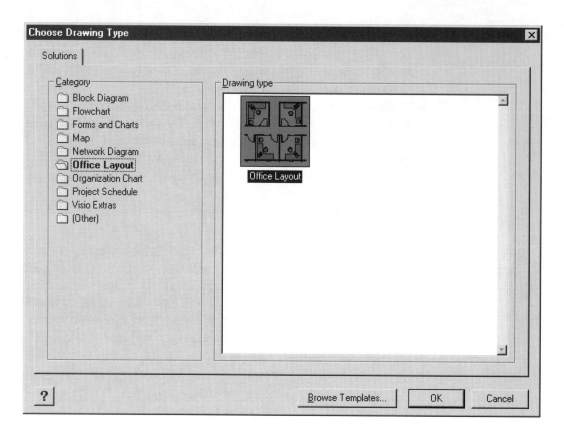

3. Click **OK**. Notice that Visio opens a new drawing and the Office Layout Shapes stencil. The page has been set up for floorplan designs. Its orientation is landscape, and its scale is 1/4"=1' (i.e., each quarter-inch on the page represents one foot in the real world).

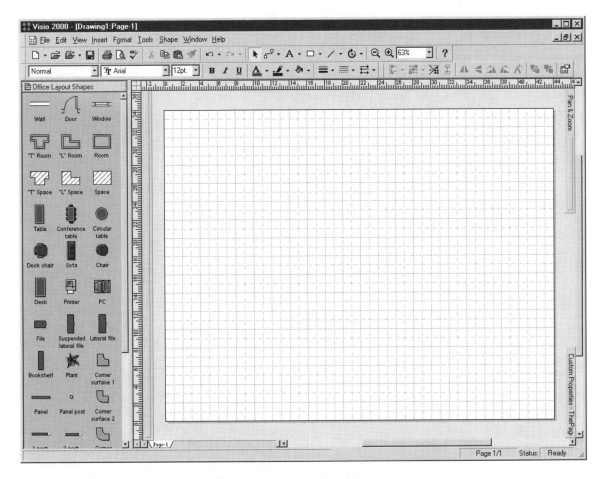

4. Drag the **Wall** shape onto the page.

5. Drag three more **Wall** shapes onto the page, connecting them together to create a square room. To make a wall shape vertical, drag the free end around until it connects with another wall end. Notice that Visio automatically *miters* (or joins) the ends of the walls, so that it looks like one continuous, four-sided wall shape.

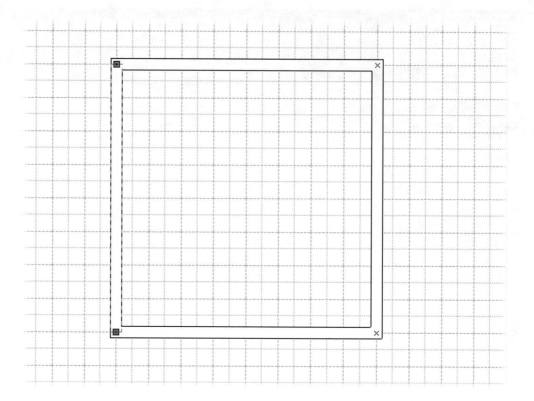

6. Here you automatically dimension a wall. Select a horizontal wall. Right-click and select **Add a Dimension** from the shortcut menu. Notice that Visio automatically places a horizontal dimension along the wall.

Tip: Dimension should always, if possible, be located outside the walls of a room. If the dimension appears on the "wrong" side (inside the room), use the control handle on the extension line to drag the dimension to the other side of the wall.

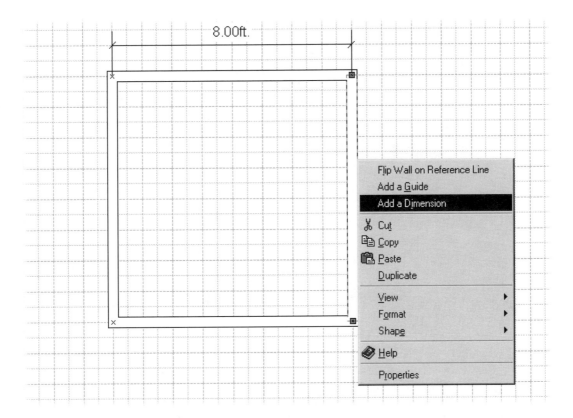

7. In this step, you automatically dimension two walls at the same time. Select a vertical wall and the remaining horizontal wall. Right-click and select **Add a Dimension** from the shortcut menu. Notice that Visio automatically places dimensions along both walls.

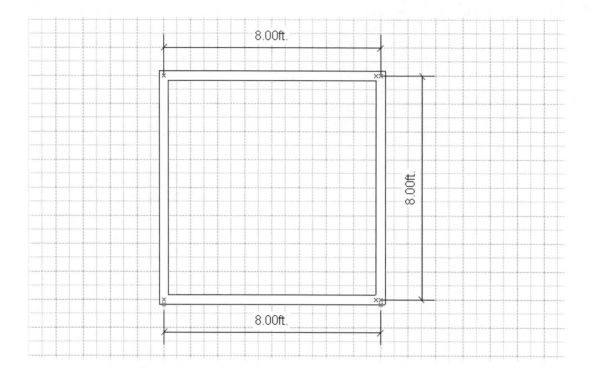

8. In the final steps of this activity, you manually dimension the remaining vertical wall. Drag the **Dimension line** shape onto the page.

9. Attach the lower end of the dimension line to the lower end of the vertical wall.

10. Drag the free end of the dimension line to the upper end of the vertical wall. Notice that the dimension clicks into place.

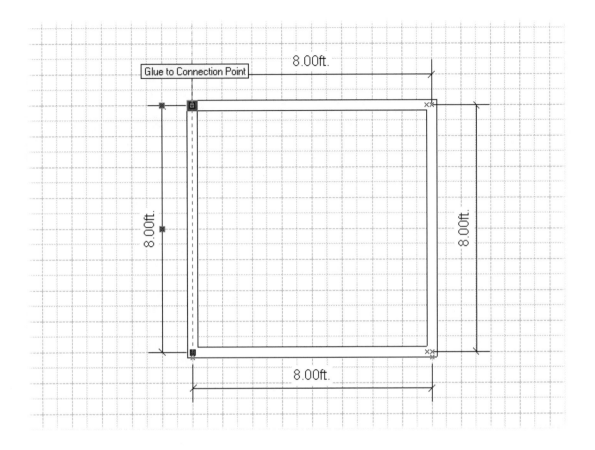

11. Press **Alt+F4** to exit Visio. Click **No** in response to the Save Changes dialog box.

This completes the hands-on activity for dimensioning.

 *Inserting Objects*

Insert | Object
Crop Tool

Uses

The insert functions, found on the **Insert** menu, are used to insert objects created by other Windows applications. From the **Insert** menu, Visio inserts the following kinds of objects: control, CAD drawing, Microsoft Graph, Data Map, object, and picture.

> **In this chapter you'll learn about:**
> ✓ **Inserting a picture**
> ✓ **Applying the Crop tool**
> ✓ **Inserting a new object**
> ✓ **Inserting an object from a file**
> ✓ **Placing a linked object**
> ✓ **Editing an object within Visio**

In general, you only view the inserted object (technically, Visio displays a raster or metafile image of the object). Visio allows you to perform some limited editing on inserted objects, such as move and copy. While Visio cannot change the content of the object, Visio can apply formatting to its frame, such as adding a shadow and cropping its boundary.

To edit the inserted object, you double-click the object and Visio launches the originating application, which then allows you to edit the object. You usually see the originating application's menu bar (and perhaps some toolbars) replace Visio's.

The options of the **Insert** menu item, as they relate to this chapter, are:

▶ **Control**: Inserts a VBA control. VBA is short for Visual Basic for Applications, which is not covered by this book.

▶ **CAD Drawing**: Inserts a drawing created by a CAD (computer-aided design) program. See Module 37 "Importing CAD Drawings" for details. Visio 2000 supports:

File Extension	Application File Format Notes
DGN	File format created by Bentley Systems' MicroStation CAD software; short for "design."
DWG	The file format created by several CAD packages, including AutoCAD, IntelliCAD, and VDraft; short for "drawing."
DXF	The file format invented by Autodesk for accessing data stored in its proprietary DWG format, and often used for exchanging drawings among CAD programs; short for "drawing interchange format."

▶ **Microsoft Graph**: Inserts a graph created by Microsoft Graph (not covered by this book).

▶ **Data Map**: Inserts a map created by an external data source, such as Microsoft Access or Excel (not covered by this book).

▶ **Object**: Inserts any OLE-aware Windows application installed on your computer, including Paintbrush, PowerPoint, WordPad, Netscape Navigator, Excel, Media Clip, and AutoCAD.

▶ **Picture**: Inserts any of these file formats:

File Extension	Application File Format Notes
AI	File format created by Adobe Illustrator, a vector-based drawing program.
BMP	The Windows standard raster format; short for "bitmap."
CDR	CorelDRAW file format, a popular Bezier-based drawing program; short for "Corel drawing."
CGM	A file format that mixes vector and raster; short for "Computer Graphics Metafile."
CMX	The file format of clip art included with the CorelDRAW package.
DIB	The "device-independent bitmap" variant of the Windows bitmap file format.
DRW	File format created by Micrografx Designer v3.1; short for "drawing."
DSF	Micrografx Designer v6 (now called iGrafx), a diagramming product similar to Visio; short for "designer format."
EMF	The Windows standard format for mixed raster and vector illustrations; short for "Enhanced Metafile."
EPS	A mixed raster-vector file format designed for PostScript-compatible printers, and understood by some software programs; short for "Encapsulated PostScript."

File Extension	Application File Format Notes
GIF	The most common raster format used on the Internet for smaller images due to its high level of lossless compression (invented by CompuServe); short for "Graphics Interchange Format."
IGES	A constantly shifting vector file format designed by a committee of CAD (computer-aided design) software companies, and meant for exchanging drawings between CAD systems (now largely superceded by STEP/PDES); short for "Initial Graphics Exchange Specification."
JPG/JPEG	Another popular format for displaying raster images on the Internet for larger images due to its very high levels of compression; short for "Joint Photographic Experts Group."
PCT	The image file format standard on Macintosh computers; short for "picture."
PCX	One of the earliest raster formats for personal computers, invented by ZSoft for its PC Paintbrush software; short for "personal computer raster."
PNG	For a time, the GIF format became less popular due to royalty issues over its compression engine; the "Portable Network Graphics" was created as an alternative royalty-free, high-compression raster file format for use on the Internet.
PS	A vector file format designed for PostScript-compatible printers, and understood by some software programs; short for "PostScript."
TIFF/TIF	The most popular raster file format for desktop publishing, and invented by Microsoft and Adobe; short for "Tagged Image File Format."
WMF	This Windows v3.x standard for mixed raster and vector illustrations was based on CGM; short for "Windows Metafile Format."

 Note: You can import additional file formats using the **File | Open** command; see Module 3 "Opening Existing Drawings." If a vector-based graphic appears jagged after being inserted in Visio, it may appear smoother by importing it with the **File | Open** command. Visio's documentation notes that this may occur with files created by Adobe Illustrator (AI), CorelDRAW (CDR), Encapsulated PostScript (EPS), and Micrografx Designer (DRW).

Using one of the Insert commands on a "foreign" file differs from using the Open command:

Open Command

Translates the file into Visio format.

Displays the translated object.

Insert Command

Keeps the object in its original format.

Displays a raster or metafile image of the object.

Open Command

Slower.

Cannot be linked.

Editable by Visio.

Insert Command

Faster.

Can be linked back to source application.

Not editable by Visio; edited by the source application with the result seen in Visio.

When you insert an object, you can instruct Visio to maintain a link back to the original file. Whenever that file is updated, the image in Visio is also updated.

Procedures

Before presenting the general procedures for inserting objects, it is helpful to know about the shortcut keys. These are:

Function	Keys	Menu	Toolbar Icon
Insert picture	Alt+II	Insert | Picture	...
Insert VBA control	Alt+IC	Insert | Control	
Insert CAD drawing	Alt+IA	Insert | CAD Drawing	...
Insert graph	Alt+IG	Insert | Microsoft Graph	...
Insert map	Alt+ID	Insert | Data Map	...
Insert OLE object	Alt+IO	Insert | Object	...
Crop object	...	...	

Inserting a Picture

Use the following procedure to insert a picture file into the Visio drawing:

1. Select **Insert | Picture**. Notice that Visio displays the Picture dialog box.

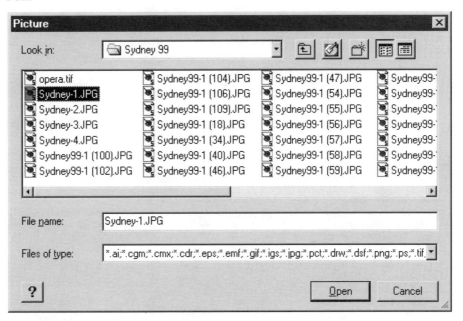

2. Select the drive and folder holding the picture you want to insert.

3. Click **Open**.

4. Depending on the file type selected, Visio may display an Import dialog box, which displays options specific to the file type. For example, the illustration shows the JPG Import dialog box with color translation options:

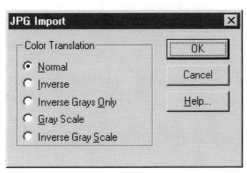

5. If required, change the type of Color Translation:

Color Translation	Meaning
Normal	Keep colors the way they appear in the file.
Inverse	Invert all colors, giving you a negative image.
Inverse Grays Only	Invert only black, white, and gray colors.
Gray Scale	Convert all colors to shades of gray.
Inverse Gray Scale	Convert all colors to shades of gray, then invert them.

The illustration shows the difference between normal (left) and inverse (right).

   ▸ If required, change the **Retain Background** option. When turned on, Visio draws a background rectangle in the image's background color.

   ▸ If required, set up the **Emulate Line Styles**. When turned on, Visio translates thick lines into polygons to help preserve visual accuracy.

6. Click **OK**. Notice that Visio takes several seconds to import the picture.

7. Notice that the picture object is placed in the center of the drawing, with green handles. You can move and resize the picture object, just like a Visio shape.

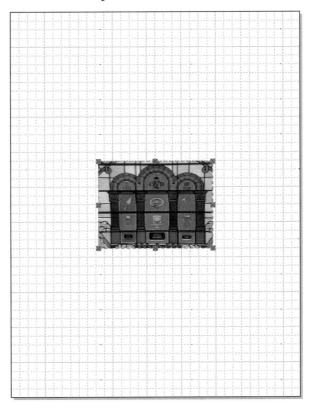

Applying the Crop Tool

Use the following procedure to crop a picture in the Visio drawing:

1. Select the picture object. Notice that Visio places handles around the picture.
2. Click the **Crop** tool; the tool may be "hidden" in the Rotation tool flyout.
3. Move the cursor over any of the handles. Notice that the cursor changes to a double-headed arrow.
4. Press the mouse button and drag the handle inward to crop the picture.

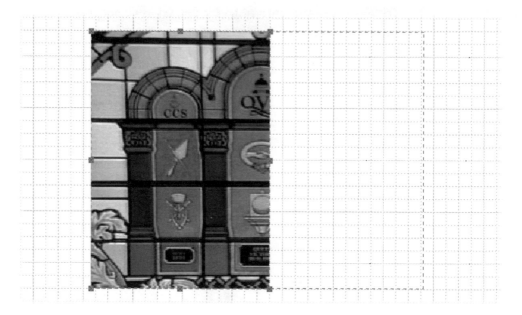

5. Let go of the mouse button, and Visio displays the smaller image. You can crop a picture object wider or narrower. When cropping wider, you don't see any more than what was present in the original image. The wider crop does, however, affect the placement of fill and shadow.

6. While the Crop tool is active, you may grab the center of the image and move it around.

Inserting a New Object

Use the following procedure to insert a new object:

1. Select **Insert | Object**. Notice that Visio displays the Insert Object dialog box.

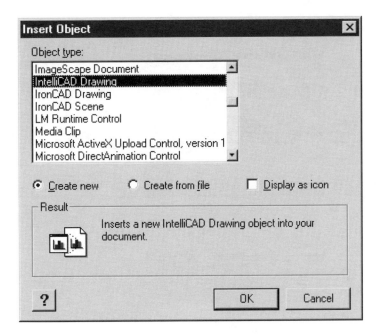

2. Click the **Create new** radio button. Notice the list of software names in the Object type list box.

3. Select a software program name from the Object type list box.

4. Click **OK**. Notice that Windows launches the application within Visio.

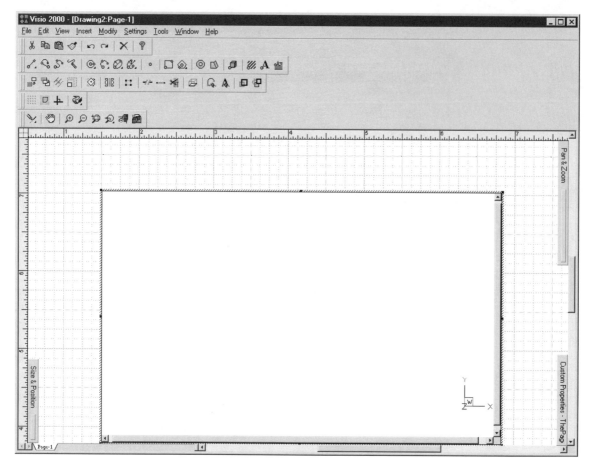

5. You can now create the new document within the application.

6. The method of exiting the application and returning to Visio varies. In some cases, select **File | Exit & Return to filename.vsd** when you are ready to return to Visio with the object. In other cases, simply pressing the **Esc** key works.

7. Notice the object is placed in the center of the Visio page.

Inserting an Object from a File

Use the following procedure to insert an object from an existing file:

1. Select **Insert | Object**. Notice that Visio displays the Insert Object dialog box.

2. Click the **Create from file** radio button. Notice the File name box and the Browse button.

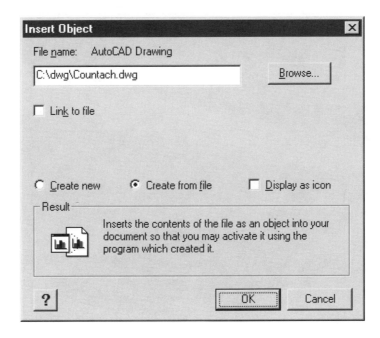

3. Type the name of the file; if you do not know it, click the **Browse** button to find it.

4. Click **OK**. Notice that Windows launches the application (called the *source* application) outside of Visio with the file you specified.

5. At the same time, the file appears in Visio, centered in the drawing.

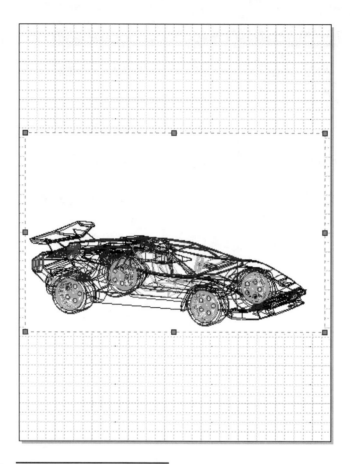

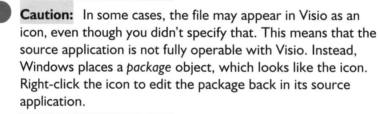

Caution: In some cases, the file may appear in Visio as an icon, even though you didn't specify that. This means that the source application is not fully operable with Visio. Instead, Windows places a *package* object, which looks like the icon. Right-click the icon to edit the package back in its source application.

6. You can exit the source application. Notice the object remains in Visio.

Placing a Linked Object

One problem with placing an object in Visio is that, after a period of time, it may no longer be up to date. For this reason, Visio allows you to insert a *linked* object. Whenever the source application makes a change to the original file, the object in Visio is also updated. Use the following procedure to insert a linked object:

1. Select **Insert | Object**. Notice that Visio displays the Insert Object dialog box.

2. Click the **Create from file** radio button.

3. Type the name of the file; if you do not know it, click the **Browse** button to find it.

4. Click the **Link to file** check box.

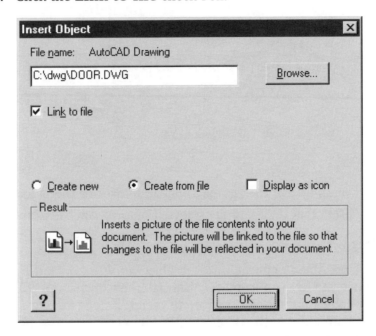

5. Click **OK**. Notice that Windows launches the application (called the *source* application) with the file you specified. At the same time, the file appears in Visio, centered in the drawing.

6. A linked object looks no different from an unlinked object. To check if the object is linked:

   ▶ Right-click the object.

   ▶ Notice the words "Linked Object" on the shortcut menu.

Although the menu may read **Linked Drawing Object | Convert**, the option <u>cannot</u> convert drawing objects to Visio shapes; see the following section for the workaround solution.

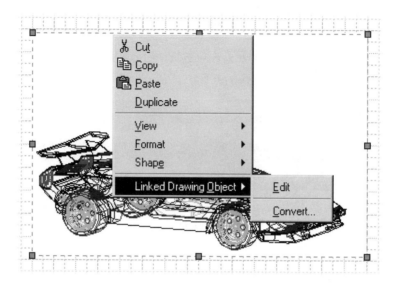

7. You may exit the source application. Notice the object remains in Visio.
8. Press **Del** to delete the selected object from the drawing.

Editing an Object within Visio

It is possible to edit an inserted object in Visio, once the object has been
converted to Visio format. (Although the Convert option appears to be
available on the object's shortcut menu, it does not work.) The
workaround described here works for vector pictures, not bitmap or raster
pictures.

1. Select the object.
2. Right-click the object. Notice the shortcut menu.

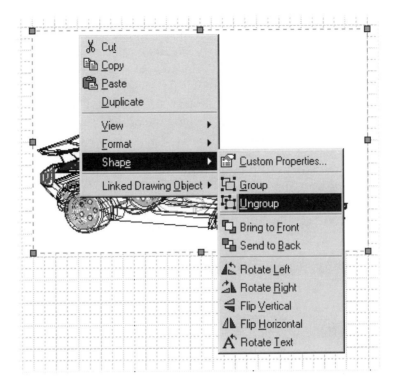

3. From the shortcut menu, select **Shape | Ungroup**. Notice that Visio displays the Convert To Group dialog box during the conversion process. Despite the name of the dialog box, Visio is <u>not</u> converting the object to a group; rather the object is converted to lines and arcs.

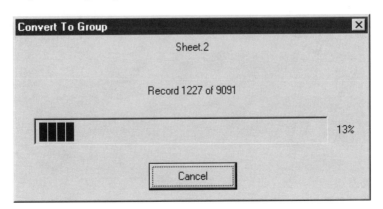

Note: If the picture is complex, it may take several minutes to ungroup the object. (Visio 2000 is better able to handle large drawings than were previous versions of Visio.) During the ungrouping process, Visio converts each vector (line or arc) to the nearest equivalent Visio object. The link (if any) back to the source application is lost. All lineweights change to the thinnest value.

4. The converted picture now consists of hundreds, or even thousands, of line and arc segments. I recommend that you group together this collection. Press **Ctrl+A** to select all shapes in the drawing, then press **Ctrl+G** to group the shapes together. See Module 17 "Creating Groups."

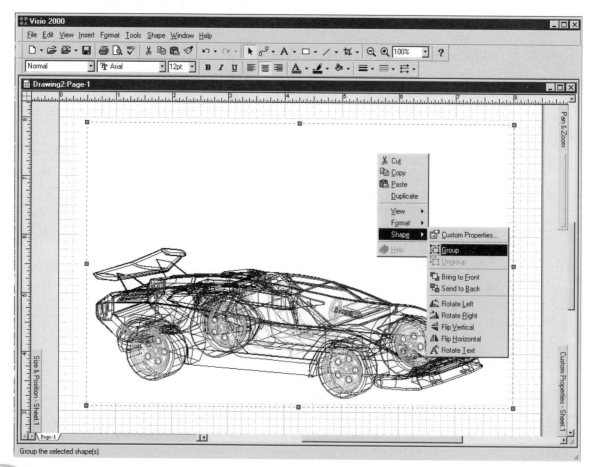

Exporting Drawings

File | Save As

Uses

The export function, found on the Save As dialog box from the **File** menu, converts the Visio drawing into other file formats. Visio drawings need to be converted since no other software program reads Visio files. You can export the current Visio page or selected shapes; you cannot export more than one page at a time (with the exception of exporting a multipage Visio drawing in HTML format).

> **In this chapter you'll learn about:**
>
> ✓ *Export options*
> ✓ *Exporting to AI and EPS*
> ✓ *Exporting to BMP and DIB*
> ✓ *Exporting to CGM*
> ✓ *Exporting to GIF*
> ✓ *Exporting to IGES*
> ✓ *Exporting to JPEG*
> ✓ *Exporting to PICT*
> ✓ *Exporting to PCX*
> ✓ *Exporting to PNG*
> ✓ *Exporting to TIFF*

 Caution: When Visio saves the drawing in another file format, it translates the drawing. This can have significant implications, since translations are never perfect.

When saving in a raster format, all Visio shapes are lost; indeed, when you see the raster image, it looks like a "grainy" photograph (the raster portion of the illustration on the following page has been exaggerated to show the effect).

When saving in a vector format or metafile format, shapes are usually saved in a similar object. For example, a line in Visio becomes a line in the other format; in some cases, however, there may be no exact match—or any match at all. For instance, Visio almost exclusively uses the elliptical arc, while older versions of AutoCAD have no native elliptical arc. In these cases, data may be changed or missing altogether.

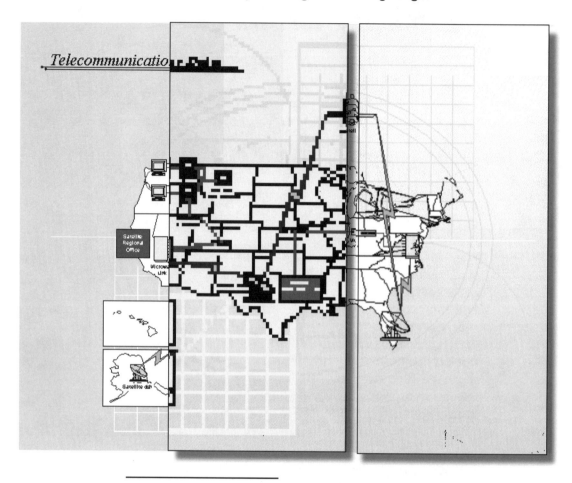

When you select **File | Save As**, Visio displays the Save As dialog box. In the **Save as type** list, you can select from the following file formats:

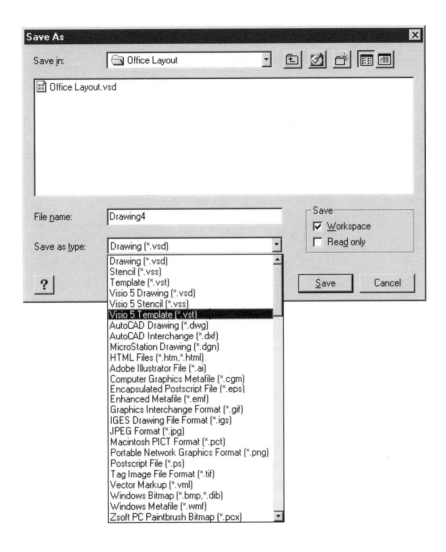

Save File As	Extension	Notes
Vector Formats		
Adobe Illustrator	AI	Also saves in EPS format.
⊠ AutoCAD Drawing	DWG	Created by AutoCAD, IntelliCAD, and other CAD (computer-aided design) systems.
⊠ AutoCAD Interchange	DXF	Drawing interchange format; used to access the data stored in DWG files and to exchange drawing files between CAD programs.
⊠ MicroStation Drawing	DGN	Created by Bentley Systems' MicroStation.

Save File As	Extension	Notes
IGES Drawing File Format	IGS	Short for "Initial Graphics Exchange Specification"; used to exchange drawing files between CAD programs; superceded by the STEP/PDES format.
PostScript File	PS	Commonly used in desktop publishing; designed to be a printer language.
⌁ Vector Markup Language	VML	Meant for displaying Visio drawings in Web pages; viewing requires Internet Explorer 5.x or higher.
Metafile Formats		
Computer Graphics Metafile	CGM	Saves in many flavors of CGM.
Encapsulated PostScript File	EPS	Commonly used in desktop publishing; also saves in AI format.
Enhanced Metafile	EMF	Standard for vector files in Windows 95/98; improves on WMF format.
Macintosh PICT Format	PCT	Picture format standard on Macintosh computers.
Windows Metafile Format	WMF	Standard for vector files in Windows 3.x; based on CGM format.
Raster Formats		
⌁ Graphics Interchange Format	GIF	Commonly used for small images on Web sites; lossless compression.
⌁ JPEG Format	JPG	Commonly used for large images on Web sites; lossy compression.
ZSoft PC Paintbrush Bitmap	PCX	The first commonly used raster file format.
⌁ Portable Network Graphics Format	PNG	Designed to replace GIF images on Web pages.
Tagged Image File Format	TIFF	Commonly used for desktop publishing.
Windows Bitmap	BMP	Standard for raster files in Windows; suffers from lack of compression.

Notes:

⌁ indicates the format is suitable for use on the Internet.

⊠ indicates the format is not available in Visio 2000 Standard Edition.

Exporting in HTML format is described in Module 36. Exporting in AutoCAD DWG and DXF file formats is described in Module 37.

Tip: When you have a choice of file formats and options, in general it is better to:

- Use a vector format since Visio is a vector format. Raster loses "resolution," which is a measure of accuracy.
- Use *compression* to reduce the file size of raster formats. Compression reduces the size of the file without losing any data.
- Not use compression when the receiving software cannot read it or when the format does not have the option.

Procedures

Before presenting the general procedures for exporting Visio files, it is helpful to know about the shortcut key. It is:

Function	Keys	Menu	Toolbar Icon
Export	F12	File | SaveAs	...

Export Options

Most formats display a dialog box of options, called **Output Filter Setup**. The content of this dialog box varies, depending on features supported by the file format and the translator. The following sections describe the options of the Output Filter Setup dialog boxes; the following file formats do not display the dialog box: VS*, EMF, VML, and WMF.

All of these dialog boxes allow you to save the settings by name, called profiles. In this way you can have several settings. For example, you might want low-resolution color output for a Web graphic, but high-resolution grayscale output for desktop publishing work. Profiles allow you to save settings by name, without needing to reselect the options.

With Visio open and a drawing loaded:

1. Select **File | Save As** from the menu bar. Notice the Save As dialog box.
2. In the **Save as type** list, select a file format other than Visio.
3. Click **Save**. After a moment, Visio displays the Output Filter Setup dialog box specific to the file format you selected.

4. Select the options in the dialog box.

5. Click **New**. Notice the New Profile Menu dialog box.

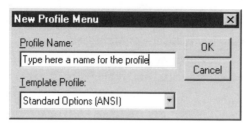

6. Type a name in the Profile Name text box. This name will appear in the Profiles list box the next time you see the Output Filter Setup dialog box.

7. Click **OK**.

8. Click **OK**. Notice that Visio's translator spends a few moments saving the drawing to disk in the translated format.

Export to AI and EPS

Convert the Visio drawing to AI (Adobe Illustrator) and EPS (Encapsulated PostScript) formats:

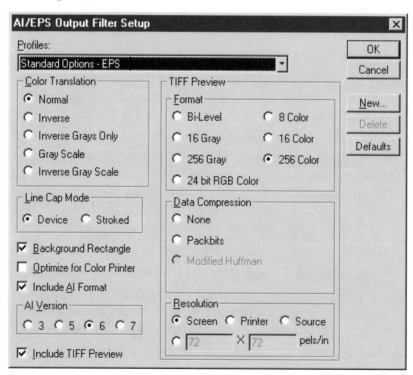

Color Translation:

- **Normal**: Keep the colors as they are in the Visio drawing.
- **Inverse**: Invert the colors (the picture looks like the strip of negatives from color film).
- **Inverse Grays Only**: Invert only white, black, and grays; keep other colors as they are.
- **Gray Scale**: Change the colors to levels of gray.
- **Inverse Gray Scale**: Change the colors to levels of gray and make a negative.

Line Cap Mode:

- **Device**: Use the line style and width capabilities of the display and printer driver.
- **Stroked**: Thick and patterned lines are drawn as polygons to more closely represent how they appear in the Visio drawing.

Other Options:

- **Background Rectangle**: Places a rectangle around the drawing as a border.
- **Optimize for Color Printer**: Optimized export format for color printers.
- **Include AI Format**: Include data for Adobe Illustrator format.
- **AI Version**: Select from version 3, 5, 6, or 7.
- **Include TIFF Preview**: Includes a small raster image for use within desktop publishing software, which cannot display AI and EPS formats.

TIFF Preview:

Format for the preview image:

- **Bi-Level**: Reduce the image to black and white; creates a smaller file size.
- **16 Gray**: Sixteen shades of gray.
- **256 Gray**: 256 shades of gray.
- **24 bit RGB Color**: 16.7 million colors.
- **8 Color**: Eight colors.
- **16 Color**: Sixteen colors.
- **256 Color**: 256 colors; the default.

Data Compression for the preview image:

▶ **None**: No compression creates a larger file but may be necessary for some applications that cannot read compressed TIFF files.

▶ **Packbits**: Best suited to black and white images.

▶ **Modified Huffman**: Best suited for gray images.

Resolution for the preview image:

▶ **Screen**: Use the screen resolution, typically 72 dpi (dots per inch) or 96 dpi.

▶ **Printer**: Use the printer's resolution, typically 300 dpi or 600 dpi; use this for the best quality hardcopy.

▶ **Source**: Let the destination application figure out the best resolution to use.

▶ **Custom**: Specify any resolution; default = 72 x 72 dpi. Visio recommends that the resolution range between 32 dpi and 400 dpi.

Export to BMP and DIB

Convert the Visio drawing to BMP (short for bitmap) or DIB (device-independent bitmap) raster file format:

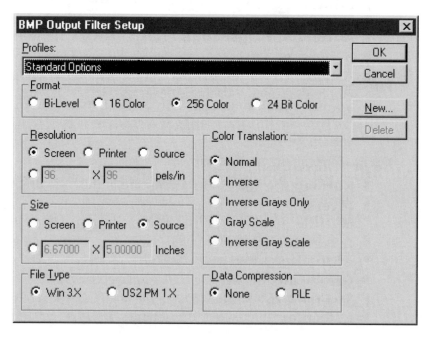

Format options:

▶ **Bi-Level**: Convert Visio drawing colors to black or white.

▶ **16 Color**: Reduce Visio drawing colors to 16 colors of the Windows standard.

▶ **256 Color**: Retain all Visio drawing colors.

▶ **24 bit Color**: Retain all colors of the original.

Resolution:

▶ **Screen**: Use the screen resolution, typically 72 dpi (dots per inch) or 96 dpi.

▶ **Printer**: Use the printer's resolution, typically 300 dpi or 600 dpi; use this for the best quality hardcopy.

▶ **Source**: Let the destination application figure out the best resolution to use.

▶ **Custom**: Specify any resolution; default = 72 x 72 dpi. Visio recommends that the resolution range between 32 dpi and 400 dpi.

Size:

▶ **Screen**: Use the screen size.

▶ **Printer**: Use the printer's page size.

▶ **Source**: Let the destination application figure out the best size to use.

▶ **Custom**: Specify a size; default = 6.67 x 5 inches.

File Type:

▶ Normally, you would keep **Win 3.X** but if you plan to use the BMP file with the OS/2 operating system, then select the **OS2 PM 1.X** option.

Color Translation:

▶ **Normal**: Keep the colors as they are in the Visio drawing.

▶ **Inverse**: Invert the colors (the picture looks like the strip of negatives from color film).

▶ **Inverse Grays Only**: Invert only white, black, and grays; keep other colors as they are.

▶ **Gray Scale**: Change the colors to levels of gray.

▶ **Inverse Gray Scale**: Change the colors to levels of gray and make a negative.

Data Compression:

▶ While the file size is greatly reduced using **RLE** (short for "run length encoding"), most applications cannot read compressed BMP files. Therefore, leave the choice at **None**.

Export to CGM

Convert the Visio drawing to CGM (short for Computer Graphics Metafile) format:

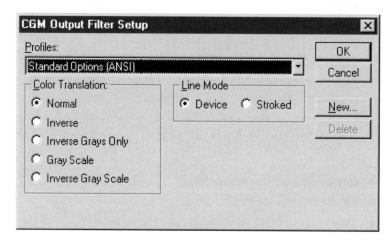

Color Translation format:

▶ **Normal**: Keep the colors as they are in the Visio drawing.
▶ **Inverse**: Invert the colors (the picture looks like the strip of negatives from color film).
▶ **Inverse Grays Only**: Invert only white, black, and grays; keep other colors as they are.
▶ **Gray Scale**: Change the colors to levels of gray.
▶ **Inverse Gray Scale**: Change the colors to levels of gray and make a negative.

Line Mode:

▶ **Device**: Use the line style and width capabilities of the display and printer driver.
▶ **Stroked**: Thick and patterned lines are drawn as polygons to more closely represent how they appear in the Visio drawing.

Export to GIF

Convert the Visio drawing to GIF (short for Graphics Interchange Format):

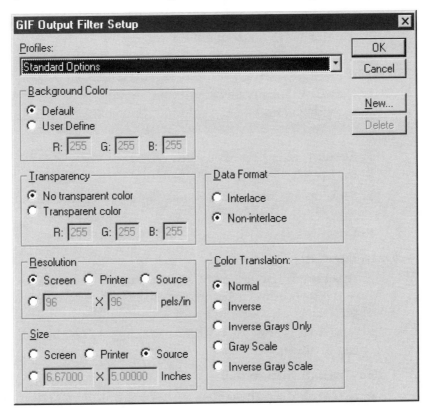

Background Color allows you to specify a different background color for the image:

▶ **Default**: Keep the background color as is.
▶ **User Define**: Specify the color via the RGB (red, green, blue) format, in which the amount of each primary color ranges from 0 (black) to 255 (full strength).

Transparency allows other images or text "underneath" the GIF image to show through the color selected as transparent:

▶ **No transparent color**: This is the default.
▶ **Transparent color**: Specify the color via the RGB (red, green, blue) format, in which the amount of each primary color ranges from 0 (black) to 255 (full strength).

Resolution:
- ▶ **Screen**: Use the screen resolution, typically 72 dpi (dots per inch) or 96 dpi.
- ▶ **Printer**: Use the printer's resolution, typically 300 dpi or 600 dpi; use this for the best quality hardcopy.
- ▶ **Source**: Let the destination application figure out the best resolution to use.
- ▶ **Custom**: Specify any resolution; default = 72 x 72 dpi. Visio recommends that the resolution range between 32 dpi and 400 dpi.

Size:
- ▶ **Screen**: Use the screen size.
- ▶ **Printer**: Use the printer's page size.
- ▶ **Source**: Let the destination application figure out the best size to use.
- ▶ **Custom**: Specify a size; default = 6.67 x 5 inches.

Data Format:
- ▶ **Interlace**: Useful for the Internet, since it shows parts of the image in the Web browser before the entire image has been delivered over the (relatively slow) telephone lines.
- ▶ **Non-interlace**: Means the entire image must be delivered before it can be displayed.

Color Translation format:
- ▶ **Normal**: Keep the colors as they are in the Visio drawing.
- ▶ **Inverse**: Invert the colors (the picture looks like the strip of negatives from color film).
- ▶ **Inverse Grays Only**: Invert only white, black, and shades of gray; keep other colors as they are.
- ▶ **Gray Scale**: Change the colors to levels of gray.
- ▶ **Inverse Gray Scale**: Change the colors to levels of gray and make a negative.

Export to IGES

IGES is a file format commonly used by high-end CAD systems to exchange drawings. Typically, these CAD packages must translate the IGES file to their own format. Convert the Visio drawing to IGES (short for Initial Graphics Exchange Specification):

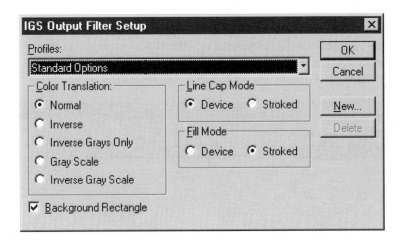

Color Translation format:

> ▶ **Normal**: Keep the colors as they are in the Visio drawing.
>
> ▶ **Inverse**: Invert the colors (the picture looks like the strip of negatives from color film).
>
> ▶ **Inverse Grays Only**: Invert only white, black, and shades of gray; keep other colors as they are.
>
> ▶ **Gray Scale**: Change the colors to levels of gray.
>
> ▶ **Inverse Gray Scale**: Change the colors to levels of gray and make a negative.

Background Rectangle:

> ▶ Draw a rectangle around the extents of the drawing.

Line Cap Mode:

> ▶ **Device**: Use the line style and width capabilities of the display and printer driver.
>
> ▶ **Stroked**: Thick and patterned lines are drawn as polygons to more closely represent how they appear in the Visio drawing.

Fill Mode:

> ▶ **Device**: Use the fill capabilities of the display and printer driver.
>
> ▶ **Stroked**: Filled areas are drawn as polygons to more closely represent how they appear in the Visio drawing.

Export to JPEG

JPEG is popular for very large images because it does a terrific job of compressing files. JPEG can make the file size smaller than any other file format; the drawback is that it is a *lossy* compression, which means some of the image may be distorted due to the compression process. JPEG is short for Joint Photographic Experts Group. Convert the Visio drawing to JPEG format:

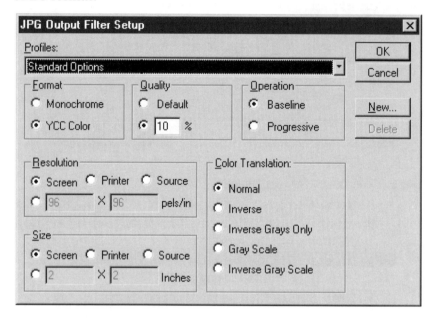

Format: Monochrome or YCC Color.

Quality: The JPEG term for "compression." The higher the quality (closer to 100%), the lower the compression and the larger the file size.

Operation: Baseline or progressive.

Resolution:
- ▸ **Screen**: Use the screen resolution, typically 72 dpi (dots per inch) or 96 dpi.
- ▸ **Printer**: Use the printer's resolution, typically 300 dpi or 600 dpi; use this for the best quality hardcopy.
- ▸ **Source**: Let the destination application figure out the best resolution to use.
- ▸ **Custom**: Specify any resolution; default = 72 x 72 dpi. Visio recommends that the resolution range between 32 dpi and 400 dpi.

Size:
- ▸ **Screen**: Use the screen size.
- ▸ **Printer**: Use the printer's page size.

> ▶ **Source**: Let the destination application figure out the best size to use.
> ▶ **Custom**: Specify a size; default = 6.67 x 5 inches.

Color Translation format:
> ▶ **Normal**: Keep the colors as they are in the Visio drawing.
> ▶ **Inverse**: Invert the colors (the picture looks like the strip of negatives from color film).
> ▶ **Inverse Grays Only**: Invert only white, black, and shades of gray; keep other colors as they are.
> ▶ **Gray Scale**: Change the colors to levels of gray.
> ▶ **Inverse Gray Scale**: Change the colors to levels of gray and make a negative.

Export to PICT

Convert the Visio drawing to Macintosh PICT (short for picture) file format:

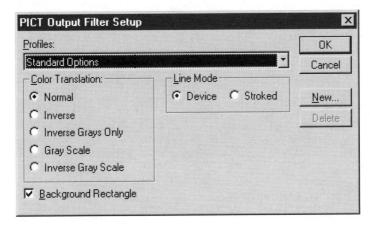

Color Translation format:
> ▶ **Normal**: Keep the colors as they are in the Visio drawing.
> ▶ **Inverse**: Invert the colors (the picture looks like the strip of negatives from color film).
> ▶ **Inverse Grays Only**: Invert only white, black, and shades of gray; keep other colors as they are.
> ▶ **Gray Scale**: Change the colors to levels of gray.
> ▶ **Inverse Gray Scale**: Change the colors to levels of gray and make a negative.

Background Rectangle draws a rectangle around the extents of the drawing.

Line Cap Mode:

▶ **Device**: Use the line style and width capabilities of the display and printer driver.

▶ **Stroked**: Thick and patterned lines are drawn as polygons to more closely represent how they appear in the Visio drawing.

Export to PCX

Convert the Visio drawing to PC Paintbrush file format:

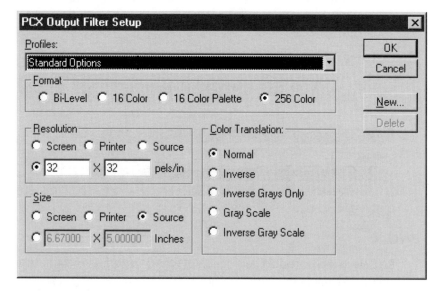

Format options:

▶ **Bi-Level**: Convert Visio drawing colors to black or white.

▶ **16 Color**: Reduce Visio drawing colors to 16 colors of the Windows standard.

▶ **16 Color Palette**: Reduce Visio drawing colors to 16 colors to the best approximation of the original.

▶ **256 Color**: Retain all Visio drawing colors.

Resolution:

▶ **Screen**: Use the screen resolution, typically 72 dpi (dots per inch) or 96 dpi.

▶ **Printer**: Use the printer's resolution, typically 300 dpi or 600 dpi; use this for the best quality hardcopy.

▶ **Source**: Let the destination application figure out the best resolution to use.

▶ **Custom**: Specify any resolution; default = 72 x 72 dpi. Visio recommends that the resolution range between 32 dpi and 400 dpi.

Size:

▶ **Screen**: Use the screen size.

▶ **Printer**: Use the printer's page size.

▶ **Source**: Let the destination application figure out the best size to use.

▶ **Custom**: Specify a size; default = 6.67 x 5 inches.

Color Translation format:

▶ **Normal**: Keep the colors as they are in the Visio drawing.

▶ **Inverse**: Invert the colors (the picture looks like the strip of negatives from color film).

▶ **Inverse Grays Only**: Invert only white, black, and shades of gray; keep other colors as they are.

▶ **Gray Scale**: Change the colors to levels of gray.

▶ **Inverse Gray Scale**: Change the colors to levels of gray and make a negative.

Export to PNG

PNG was invented to replace GIF, which requires royalty payments under certain situations. Convert the Visio drawing to PNG (short for Portable Network Graphics) format:

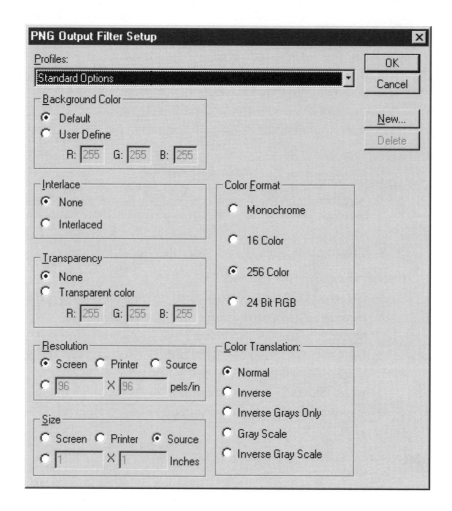

Background Color:

▶ **Default**: White.

▶ **User Define**: Specify another color using the RGB (red, green, blue) method. Here are some examples of the colors created by the RGB system:

R (Red)	G (Green)	B (Blue)	Result
0	0	0	Black
255	0	0	Red
0	255	0	Green
0	0	255	Blue

R (Red)	G (Green)	B (Blue)	Result
191	191	191	Medium Gray
255	255	255	White

The RBG method allows you to specify 16.7 million colors by varying the amount of red, green, and blue in 256 increments (0 to 255).

Interlace:

> ▶ **None** means the entire image must be delivered before it can be displayed.

> ▶ **Interlaced** is useful for the Internet, since it shows parts of the image in the Web browser before the entire image has been delivered over the (relatively slow) telephone lines.

Transparency allows other images or text "underneath" the GIF image to show through the color selected as transparent.

Resolution:

> ▶ **Screen**: Use the screen resolution, typically 72 dpi (dots per inch) or 96 dpi.

> ▶ **Printer**: Use the printer's resolution, typically 300 dpi or 600 dpi; use this for the best quality hardcopy.

> ▶ **Source**: Let the destination application figure out the best resolution to use.

> ▶ **Custom**: Specify any resolution; default = 72 x 72 dpi. Visio recommends that the resolution range between 32 dpi and 400 dpi.

Size:

> ▶ **Screen**: Use the screen size.

> ▶ **Printer**: Use the printer's page size.

> ▶ **Source**: Let the destination application figure out the best size to use.

> ▶ **Custom**: Specify a size; default = 6.67 x 5 inches.

Color Format: Monochrome (black and white), 16 colors, 256 colors (the default), or 24-bit RGB (16.7 million colors).

Color Translation format:

> ▶ **Normal**: Keep the colors as they are in the Visio drawing.

> ▶ **Inverse**: Invert the colors (the picture looks like the strip of negatives from color film).

▶ **Inverse Grays Only**: Invert only white, black, and shades of gray; keep other colors as they are.

▶ **Gray Scale**: Change the colors to levels of gray.

▶ **Inverse Gray Scale**: Change the colors to levels of gray and make a negative.

Export to TIFF

Convert the Visio drawing to TIFF (short for Tagged Image File Format):

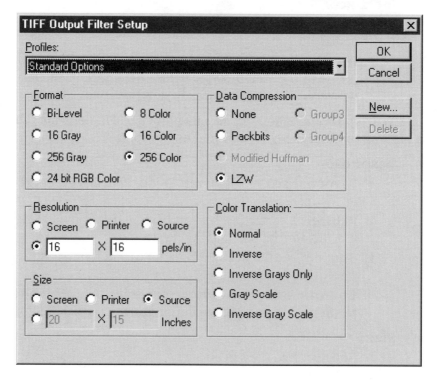

Format:

▶ **Bi-Level**: Reduce the image to black and white; creates a smaller file size.

▶ **16 Gray**: Sixteen shades of gray.

▶ **256 Gray**: 256 shades of gray.

▶ **24 bit RGB Color**: 16.7 million colors.

▶ **8 Color**: Eight colors.

▶ **16 Color**: Sixteen colors.

▶ **256 Color**: 256 colors; the default.

Resolution:
- ▶ **Screen**: Use the screen resolution, typically 72 dpi (dots per inch) or 96 dpi.
- ▶ **Printer**: Use the printer's resolution, typically 300 dpi or 600 dpi; use this for the best quality hardcopy.
- ▶ **Source**: Let the destination application figure out the best resolution to use.
- ▶ **Custom**: Specify any resolution; default = 72 x 72 dpi. Visio recommends that the resolution range between 32 dpi and 400 dpi.

Size:
- ▶ **Screen**: Use the screen size.
- ▶ **Printer**: Use the printer's page size.
- ▶ **Source**: Let the destination application figure out the best size to use.
- ▶ **Custom**: Specify a size; default = 6.67 x 5 inches.

Data Compression:
- ▶ **None**: No compression creates a larger file but may be necessary for some applications that cannot read compressed TIFF files.
- ▶ **Packbits**: Best suited to black and white images.
- ▶ **Modified Huffman**: Best suited for gray images.
- ▶ **LZW**: Best suited for color images.

Color Translation format:
- ▶ **Normal**: Keep the colors as they are in the Visio drawing.
- ▶ **Inverse**: Invert the colors (the picture looks like the strip of negatives from color film).
- ▶ **Inverse Grays Only**: Invert only white, black, and shades of gray; keep other colors as they are.
- ▶ **Gray Scale**: Change the colors to levels of gray.
- ▶ **Inverse Gray Scale**: Change the colors to levels of gray and make a negative.

Hands-On Activity

In this activity, you use the export functions. Begin by starting Visio. Choose **Browse existing files**.

1. Open the **Perspective Block Diagram.Vsd** document supplied in the Block Diagram folder.
2. Select **File | Save As**.
3. Click on the **Save as type** list box and select the **GIF** file format.
4. If necessary, type a filename in the File name text box and select the destination subdirectory.
5. Click **Save**. Notice the GIF Output Filter Setup dialog box.
6. Select **Visio HTML Export** option from the Profiles list box. This action pre-selects all other options on your behalf.
7. Click **OK**. Visio converts the drawing and saves it in GIF format.
8. Let's bring the exported Visio drawing into a raster editor. Start **Windows Paintbrush** (or another raster editor) by double-clicking on its icon in the Windows desktop or from the Windows Start menu.
9. Select **File | Open** from the menu and open **Perspective Block Diagram.Gif**. Notice the raster version of the Visio drawing.
10. Press **Alt+F4** to exit Paintbrush.
11. Click on Visio and press **Alt+F4** to exit Visio. Click **No** in response to the Save Changes dialog box.

This completes the hands-on activity for exporting Visio drawings in other file formats.

Special Selections

Edit | Select Special

Uses

Usually, you click a shape to select it. To select more than one shape, you hold down the **Shift** key while clicking the shapes. To select all shapes on the page, you press **Ctrl+A**. But what do you do when you don't want to select everything, yet need to select specific object types in the drawing? Or what about the situation where you want to select all guidelines?

> ### In this chapter you'll learn about:
> ✓ **Using Select Special**

The answer is the **Select Special** selection of the **Edit** menu. It lets you select shapes on the basis of what they are, or by the name of the layer they reside on. You choose shapes and objects in either of two categories: shapes and other objects in the drawing or layer name.

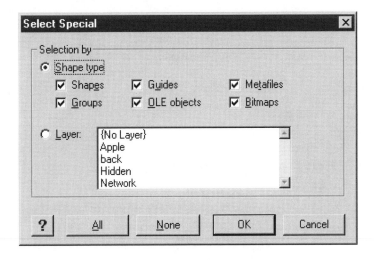

The **Shape type** options are:
- ▶ **Shapes**: Selects all shapes on the current page.
- ▶ **Groups**: Selects all grouped objects on the page.
- ▶ **Guides**: Selects all guidelines and guide points on the page.
- ▶ **OLE objects**: Selects all linked and embedded objects.
- ▶ **Metafiles**: Selects all objects pasted in WMF format.
- ▶ **Bitmaps**: Selects all objects pasted in BMP format.
- ▶ **All**: Selects all shape types.
- ▶ **None**: Selects no shape types.

The **Layer** options are:
- ▶ **Layer**: Selects all objects assigned to a specific layer name; hold down **Ctrl** to select more than one layer.
- ▶ **All**: Selects all layers.
- ▶ **None**: Selects no layers.

Procedures

Before presenting the general procedures for special selections, it is helpful to know about the shortcut keys. These are:

Function	Keys	Menu	Toolbar Icon
Select	...	...	▶
Select Special	Alt+EI	Edit | Select Special	...
Select All	Ctrl+A	Edit | Select All	...

Using Select Special

Use the following procedure to select objects:

1. Select **Edit | Select Special**. Notice the Select Special dialog box.
2. Choose **Shape type** or **Layer**.
   - ▶ Within the Shape type area, select any combination of shapes, groups, guides, OLE objects, metafiles, or bitmaps.
   - ▶ Or, within the Layer area, select a layer name from the list box.
3. Click **OK**. Notice that Visio highlights the objects that match your search criteria.

Hands-On Activity

In this activity, you use the special selection function. Begin by starting Visio. Select **Browse existing file**.

1. Open the document **Basic Network Diagram.Vsd** found in the Network Diagrams folder.

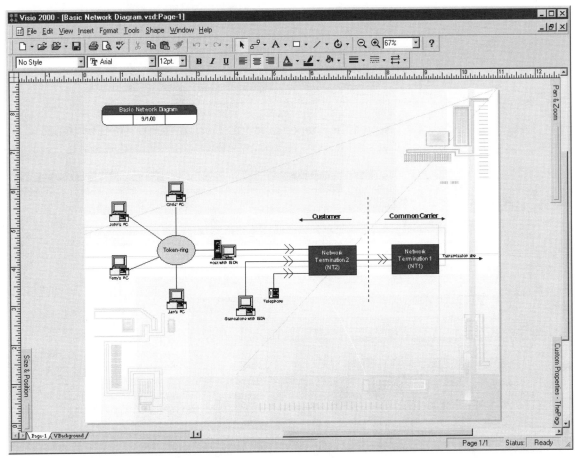

2. Select **Edit | Select Special**. Notice the Select Special dialog box.
3. Click the **Shape type** radio button.
4. Click **None** to turn off all options.
5. Click **Shapes** to turn on the option.

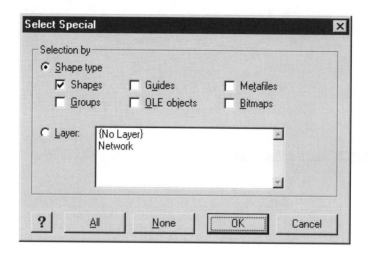

6. Click **OK**. Notice the shapes that are selected, surrounded by handles. Some objects that appear to be shapes are not selected; these are groups.

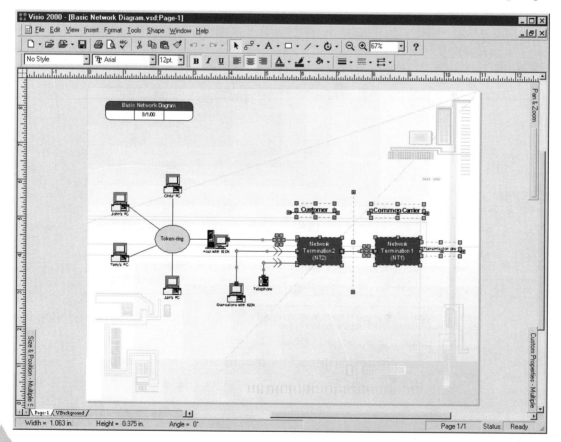

7. Select **Edit | Select Special** again.

8. Click the **None** button to remove all selected options.

9. Click **Groups**.

10. Click **OK**. Notice that this time the groups are selected, surrounded by handles.

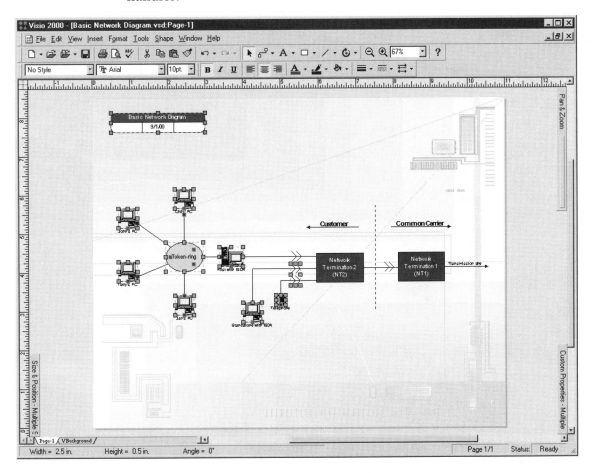

11. Click anywhere on the page to deselect the shapes.

12. Press **Alt+F4** to exit Visio. Click **No** in response to the Save Changes dialog box.

This completes the hands-on activity for special selections.

Module 31 | *Drawing Explorer*

View | Windows | Drawing Explorer

Uses

Visio provides you with three ways to view the drawing. One is the drawing page, which you have been working with all through this book. Another view is the underlying ShapeSheet, as discussed in detail in *Learn Visio 2000 for the Advanced User* (also from Wordware Publishing). The third view is new to Visio 2000, and is called the **Drawing Explorer**.

> **In this chapter you'll learn about:**
>
> ✓ **Navigating the Drawing Explorer**

The Drawing Explorer allows you to view the drawing hierarchically, in much the same manner as the Windows Explorer provided by Windows 95/98/2000. Instead of showing you drives, folders, and files, though, Visio's Drawing Explorer shows you foreground and background pages, shapes, layers, styles, masters, fill patterns, line patterns, and line ends. You can add, delete, edit, and highlight objects in your drawing. As you do, the Drawing Explorer updates the drawing—and vice versa.

Procedures

Before presenting the general procedures for navigating the Drawing Explorer, it is helpful to know about the shortcut keys. These are:

Function	Keys	Menu	Toolbar Icon
Drawing Explorer	Alt+VND	View | Windows | Drawing Explorer	
🗀 Rename	F2	…	…
🗀 Undo renaming	Esc	…	…

Note:

🗀 Indicates the function operates only within the Drawing Explorer.

Navigating the Drawing Explorer

The Drawing Explorer presents a new interface to the Visio user.

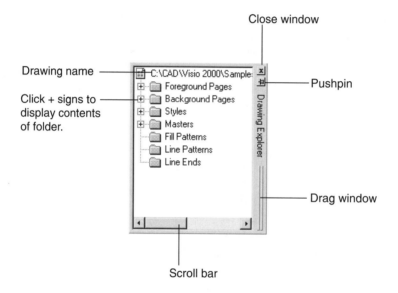

Close window

Drawing name

Click + signs to display contents of folder.

Pushpin

Drag window

Scroll bar

The Drawing Explorer window normally stays open. You can have it roll open and closed when the cursor passes over it. Click the pushpin (so that it no longer looks depressed) to minimize the window.

The window is normally docked to the side of the Visio drawing area. Drag the window's title bar away to make the window float. When floating, double-click the title bar to re-dock the window.

Click the + (plus) sign to open a folder. When the folder is open, the + is replaced by a − (minus) sign; click the − sign to close the folder.

When the window is too small to display all its data, horizontal and vertical scroll bars appear. Click the scroll bars to see the data that isn't in view.

The Drawing Explorer window shows the content of each drawing, using the following hierarchical structure:

Drawing filename: The full pathnames of drawings currently open in Visio. Within each drawing are the following folders:

> ▶ **Foreground Pages and Background Pages**: The pages used in the drawing; every drawing has at least one foreground page. Within each page are the following folders:
>
>> ▶ **Shapes**: The names of shapes on the page; when a "shape" is a group, then additional Shapes and Layers folders appear within it; see illustration below.
>>
>> ▶ **Layers**: The names of layers on the page.
>
> ▶ **Styles**: The names of text styles, if any.
> ▶ **Masters**: The names of master shapes used in the drawing.
> ▶ **Fill Patterns**: The names of fill pattern styles, if any.
> ▶ **Line Patterns**: The names of line pattern styles, if any,
> ▶ **Line Ends**: The names of line end styles, if any.

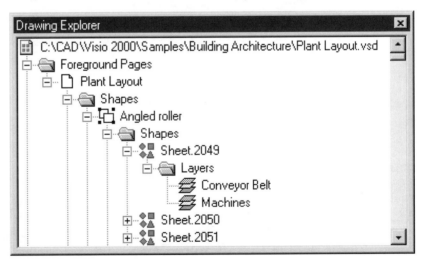

The Drawing Explorer has a multitude of shortcut menus associated with it. You can right-click any item in the window and get a context-specific shortcut menu. The illustration on the following page shows some of the shortcut menus.

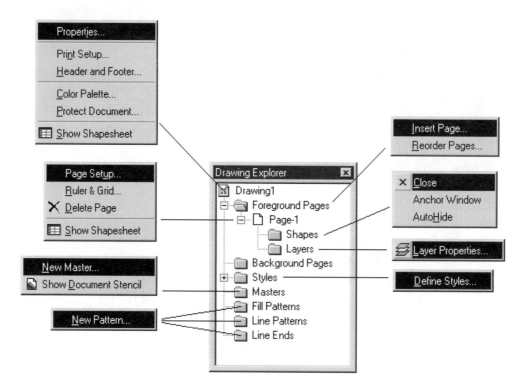

When an option on a shortcut menu has an ellipsis (...), this means the option displays a dialog box. For example, **Properties...** displays the Properties dialog box.

Tip: When you move the cursor over a rollout window set to AutoHide, you can hear a sound as the window opens and closes. To add the sounds to Visio 2000's rollout windows, from the Windows toolbar, select **Start | Settings | Control Panel | Sounds**. In the **Events | Windows** list, select **Restore Up** or **Restore Down**. In the Sound area, select a WAV file from the Name list. Test the sound in the Preview area. Click **OK** to dismiss the dialog box.

When the sound becomes annoying to you, you can return to the Sounds Properties dialog box, and select **(None)** for the sound.

Hands-On Activity

In this activity, you use the Drawing Explorer. Begin by starting Visio.

1. In the Welcome to Visio 2000 dialog box, select **Browse existing files** and click **OK**.

2. In the Open dialog box, select **Perspective Block Diagram.Vsd**, which you can find in the Visio 2000\Samples\Block Diagram folder.

3. Open the Drawing Explorer:

   ▸ If you do not see Drawing Explorer, select **View | Windows | Drawing Explorer** from the menu bar.

   ▸ If you see just the title bar of Drawing Explorer, it is "rolled up." Move your cursor over the title bar to "roll out" the window.

   ▸ To keep the Drawing Explorer window from rolling up, click the pushpin icon.

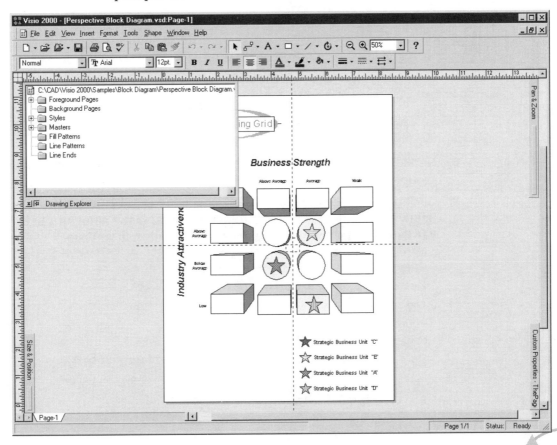

4. Open the Foreground Pages folder and click the + next to the folder. Notice that it contains a single page, called Page-1.

5. Open **Page-1**. Notice it contains a pair of folders called **Shapes** and **Layers**.

6. Open the **Shapes** folder. Notice it contains a long list of shape names, such as Block and Block.10.

7. Select the **Block.10** shape. Notice that a shape is highlighted in the drawing.

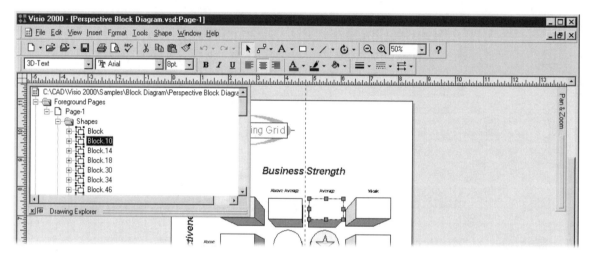

8. Notice the + next to **Block.10**. This indicates the "shape" is actually a group. Click the + to open the group; another **Shapes** folder appears

9. Click the + to see the name of the shape, **Sheet.11**, in the group. Below the shape is the Layers folder. It contains the name of the layer, **3D Depth**, that the shape resides on. (Recall that, in Visio, a shape can reside on more than one layer.)

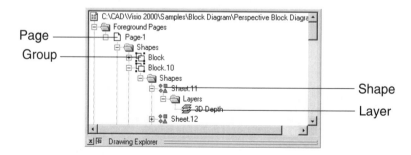

Page ———
Group ———

Shape ———
Layer ———

10. Right-click layer **3D Depth**. From the shortcut menu, select **Visible** so that it turns off (no check mark). Notice that some objects disappear from the drawing. Make the layer visible again.

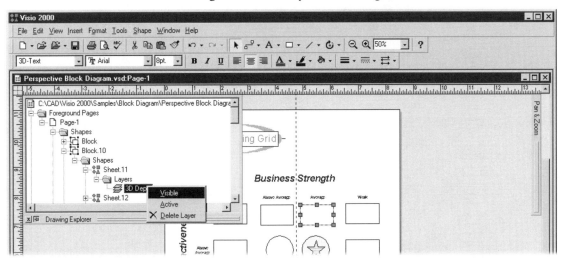

11. Scroll down the Drawing Explorer. Right-click **Masters**, and select **Show Document Stencil** from the shortcut menu. Notice that Visio opens a green stencil called **Document Stencil**. This stencil is special because it shows all the masters used by the drawing. (Recall that when you drag a shape into a page, the shape is a copy of the *master* stored in the stencil.)

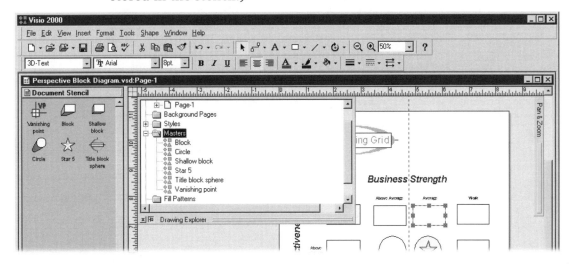

12. Press **Alt+F4** to exit Visio. Click **No** in response to the Save Changes dialog box.

This completes the hands-on activity for using the Drawing Explorer.

Double-clicking the Mouse Button

Format | Behavior | Double-Click

Uses

In this chapter you'll learn about:
✓ **Double-click tab options**
✓ **Assigning double-click action to a shape**

Most software programs perform a single action (or no action at all) when you double-click an object. For example, double-clicking in Word usually selects a word; double-clicking an icon on the Windows desktop opens the program or document.

By default, double-clicking a Visio shape lets you edit the shape's text. Unlike most other programs, though, Visio allows you to choose from as many as ten options from the **Double-Click** tab.

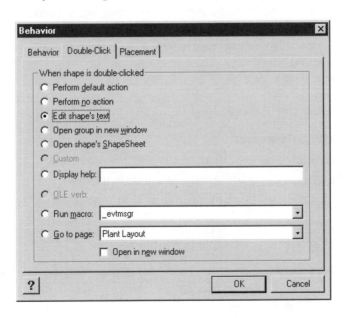

Tip: To double-click, press the left mouse button twice quickly. If nothing happens, it could be you are double-clicking too slowly—or too fast. To check your double-click speed, from the Windows taskbar, select **Start | Settings | Control Panel | Mouse**. In the Buttons tab, an option allows you to adjust and test your double-click speed.

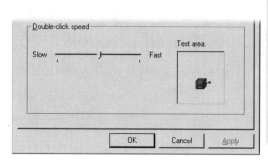

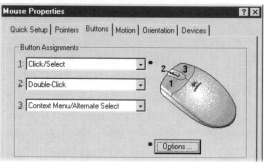

If you have a three-button mouse, you may find it useful to define the center button to execute a double-click. When reconfigured like this, you press the middle button once, but the computer interprets it as a double-click; I find this saves a lot of wear on my index finger! (If your computer's mouse does not include software for defining the function of buttons, you may be able to download such software from the mouse vendor's Web site.)

The **Double-Click** tab's options are:

Perform default action:

▶ For a *shape*, allow editing of the shape's text block.

▶ For a *group*, open the group in a new window.

▶ For an *OLE object*, launch the linked application.

Perform no action:

▶ Nothing happens when you double-click.

Edit shape's text:

▶ Goes into text editing mode.

▶ Applies to shapes only; other objects are ignored.

Open group in new window:
▶ Displays the group in an independent window for editing.
▶ Applies to groups only.

Open shape's ShapeSheet:
▶ Displays the numbers that control the look and size of the shape in a spreadsheet-like interface.
▶ This option is useful for developers who work with the ShapeSheet.

Custom:
▶ Performs a custom (user-defined) behavior.
▶ Available only when the object's ShapeSheet contains an action defined in the EventDblClick cell of the Events section.

Display help:
▶ Displays a topic from an HLP help file.
▶ The help filename and topic must be specified in the following formats: **filename.chm!keyword** or **filename.chm!#Number**.

Metaname	Meaning
filename.chm	Name of a Windows help file, such as Shape.Chm.
!keyword	Index term associated with the help topic, such as "Basic Shape."
!#number	Numeric ID referenced in the map section of the help project file.

OLE verb:
▶ Typically executes a command like Edit or Open.
▶ Applies to an inserted object only.

Run macro:
▶ Runs one of the macros installed with Visio.
▶ The name of the macro program can be selected from the list box.
▶ This option was called "Run Add-on" in previous versions of Visio.

Go to page:
▶ Switches to another page in the drawing.
▶ The name of the page can be selected from the drop list.

Open in new window:
▶ Opens the page, shape, group, OLE object, etc., in a new window.
▶ This option applies to some of the double-click options listed above.

Caution: The option of the **Double-Click** tab applies only to the shape you select. In fact, you cannot access the Double-Click tab unless you first select a shape. You cannot assign double-click behavior to a page.

Procedures

Use the following procedure to change the double-click action assigned to a shape:

1. Select the shape.
2. From the menu, select **Format | Behavior**.
3. In the Behavior dialog box, select the **Double-Click** tab.
4. Click an option from the Double-Click dialog box.
5. Click **OK**.
6. Double-click on the shape to test the action.

Hands-On Activity

 In this activity, you use one of the double-clicking functions. Begin by starting Visio.

1. Open a new, blank drawing.
2. Open the **Symbols.Vss** stencil file from the **Visio Extras** folder.
3. Drag the **Coffee** shape into the drawing.

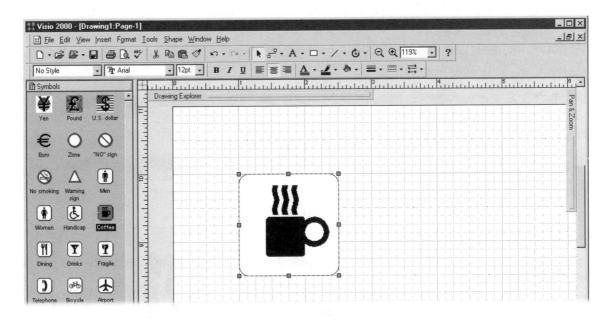

4. Double-click the coffee symbol. Notice that Visio switches to text mode.

5. Select **Format | Behavior | Double-Click**. Notice that the Double-Click tab has the **Edit shape's text** option selected.

6. Select **Open group in new window**.

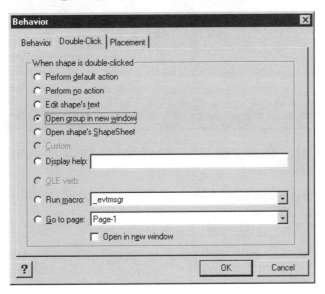

7. Click **OK**.

8. Double-click on the coffee cup. Notice that the group is displayed in a separate window.

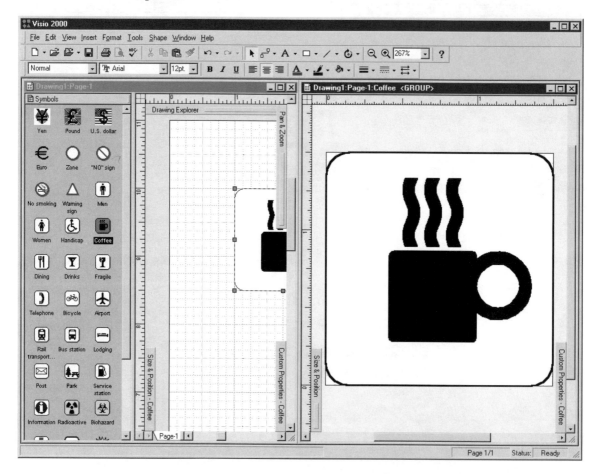

9. Press **Alt+F4** to exit Visio. Click **No** in response to the Save Changes dialog box.

This completes the hands-on activity for changing the double-click action assigned to a shape.

Behavior

Format | Behavior
Format | Special

Uses

The **Behavior** and **Special** selections of the **Format** menu are used to change how shapes and groups act and display. The Behavior dialog box controls the behavior of each shape. The Special dialog box displays basic information and lets you attach data to the shape.

> **In this chapter you'll learn about:**
> ✓ **The Behavior dialog box**
> ✓ **The Placement tab**
> ✓ **The Special dialog box**

The Behavior Dialog Box

The Behavior dialog box controls the interaction, highlighting, resize, and group behaviors:

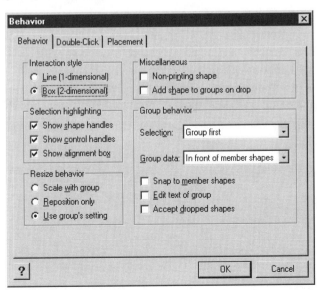

Interaction style: Visio treats lines as one-dimensional, while nearly all other shapes are treated as two-dimensional. By selecting **Line** for a 2D shape, you change how the shape reacts to resizing and rotation.

▶ **Line (1-dimensional)**: Shape can stretch and move, but cannot be widened.

▶ **Box (2-dimensional)**: Shape can also be widened.

Selection highlighting: Determines which of three indicators—shape handles, control handles, and alignment box—display when an object is selected, as the illustration below shows.

▶ **Show shape handles**: Displays handles when the shape is selected.

▶ **Show control handles**: Displays control handles.

▶ **Show alignment box**: Displays the alignment box.

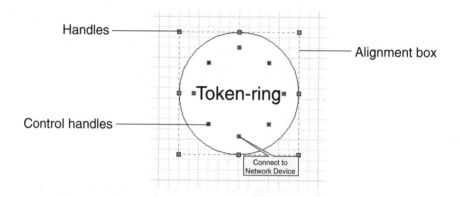

Tips: The control handles allow you to change specific aspects of a shape without affecting the shape overall. For example, in the door shape, one control handle changes the width of the door, while the other control handle changes the angle of the swing.

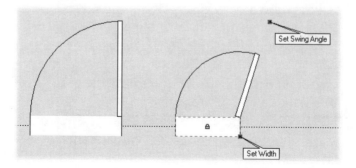

When the handle looks like a padlock, the shape cannot be resized.

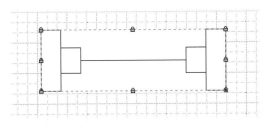

Resize behavior: These three settings affect a shape only when it is part of a group:

▶ **Scale with group**: The shape scales with the group.

▶ **Reposition only**: The shape can be moved but not scaled.

▶ **Use group's setting**: The shape reacts the same way as the group.

Miscellaneous:

▶ **Non-printing shape**: The shape is not printed.

▶ **Add shape to groups on drop**: When a shape is dropped on a group, the shape is added to the group.

Group behavior: Controls the behavior of groups and their components (new to Visio 2000).

▶ **Selection**: Specifies what happens when you select a group.

  ▶ Group only specifies that individual shapes within the group cannot be selected.

  ▶ Group first specifies that the first click selects the group; a second click selects the shape.

  ▶ Members first specifies that individual shapes are selected; click the bounding box to select the group.

▶ **Group data**: Determines the group's display order of text and shapes created with drawing tools:

  ▶ Hide hides the group's text and shapes, except for connection points and control handles.

  ▶ Behind member shapes displays the group's components behind the drawing tool-created shapes.

  ▶ In front of member shapes displays the group's components in front of the drawing tool-created shapes.

▶ **Snap to member shapes**: Determines whether shapes within the group can be snapped and glued to.

▶ **Edit text of group**: Determines whether group text can be edited.

▶ **Accept dropped shapes**: The group incorporates the shape dropped onto the group.

The Placement Tab

The **Layout Behavior** option found in earlier versions of Visio has been replaced by the **Placement** tab of the Behavior dialog box. A shape becomes placeable when you glue a dynamic connector shape to it. Placeable shapes are detected by dynamic connectors, and are included in automatic layouts.

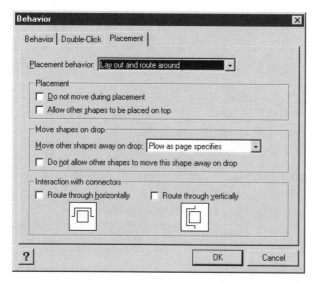

Placement behavior: Determines how the selected 2D shape interacts with dynamic connectors:

▶ **Let Visio decide**: The shape is placeable depending on the type of connector glued to the shape.

▶ **Lay out and route around**: The 2D shape is always placeable.

▶ **Do not lay out and route around**: The 2D shape is never placeable.

Placement: Determines the behavior of the selected 2D shape during the Lay Out Shapes command.

▶ **Do not move during placement**: The shape does not move.

▶ **Allow other shapes to be placed on top**: Other shapes can be placed on top of the selected shape.

Move shapes on drop:

▶ **Move other shapes away on drop**: When a shape is dropped in the drawing, determines whether other shapes *plow* (automatically move out of the way).

    ▶ Plow as page specifies: Shapes move out of the way based on the page's setup.

    ▶ Plow no shapes: Shapes do not move out of the way.

    ▶ Plow every shape: All shapes move out of the way.

▶ **Do not allow other shapes to move this shape away on drop**: The selected shape does not move when another shape is dropped on the page, regardless of the setting of the Move other shapes away on drop option.

Interaction with connectors:

▶ **Route through horizontally**: Dynamic connectors are allowed to go through the selected 2D shape horizontally.

▶ **Route through vertically**: Dynamic connectors are allowed to go through the selected 2D shape vertically.

The Special Dialog Box

The **Special** dialog box displays some basic information about the shape and lets you attach data to the shape. The data fields, such as **Data 1**, contain a field, which can be inserted with the **Field** command (see Module 24 "Placing Text and Fields").

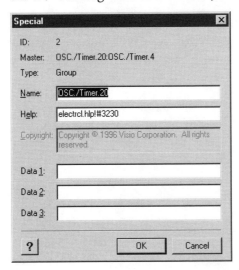

ID: Specifies the number assigned by Visio to the shape; the first shape created in the drawing is 1, etc.

Master: Specifies the name of the shape's master; name is displayed only if the shape is an instance of a master.

Type: Specifies the type of shape, such as group, etc.

Name: Specifies the shape's name of up to 31 characters long.

Help: Specifies the help reference, in the format of *filename*.chm!*keyword* or *filename*.chm!*#number*.

Copyright: Displays copyright information.

Data 1, **Data 2**, and **Data 3**: Allow you to enter up to 64KB of data for the shape.

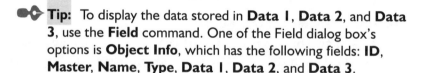

Tip: To display the data stored in **Data 1**, **Data 2**, and **Data 3**, use the **Field** command. One of the Field dialog box's options is **Object Info**, which has the following fields: **ID**, **Master**, **Name**, **Type**, **Data 1**, **Data 2**, and **Data 3**.

Hands-On Activity

In this activity, you use the behavior functions. Begin by starting Visio.

1. Open a new, blank drawing.

2. Open the **Basic Network Shapes.Vss** stencil file, which is found in the Network Diagram folder.

3. Drag the **Ethernet** shape into the drawing. Notice its handles (small green squares at the corners of the shape) and alignment box (green dashed rectangle surrounding the entire shape). The three "handles" on the word "Ethernet" are control handles.

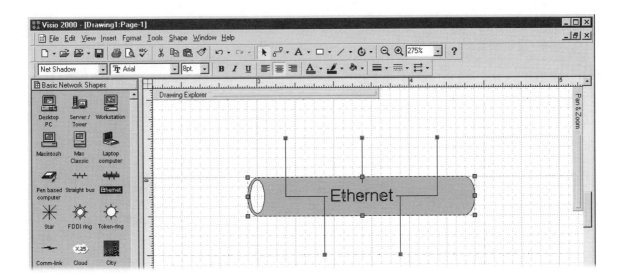

4. Select **Format | Behavior** from the menu. In the Behavior dialog box, ensure the **Behavior** tab is showing.

5. Turn off all three **Selection highlighting** options.

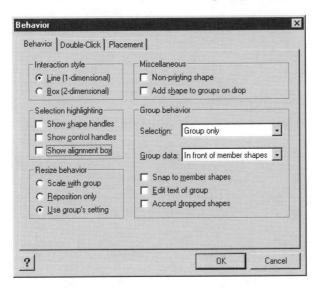

6. Click **OK**. Notice that the selection cues disappear from the shape.

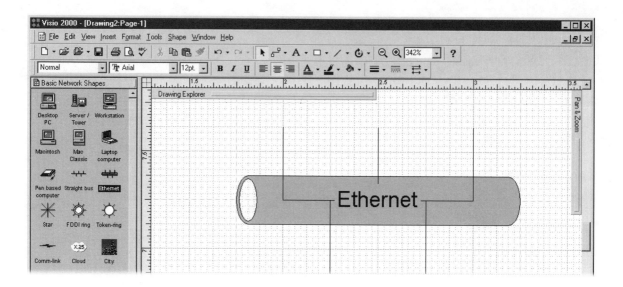

7. Press **Alt+F4** to exit Visio. Click **No** in response to the Save Changes dialog box.

This completes the hands-on activity for changing the behavior of shapes.

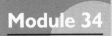 # *Custom Properties*

Shape | Custom Properties
Tools | Macros | Custom Property Editor
Tools | Macros | Visio Extras | Property Reporting Wizard

Uses

The **Custom Prop-erties** selection of the **Shape** menu is used to edit the custom (defined by you) properties defined in the shape. The properties are not color or linetype; rather, they are data attached to a shape, such as its name,

In this chapter you'll learn about:

✓ **The Define Custom Properties dialog box**

✓ **Editing a shape's custom properties**

✓ **Adding a custom property**

✓ **Editing custom property fields**

✓ **Summarizing custom property data**

model number, and price. CAD software sometimes refers to properties as "attributes" or "tag data." In Visio, a custom property has three parts:

Label: The name of the property, such as "Cabinet Width."

Value: The value of the property, such as "33 inches."

Prompt: The message describing the property to the user, such as "Select a standard width from the list."

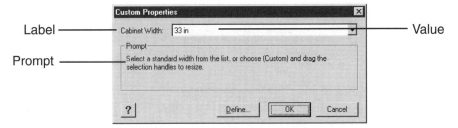

Custom properties are fully editable. The data itself is edited with the **Custom Properties** command; the data fields are edited with the **Custom**

Property Editor command. New custom properties are created with **Define Custom Properties**.

Some custom properties, such as price or model number, do not affect the shape; other custom properties can be made to change the shape. For example, the custom property of a cabinet can determine its width. The Custom Properties dialog box can be made to limit the range of acceptable values. The custom property can appear on the shape's shortcut menu.

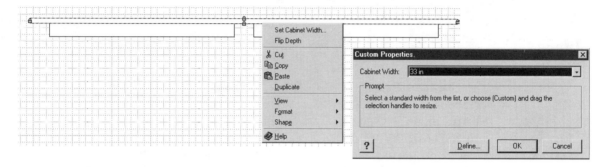

You summarize the information using the Property Reporting Wizard, which places the report on a separate layer in the current drawing page. These reports are excellent for counting all shapes in a drawing, producing a bill of material, or creating an inventory report. Unfortunately, the three Custom Property related tools are not gathered together in one menu, which makes it a bit hard to use them.

 Note: Most shapes do <u>not</u> have custom properties defined. When you use the Custom Properties command, older versions of Visio display a warning dialog box. Visio 2000, on the other hand, asks if you would like to create custom properties for the shape.

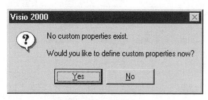

Define Custom Properties Dialog Box

You use this dialog box to add custom properties to a shape. As mentioned above, a custom property consists of just three parts: label, value, and prompt. The label and prompt are straightforward; the value is somewhat more involved.

When it comes to defining the value, Visio allows you to constrain acceptable responses. In a door shape, for example, you may want to limit the width to standard values, such as 24", 27", 30", 33", and 36". For this reason, there are three parameters to value: type, format, and initial value.

The upper half of the Define Custom Properties dialog box allows you to define the five parameters (label, value type, value format, initial value, and prompt). The illustration shows how the areas of the dialog box relate to the Custom Property dialog box seen by the user.

The lower half summarizes the custom properties; recall that a shape can have more than one custom property.

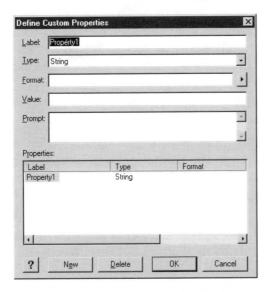

Label: Specifies the descriptive name for the custom property, such as "Cabinet Width" or "Model Number." The label appears next to where you enter the data.

Type: Specifies the type of data permitted for the custom property value; it can be up to 65,536 characters long.

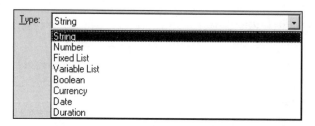

▶ **String**: Accepts all input as text; text input by the user will be formatted according to the Format options (Normal, UPPERCASE, lowercase).

▶ **Number**: Expects a number, date, time, duration, currency, scalar, dimension, or angle; data input by the user will be formatted according to the Format options (General, General units, Whole number, Whole number with units, Floating point, Floating point with units, Fraction, Fraction with units).

▶ **Fixed List**: Displays a drop list from which the user can select a value specified by the Format field. The values in the list are separated by semicolons. For example, the width of a door is limited to 24", 30", and 36". The Format section would be: **24 in;30 in;36 in**.

▶ **Variable List**: Displays a drop list from which the user can select a value (as specified by the Format field) or the user can type a value.

▶ **Boolean**: Restricts the user to selecting either True or False.

▶ **Currency**: Accepts input as currency; data input by the user will be formatted according to the Format options (System settings, $x, $x.xx, x.xx dollar, x.xx USD).

▶ **Date**: Seconds, minutes, hours, days, months, and/or years; data input by the user will be formatted according to the Format options.

▶ **Duration**: Displays elapsed time; data input by the user will be formatted according to the Format options (Weeks, Days, Hours, Minutes, Seconds, HH:MM, MM:SS).

Format: Specifies the format of the value, as well as specific values.

▶ **String**: Formats the text as normal (upper- and lowercase as typed by the user), converted to all uppercase, or converted to all lowercase.

▶ **Number**: Formats the number as follows:

  ▶ **General**: Any number can be entered; units.

- ▶ **General Units**: Any number can be entered with units; if units are left out, the page's units are used.
- ▶ **Whole Number**: Numbers are rounded up to the nearest whole numbers; units are omitted.
- ▶ **Whole Number With Units**: (1 cm) The user can enter whole numbers followed by a unit (such as cm), but not fractions or decimals.
- ▶ **Floating Point Number**: (1.23 cm) The user can enter whole numbers and decimal numbers with units.
- ▶ **Fraction**: (15/16) The user can enter whole numbers and fractions, but not decimal numbers.
- ▶ **Fraction With Units**: (15/16 in.) The user can enter whole numbers and fractions followed by a unit (such as cm), but not decimal numbers.

▶ **Currency**: Formats the number entered by the user to one of the following: System settings, $x, $x.xx, x.xx dollar, or x.xx USD; the currency is specified by the Regional Settings set with Windows (to change, select **Start | Settings | Control Panel | Regional Settings | Currency** from the taskbar).

▶ **Date**: Formats the number entered by the user to one of the following:

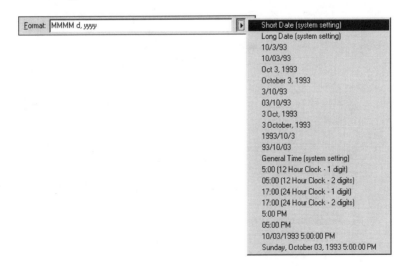

▶ **Duration**: Formats the number entered by the user to one of the following: Weeks, Days, Hours, Minutes, Seconds, HH:MM, or MM:SS.

Value: Specifies the initial (default) value; when the user enters a value in the Custom Properties dialog box, that value overwrites the default value.

Prompt: Specifies an instruction to the user for this custom property.

Properties: Displays a summary of custom property data for the shape.

> **Tip:** Developers can specify additional parameters for the custom property via its ShapeSheet. These include **SortKey** (specifies the order in which multiple custom properties appear), **Invisible** (hides the custom property from the user), and **Ask** (displays the Custom Properties dialog box when the shape is dragged onto the page).

Editing a Shape's Custom Properties

Use the following procedure to edit a shape's custom properties:

1. Select a shape. (Note that not all shapes contain custom properties.)
2. Select **Shape | Custom Properties**. Notice the Custom Properties dialog box.

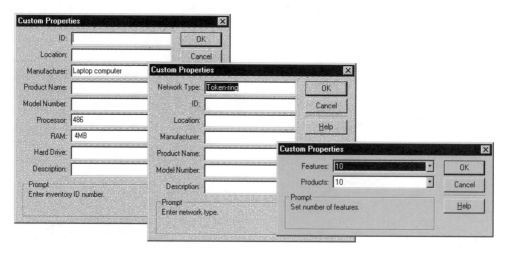

3. Add or change data in the text fields displayed by the Custom Properties dialog box.
4. Click **OK**.

Adding a Custom Property

Whether or not a shape already has custom properties, you can always add one more. Use the following procedure to add a custom property to a shape:

1. Select a shape.

2. Select **Shape | Custom Properties**.

    ▶ When the shape already has at least one custom property, notice that Visio displays the Custom Properties dialog box. Click **Define**.

    ▶ When the shape doesn't have any custom properties, notice that Visio displays a warning dialog box. Click **Yes**.

3. In either case, Visio then displays the Define Custom Properties dialog box.

    ▶ When the shape already has at least one custom property, notice that Visio displays data in the Define Custom Properties dialog box. Click **New**.

    ▶ When the shape doesn't have any custom properties, notice that Visio displays no data in the dialog box. Don't click anything, yet!

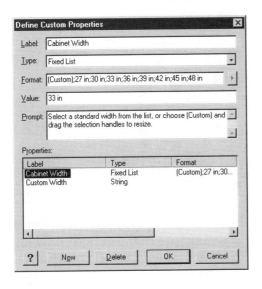 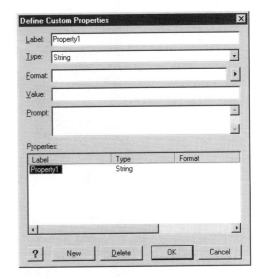

4. In the Label field, type a one- or two-word label for the property. For a door shape, you could enter **Door Width**.

5. In the Type field, select the type of data you want represented. In most cases, this will likely be **String** (which accepts all input as text) or **Number**. For Door Width, you could select **Number**.

6. In the Format field, specify the format for the data; this is optional. In most cases, you will likely want to format dates, currencies, and numbers. For Door Width, you could select **Whole Number with Units**.

7. In the Value field, specify the default value; this is optional and you may leave it blank. For Door Width, you could specify **30 in**.

8. In the Prompt field, type a one- or two-sentence description of the custom property; this is optional, and you may leave it blank. For Door Width, you could enter **Specify the width of the door in inches**.

9. Click **OK**, and test your new custom property by entering a value.

Editing Custom Property Fields

Use the following procedure to edit custom property fields:

1. Select **Tools | Macros | Custom Properties Editor** from the menu bar. Notice that Visio loads the Custom Properties Editor dialog box, which looks a lot like a wizard.

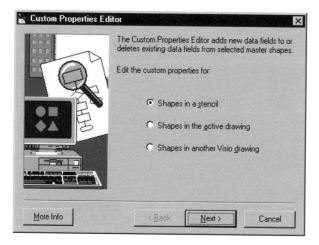

2. The dialog box allows you to edit the custom properties for either: (1) all shapes in a VSS stencil file; (2) all shapes in the current drawing; or (3) shapes stored in another VSD Visio drawing. Select the **Shapes in the active drawing** option. Click **Next**.

3. Notice that Visio searches the drawing for master shapes. Select the shape(s) names you want to edit.

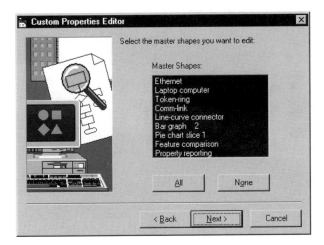

4. Click **Next**. Select the property to edit, add, or remove. To add a custom property, click **Add**.

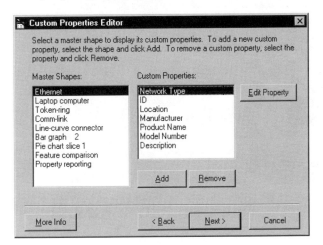

5. Click **Next**. You have a chance to review your changes. Or not. Click **Next**.

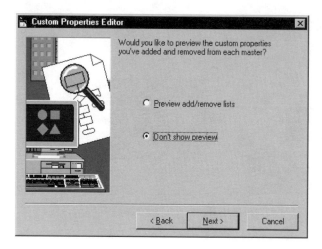

6. Click **Finish**. You're done!

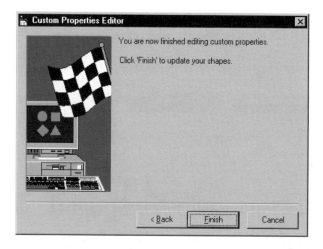

7. Use the Custom Properties command to see the changes to custom properties.

Summarizing Custom Property Data

Use the following procedure to create a report from property fields:

1. Select **Tools | Macro | Visio Extras | Property Reporting Wizard**. Notice the Property Reporting Wizard dialog box.

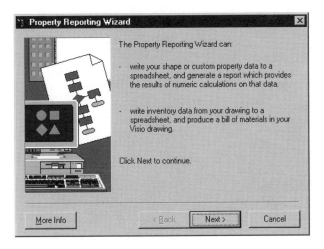

2. Click **Next**. Here you decide which shapes the report is based on:

   Range: In the whole document (when it contains more than one page) or just the current page.

   Include: All shapes, selected shapes, or shapes with specific custom properties.

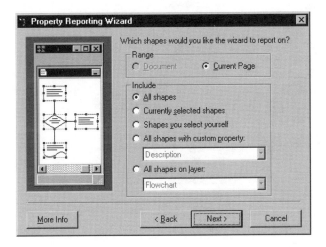

3. Click **Next**. Choose the custom properties you want included in the report.

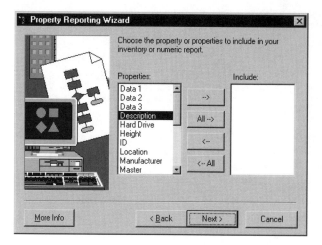

4. Click **Next**. In this dialog box, Visio indicates that you can perform several calculations, such as finding the average value. However, due to a bug in the wizard, the calculation does not take place.

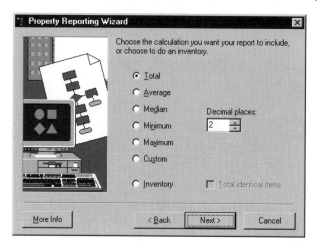

5. Click **Next**. Type in the name for the report and select a drawing page for the report.

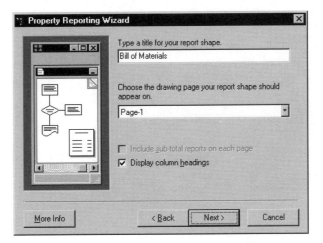

6. Click **Next**. Not done yet. You get to choose if you want even more text in the report. For fun, click all check boxes.

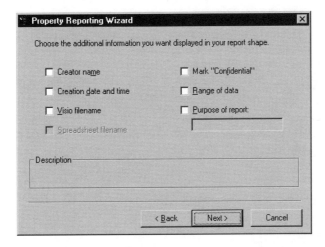

7. Click **Next**. Visio notes you have answered all questions necessary.

351

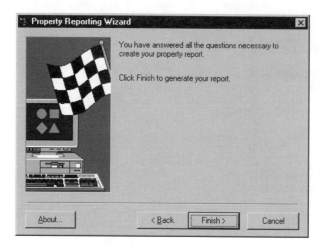

8. Click **Finish**. Watch the blue squares as they march across the dialog box.

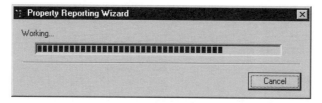

9. Zoom out to the entire page to view the property report. (From **Zoom** on the toolbar, select **Page**.)

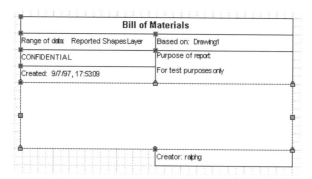

This completes the procedures for working with custom properties.

Internet Tools

Insert | Hyperlink

Uses

Visio allows you to create hyperlinked versions of drawings in two different environments:

> In this chapter you'll learn about:
> ✓ *Adding a hyperlink to a shape or page*
> ✓ *Editing a hyperlink*
> ✓ *Jumping to a hyperlink*

> ▶ Hyperlinks can be added to the Visio drawing, allowing you to jump from document to document on your own computer system.

> ▶ Visio drawings can be saved in HTML and VML format for viewing by Web browsers. See Module 36 "Creating a Web Document."

The **Hyperlinks** selection of the **Insert** menu places hyperlinks in the Visio drawing. A *hyperlink* is a filename with reaction: Click the hyperlink and Visio loads the file specified by the hyperlink. Visio calls the hyperlink the *address*. (A hyperlink is also known as a URL, short for "uniform resource locator," the universal file naming system used by the Internet.)

Typical hyperlinks (or URLs) look like this:

Hyperlink	File or location
c:\visio\samples\block diagram.vsd	Visio drawing file.
c:\visio\solutions\basic blocks.vss	Visio stencil file.
c:\folder\index.htm	HTML document located on your computer.
c:\graphics\filename.gif	Graphic file in GIF format.
http://www.visio.com	Visio's Web site.
http://www.wordware.com	Wordware Publishing's Web site.
http://www.upfrontezine.com	Author Ralph Grabowski's Web site.

As you can see from the list, you can add a hyperlink to <u>any</u> kind of file in a Visio drawing—whether on your computer or on the Internet. When you pause the cursor over a hyperlinked shape in a Visio drawing, the cursor changes to show a tiny earth and a three-link chain.

When Visio is unable to display the file, it launches the appropriate application. For example, to display an HTML document, Visio launches your Web browser; to display a graphic file, Visio launches your image editing program. Visio searches the Windows registry to determine which program to launch, based on the filename's extension.

In addition to linking to a filename, you can also select the page to display. Visio calls this the *sub-address*. In a multipage Visio drawing, you can specify the page name.

You can also create internal hyperlinks, where the Visio drawing links to other parts of itself. New to Visio 2000 is the ability to attach more than one hyperlink to a shape.

Procedures

The shortcut key for inserting hyperlinks is:

Function	Keystroke	Menu	Toolbar Icon
Insert Hyperlinks	Ctrl+K	Insert | Hyperlinks	

Adding a Hyperlink to a Shape or Page

Use the following procedure to insert a hyperlink in a Visio shape or page:

1. Select a shape.
2. Select **Insert | Hyperlinks** from the menu bar. Notice the Hyperlinks dialog box.

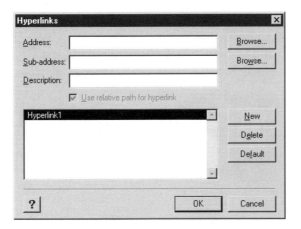

3. There are four areas to fill out in this dialog box, but only the first is required. Type a filename (or URL) in the Address text box.

4. If you don't remember the filename, click the **Browse** button. Notice the menu listing two choices: **Internet Address** and **Local File**.

    ▶ Selecting **Internet Address** launches your computer's Web browser, and connects to the www.visio.com Web site.

    ▶ Selecting **Local File** displays the Link to File dialog box, which lets you select a file from your computer and networked drives.

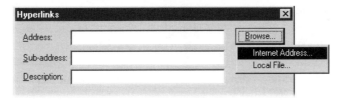

5. When the URL points to a Visio drawing, you have the option of specifying a specific page within the drawing by typing an address in the **Sub-address** box. Although the Visio documentation states that you can also link to a location (also called an *anchor*) within an HTML file, attempting to do this results in a warning dialog box:

Tip: To link another drawing page, leave the Address field blank. Click the **Browse** button located next to the Sub-address field. Visio displays another Hyperlink dialog box:

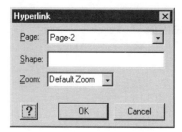

- Select a page name from the Page list box.
- (*Optional*) Specify the name of a shape in the Shape field.
- (*Optional*) Select a **Zoom** level; this will cause Visio to zoom in on the shape.
  Click **OK**.

 Note: The Hyperlink dialog box does not list the names of shapes in the Shape field, so you have to determine the name yourself. Visio assigns the name when you drag a shape from the stencil onto the page. The name is *name.n*. The *name* is a name, such as Sheet or Square, while *n* is a number incremented each time a shape is dragged onto the page, such as **Sheet.4**.

There are several ways to determine the name of a shape. One way is to select **Format | Special** from the menu bar. The Special dialog box displays the shape's name in the Master field. For example:

  Master: Process:Sheet.4

"Process" is the name of the master, while "Sheet.4" is the name of the shape. (Recall that when you drag a shape from the stencil to the page, Visio makes a copy of the master.)

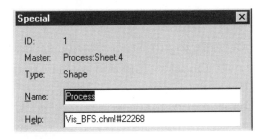

6. When you pause the cursor over a hyperlinked shape, the cursor changes and a tooltip displays the address. As an alternative, you can type in a descriptive name of the link in the **Description** box, which is displayed instead.

7. When **Use relative path for hyperlink** is turned on, you can move the Visio drawing and its linked files together to other folders and drives and the links will still work.

8. Click **New** to add another hyperlink to the shape. The **Delete** button removes the selected hyperlink. The **Default** button changes the list name from "Hyperlink 1" to the text in the Description field; this button also selects the default hyperlink, which is used by applications that recognize a single hyperlink only.

9. Click **OK**. Right-click the shape, and then choose the hyperlink to test the link.

Editing a Hyperlink

Use the following procedure to edit the URL and wording of a hyperlink:

1. Move the cursor over shapes to find one with a hyperlink. Notice how the cursor changes.

2. From the menu, select **Insert | Hyperlinks**. Notice the Hyperlinks dialog box.

3. Select a hyperlink from the list in the lower half of the dialog box.

4. Edit the entries in the Address, Sub-address, and Description fields.

5. Click **OK**.

6. Right-click the shape, and then choose the hyperlink to test the changes you made to the link.

Jumping to a Hyperlink

Use the following procedure to jump to a location specified by a hyperlink:

1. Move the cursor over shapes to find one with a hyperlink. Notice how the cursor changes.

2. Right-click the shape. Notice that the menu includes the name(s) of the hyperlink(s).

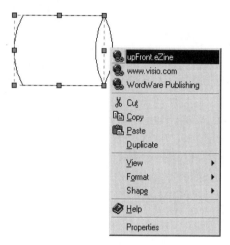

3. Select a hyperlink. Notice that Visio opens the file, or opens the related application to display the file or Web site.

Hands-On Activity

In this activity, you insert a hyperlink in a drawing. (This activity assumes that Excel or another spreadsheet program is installed on your computer.) Start Visio.

1. From the Welcome to Visio 2000 dialog box, double-click **Choose drawing type**.

2. Click **Flowchart**, and then double-click **Basic Flowchart**.

3. Drag the **Stored Data** shape onto the page.

4. Press **Ctrl+K** or select **Insert | Hyperlinks** from the menu. Notice the Hyperlinks dialog box.

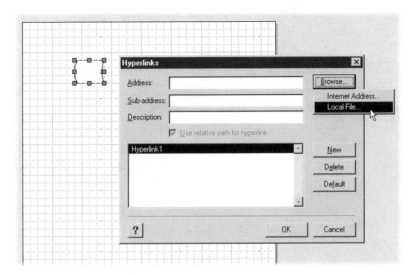

5. Click **Browse** (next to the Address field). Select **Local File**. Notice that Visio displays the Link to File dialog box:

Look in: **\Visio 2000\Samples\Project Schedule**

File name: **Sample Gantt Chart Data.xls**

Files of type: **Office Files**

Click **Open**.

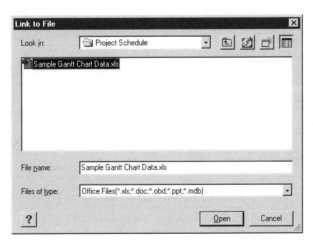

6. For the Description field, type **Sample Gantt Chart Data**.

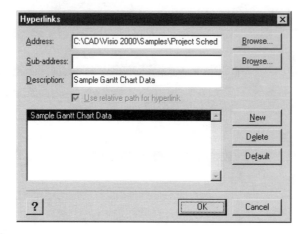

7. Click **OK**. Notice that the shape looks no different.

8. Pause the cursor over the shape. Notice the cursor changes and a tooltip displays the description, "Sample Gantt Chart Data." The change in cursor alerts you that the shape contains a hyperlink. When the shape contains more than one hyperlink, the tooltip reads "Multiple Hyperlinks."

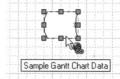

9. Right-click the shape. Notice that the shortcut menu lists the hyperlink.

10. Select **Sample Gantt Chart Data**. Notice that Visio opens Excel with the spreadsheet.

11. Exit Visio and Excel with **Alt+F4**.

This completes the hands-on activity for creating and using hyperlinks.

Creating a Web Document

File | Save As | HTML

Uses

In this chapter you'll learn about:

✓ *Saving a drawing as an HTML file*

Visio drawings can be saved in HTML and VML format for viewing by Web browsers:

▶ HTML format for viewing by Web browsers on your firm's intranet or by everyone on the Internet. The Visio drawing itself is converted to GIF, JPG, PNG, or VML file formats.

▶ VML format for viewing by Internet Explorer 5.0. VML is short for "Vector Markup Language" and is new to Visio 2000; the DWF (drawing Web format) introduced by Visio 5.0 is no longer supported.

Each page in the Visio drawing becomes a Web page. When you insert hyperlinks in the Visio drawing, they are preserved in the Web documents. Your Visio drawing cannot be edited when displayed by the Web browser.

When Visio exports the drawing page as an HTML document, it generates more than one file. In the table, the *filename* refers to the Visio drawing filename, such as "Global Organization Chart":

File	Purpose
filename.htm	The primary HTML page; this file uses the following files:
filename_frame.htm	Defines the frames (see illustration).
filename1_raster.htm	The HTML code that displays the raster image.
filename1_raster.gif	The raster image generated from the Visio page (GIF, in this case).
filename1_vml.VML	The VML image generated from the Visio page.
filename_nav.htm	The navigation frame; this file uses the following files:
filename_utils.js	The JavaScript code that activates the page turning.
lt_off.gif	Left arrow.

File	Purpose
lt_over.gif	Left arrow displayed when selected.
rt_off.gif	Right arrow.
rt_over.gif	Right arrow displayed when selected.

The filenames generated by Visio, such as Global Organization Chart1_raster.gif, can be decoded as follows:

▸ **Global Organization Chart**: Specifies the name of the source Visio drawing.

▸ **1_**: Specifies the Visio drawing page number.

▸ **raster**: Specifies the file is in raster format.

▸ **.gif**: Specifies the type of raster format, GIF in this case.

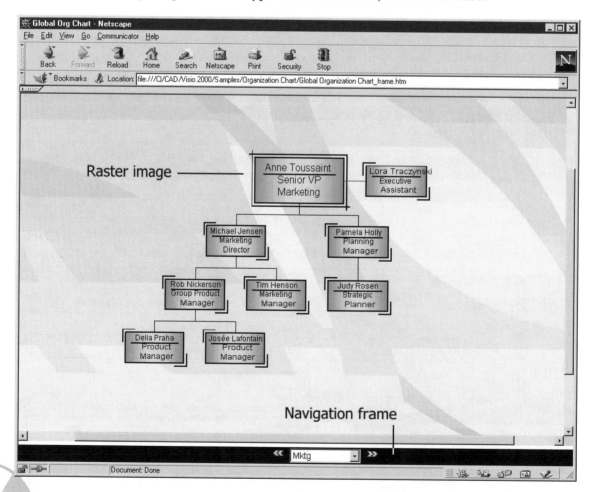

> **Tip:** To view the source code of the HTML files generated by Visio, select **View | Page Source** in Netscape Navigator (or **View | Source** in Internet Explorer).

```
Source of: file:///C|/CAD/Visio 2000/Samples/Organization Chart/Global Organization Chart_frame.htm - Netscape

<html>
<head>
<title>Global Org Chart</title>
<script src="Global Organization Chart_utils.js">

</script>
<script>
<!--
var g_NavBarLoaded = g_TitleBarLoaded = false;

function FileEntry(pageName, vmlImage, rasterImage) {
        this.PageName = pageName;
```

Procedures

The shortcut keys for saving Visio drawings in HTML or VML format are:

Function	Keystroke	Menu	Toolbar Icon
Save as HTML	...	File | Save As | HTML Files	...
Save As VML	...	File | Save As | Vector Markup	...

Saving as an HTML File

Use the following procedure to save the Visio drawing in HTML format:

1. Select **File | Save As** from the menu bar. Notice the Save As dialog box.
2. From the Save as type list box, select **HTML Files (*.htm,*.html)**.
3. If necessary, specify a different filename, and select another folder and drive.
4. Click **Save**. Notice the Save As HTML dialog box.

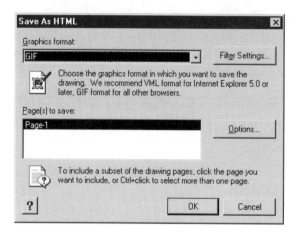

5. Select a format from the Graphics format list box. The Visio drawing is converted to one of the file formats commonly used by Web browsers. Although you have a choice of three raster formats (GIF, JPEG, and PNG) and one vector format (VML), you should choose GIF for two reasons:

    ▶ GIF is understood by all Web browsers; PNG and VML are not.

    ▶ GIF does not corrupt the image; JPEG performs *lossy compression*, which means that fine lines found in Visio drawings might become blurry.

6. Click **Filter Settings**. Notice that Visio displays the Filter Settings dialog box. The dialog box varies, depending on whether you selected a raster format or VML.

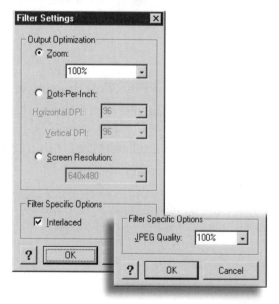

7. The Output Optimization area specifies how the Visio drawing will appear in the HTML document. You have three options:

   ▶ **Zoom**: Reduces (such as 25%) or enlarges (such as 200%) the drawing from its current size.

   ▶ **Dots-Per-Inch**: Specifies the resolution in horizontal and vertical dpi (dots per inch), ranging from 32 dpi to 96 dpi.

   ▶ **Screen Resolution**: Selects a target screen resolution, ranging from 640 x 480 to 1920 x 1200.

8. The Filter Specific Options area specifies options specific to the raster format you selected:

Format	Filter Specific Option
GIF	**Interlaced**: When on, alternating raster lines of the image are displayed by the Web browser, which makes the image appear sooner on a slow Internet connection.
JPEG	**JPEG Quality**: The higher the compression, the lower the quality of image; 100% is highest quality, while 10% is lowest quality.
PNG	No options.

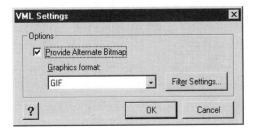

9. If you chose VML in the Save As HTML dialog box, the VML Settings dialog appears when you click **Filter Settings**. Its options are:

   Provide Alternate Bitmap: If the Web browser cannot display the VML file, it will display a raster image instead.

   Graphics format: Select a raster (bitmap) format; GIF is the best choice, as noted earlier.

   Filter Settings: Display the same dialog box as for GIF, JPEG, and PNG.

10. When the Visio drawing contains more than one page, you can select which pages you want exported in the Page(s) to save area:

    ▶ Click to select a single page.

▶ Hold down the **Ctrl** key and click to select more than one page.

There is usually no need to select the background page, since it is automatically placed in the background of each related foreground page.

11. Click **Options**. Notice that Visio displays the Export Options dialog box.

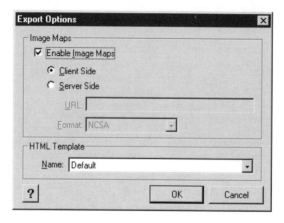

Image maps are those images you see at a Web site that have one or more areas you click to jump somewhere. When a Visio drawing contains hyperlinks, the drawing becomes an image map when you select the **Enable Image Maps** option.

Image maps work two ways: client or server. The *client* is your Web browser; the *server* is the Web site that serves up your HTML sites. In most cases, you want the Web browser to handle the hyperlinking of image maps. In some corporate environments, however, the Web server is in charge of image maps. In that case, select **Server Side** and ask your network manager for the URL and Format data.

By default, Visio exports the drawing to a generic-style HTML page. You can, however, instruct Visio where to place elements in the HTML page via a *template*. Use an HTML template that contains *substitution codes*. Create the HTML file with a text editor, giving it an HTM extension. Visio recognizes the following substitution codes:

Codes	Meaning
<!--IMAGE-- >	The Visio drawing.
<!--CS_IMAGE_MAP-- >	Map data containing hyperlinks.

Codes	Meaning
Navigation Buttons	
<!--NEXT_ANCHOR-- >	Makes the Next button a navigational link to the next page.
<!--NEXT_PAGE_BTN-- > <IMG SRC="Next.GIF" >	Tags for the Next button graphic.
<!--NEXT_ANCHOR_END >	Ending anchor tag for the Next button.
<! --BACK_ANCHOR-- >	Makes the Back button a navigational link to the previous page.
<!--BACK_PAGE_BTN-- > <IMG SRC="Back.GIF" >	Back button graphic.
<!--BACK_ANCHOR_END >	Ending anchor tag for the Back button.
File | Properties Data	
<!--FILE_NAME-- >	Visio drawing filename.
<!--FILE_PATH-- >	Visio drawing pathname.
<!--FULL_NAME-- >	Visio drawing drive, path, and file name.
<!--CREATOR-- >	Creator.
<!--DESCRIPTION-- >	Description.
<!--KEYWORDS-- >	Keywords.
<!--SUBJECT-- >	Subject.
<!--TITLE-- >	Title.
<!--x-- >	x = Category, Company, Manager, or Hyperlink_Base.
Page Numbering	
<!--PAGE_COUNT-- >	Total number of pages in the Visio drawing.
<!--PAGE_INDEX-- >	Page number relative to other pages in the Visio drawing.
<!--PAGE_NAME-- >	Name of Visio page saved in HTML format.
<!--HTML_PAGE_COUNT-- >	Total number of HTML pages.

Notes: <! ... > is the HTML tag for a comment; this allows substitution codes to be ignored by the Web browser.

Visio retrieves some of the information from the File | Properties dialog box.

12. Click **OK**. Visio converts the drawing pages to raster and/or VML files. (The **Cancel** button does not work on the Exporting dialog box.)

13. Visio offers to let you view the HTML file. Click **Yes**. Notice that Visio launches your Web browser and loads the HTML file.

 Note: When you select **File | Save As | Vector Markup**, Visio saves the drawing as a VML file without displaying any dialog boxes.

Hands-On Activity

In this activity, you export a drawing in HTML format. Start Visio.

1. From the Welcome to Visio 2000 dialog box, select **Browse existing files**.
2. In the Open dialog box, select the **Global Organization Chart.Vsd** file found in the \Samples\Organization Chart folder.
3. From the menu bar, select **File | Save As**. Notice the Save As dialog box.
4. From the dialog box, click the **Save as type** list box, and select **HTML Files (*.htm,*.html)**.
5. Click **Save**. Notice the Save As HTML dialog box.
6. In the Graphics format list box, select **VML**.

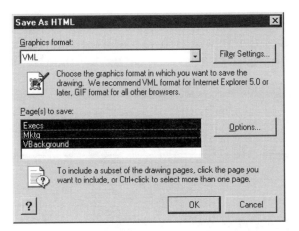

7. Click **Filter Settings**. Notice the VML Settings dialog box.

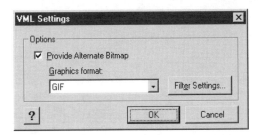

8. In the VML Settings dialog box, check **Provide Alternate Bitmap** to turn that option on, and enter **GIF** in the Graphics format box. Click **OK**.

9. Back in the Save As HTML dialog box, hold down the **Ctrl** key and select all three pages in the **Page(s) to save** list.

10. Click **OK**. Notice that Visio converts the three pages to GIF and VML files.

11. When finished converting the pages to HTML, Visio asks if you want to see the result. When you click **Yes**, Visio launches your computer's default Web browser and loads the files.

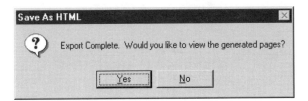

12. The Web browser displays the Visio drawing, with page controls at the bottom. Click the double arrows to move forward and backward through the pages, or select a page name from the list box.

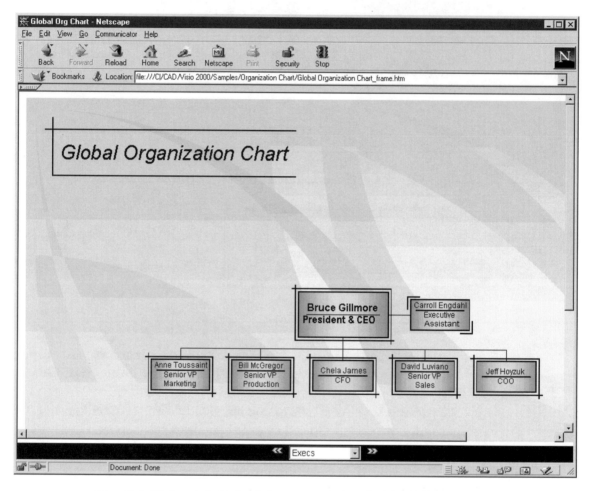

13. Exit Visio and the Web browser with **Alt+F4**.

This completes the hands-on activity for exporting a Visio drawing as a Web document.

Module 37 *Importing CAD Drawings*

Uses

In this chapter you'll learn about:

✓ *Importing a CAD drawing*

Visio is sometimes used together with CAD (computer-aided design) software. Visio can display certain types of CAD drawings. You can place Visio shapes on the CAD drawing, which "snap" to the CAD geometry.

Visio reads CAD drawings in these formats:

DWG: The file format for drawings created by all versions of IntelliCAD, and all versions of AutoCAD going back to version 2.5 (DWG is short for "drawing").

DGN: The file format for drawings created by Bentley Systems' MicroStation (DGN is short for "design").

DXF: A file format used to exchange drawings between CAD programs, as well as non-CAD programs (DXF is short for "drawing interchange format").

IGES: Another file format used to exchange drawings between CAD systems (IGES is short for "Initial Graphics Exchange Specification").

After the drawing is placed on the page:

▶ Shapes snap automatically to the underlying geometry. For example, electrical outlets, HVAC ducts, and furniture shapes automatically rotate and snap into place.
▶ You can select layers to convert into Visio objects.
▶ The CAD drawing can be edited from within Visio using the OLE capabilities of the originating CAD package.

Caution: CAD drawings contain a great deal of information in addition to the lines and arcs that make up a typical Visio drawing. Even the color, line style, and layer name of a CAD drawing can contain legal information. For example, a property line might be shown in a specific color and linetype. The translation of a CAD drawing to a foreign program, unfortunately, often results in the loss of some data and the modification of other data.

CAD objects are erased when Visio is unable to convert them. Specifically, when importing an AutoCAD drawing, Visio does not display the following:

- Paper space (called "layouts" in AutoCAD 2000).
- Multiple model space viewports (only one model space viewport is displayed).
- Proxy objects (or "zombie" objects).
- OLE object images.
- 3D ACIS solids.
- 2D ACIS regions.

  For example, if the AutoCAD drawing consists solely of ACIS solid models, the drawing will appear blank when opened in Visio 2000.

  Other AutoCAD objects are partially displayed. Visio is able to display some of the object, but not all of it. The following are partially displayed:

- Raster image: Only the border is displayed.
- Complex linetypes: Only the straight line portions are displayed.
- TrueType fonts: AutoCAD's SHX fonts are substituted.
- Some text justification problems, which seems related to Visio's inability to display TrueType fonts in the CAD drawing.
- Variable-width, splined polylines show some imperfection.
- Lineweights are not shown (the lines are displayed one pixel wide).
- 3D models are flattened to 2D, but 3D viewpoint is preserved.

> **Tip:** If your CAD program is not supported directly by Visio, it might be able to save drawings in one of the four formats listed above.

Procedures

As you can see from the above list, translation is <u>never</u> 100% accurate. With this caveat in mind, here are the procedures for importing and exporting AutoCAD DWG files. The shortcut keys are:

Function	Keystroke	Menu	Toolbar Icon
Open CAD File	...	File | Open | AutoCAD Drawing	...
Insert CAD File	Alt+IA	Insert | CAD Drawing	...

Import a CAD Drawing

Use the following procedure to import an AutoCAD drawing into Visio for viewing only:

1. Select **File | Open** from the menu bar. Notice the Open dialog box.
2. From the Files of type list box, select a CAD drawing format:
   ▸ AutoCAD drawing (*.dwg,*.dxf)
   ▸ MicroStation drawing (*.dgn)
   ▸ IGES drawing file format (*.igs)

> **Tip:** The procedure for importing DXF files is identical to DWG. To add a CAD drawing to an existing Visio page, select **Insert | CAD Drawing**; the IGES format, however, is not available.

3. Select the CAD drawing file. If necessary, change folders and drives.
4. Click **Open**. Notice the CAD Drawing Properties dialog box. The options of the General tab are:

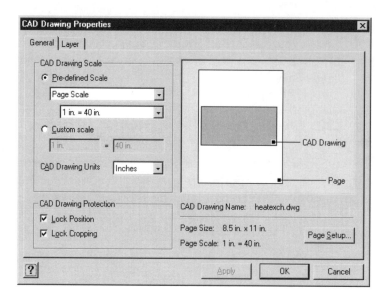

CAD Drawing Scale: Specifies the size of the CAD drawing relative to the Visio page. If you plan to place Visio shapes in the drawing, then you must scale the CAD drawing to fit the scale of the shapes. You can set the scale three ways:

▶ **Pre-defined Scale** causes Visio to scale the CAD drawing automatically; the extents of the drawing is scaled to fit the page ("extents" refers to a rectangle that encompasses all entities in the drawing). Click the **Page Scale** drop list to select a discipline: Architectural, Civil engineering, Mechanical engineering, or Metric.

▶ **Custom scale** lets you specify any scale factor. The first number refers to the Visio page, while the second number refers to the CAD drawing. For example, **1 in. = 40 in**. means that one inch in the Visio page represents 40 inches in the CAD drawing.

▶ **Page Setup** lets you change the size and scale of the Visio page. See Module 4 "Setting Up Pages and Layers."

CAD Drawing Units: Specifies how to interpret CAD drawing units. (CAD software uses unitless units that are interpreted as real-world units.) Select a measurement unit, if you know what it should be.

CAD Drawing Protection has two options:

▶ **Lock Position**: Locks the CAD drawing so that it cannot be moved.

> ▶ **Lock Cropping**: Locks the CAD drawing so that it cannot be cropped.

Tip: After the drawing is inserted on the page, you can change these properties. Right-click the drawing, and select **CAD Drawing Object | Properties**.

5. Click the **Layer** tab. It lets you specify some options related to layers in the CAD drawing:

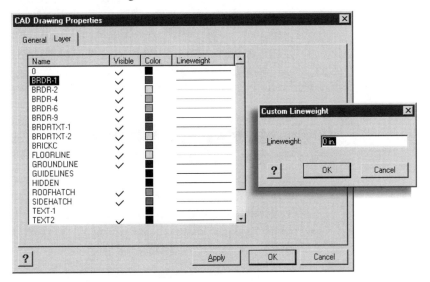

Name: Specifies the names of all layers found in the drawing, including externally referenced layers.

> ▶ Click the **Name** header to sort layer names in alphabetical order; click a second time to sort in reverse (Z to A) order.
> ▶ You cannot edit layer names.

Visible: Specifies whether entities on the layer are displayed; the default visibility is based on each layer's setting in the CAD drawing.

> ▶ A check mark means the layer is visible; click the check mark to turn off visibility.
> ▶ Click the **Visible** header to sort layers by visibility.

Color: Specifies the color of entities on the layer; the default color is based on the setting in the CAD drawing.

> ▶ Click a color square to display the Color dialog box, which lets you change the color of entities on the layer.

▶ Click the **Color** header to sort layer names by color, starting with red; click the header a second time to sort in reverse order, starting with white.

Lineweight: Specifies the weight (width) of lines making up entities; the default weight is 0, which means lines are drawn as thin as possible. Visio ignores lineweights specified in the CAD drawing.

▶ Click a line to display the Custom Lineweight dialog box, and specify a new weight.

▶ Click the **Lineweight** header to sort layer names by lineweight, starting with the lightest weight; click the header a second time to sort in reverse order, starting with the heaviest weight.

6. Click **OK**. Notice that Visio displays the CAD Drawing dialog box. This gives you another chance to match the CAD drawing scale to the Visio page scale. Select an option, and click **OK**. Notice the CAD drawing on the page.

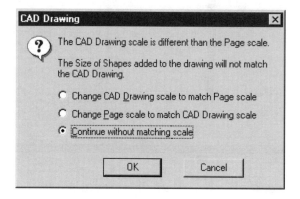

Tip: If you do not see the CAD drawing, Visio may have located it off the page. To find the drawing, change the zoom to 1%, and look for the drawing on the pasteboard.

This concludes the procedures for inserting a CAD drawing in Visio 2000.

Toolbar Customization

View | Toolbars | Customize

Uses

In this chapter you'll learn about:

✓ **Changing toolbar options**

✓ **Creating a new toolbar**

All Windows programs, including Visio, have toolbars. The toolbar holds buttons and drop lists that allow you to directly select commands. Generally, it is quicker to select a command from a toolbar than from the menus because fewer mouse clicks are required.

The drawback to toolbars is that the button icons, such as on the **Snap & Glue** toolbar, can sometimes be confusing.

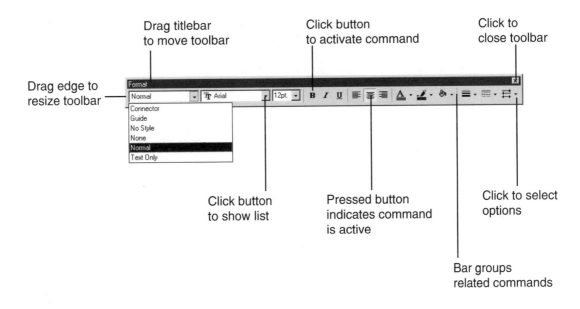

Drag titlebar
to move toolbar

Click button
to activate command

Click to
close toolbar

Drag edge to
resize toolbar

Click button
to show list

Pressed button
indicates command
is active

Click to select
options

Bar groups
related commands

Drag to move toolbar

ScreenTip

●❯ **Tip:** When you drag a toolbar near the edge of the Visio window, the toolbar automatically docks. To prevent the toolbar from docking, hold down the **Ctrl** key while dragging the toolbar.

As of Visio 2000, you can fully customize the toolbars. That means you can create new toolbars, edit them to hold any Visio command, and delete toolbars.

Procedures

The shortcut key for customizing toolbars is:

Function	Keystroke	Menu	Toolbar Icon
Customize Toolbars	Alt+VTC	View | Toolbars | Customize	...

▲ **Note:** You can right-click any toolbar, and select **Customize** from the shortcut menu.

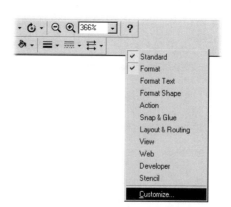

Changing Toolbar Options

Use the following procedure to change the "look and feel" of Visio toolbars:

1. Select **View | Toolbars | Customize** from the menu bar. Notice the Customize dialog box.

2. Select the **Options** tab.

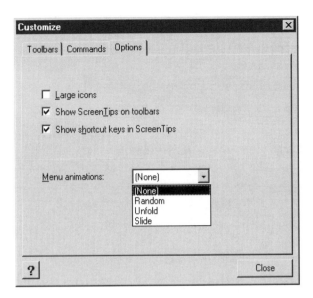

3. Change any of the options:

   Large icons: When on, displays toolbar icons at twice their normal size.

   Show ScreenTips on toolbars: When on, Visio displays a tooltip when the cursor lingers over a toolbar button. The tooltip describes the name of the toolbar button.

   Show shortcut keys in ScreenTips: When on, the tooltip includes the shortcut keystroke, if one is available for the tool.

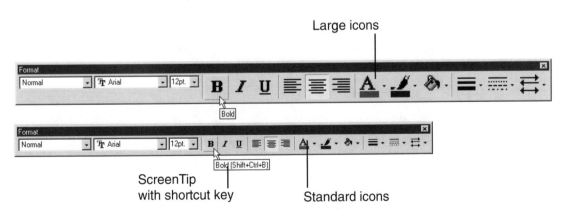

   Menu animations: Determines how the menus open:

   ▶ **None**: The menu opens normally.

> ▶ **Random**: The menu opens by unfolding or sliding.
> ▶ **Unfold**: The menu opens by sliding open sideways and downwards.
> ▶ **Slide**: The menu opens by sliding down.

4. Click **Close** to see the effect of the options you changed.

●◆ **Tips:** Large icons are easier to see on a high-resolution screen, but take up more screen "real estate." ScreenTips with shortcut keys are useful enough to always keep turned on. On a fast computer, menu animations are not noticeable.

Creating a New Toolbar

Use the following procedure to create a new toolbar:

1. Select **View | Toolbars | Customize** from the menu bar. Notice the Customize dialog box.

2. Click **New** on the Toolbars tab. Notice the New Toolbar dialog box.

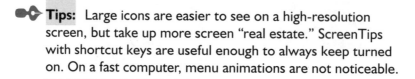

3. Enter a descriptive name for the toolbar. This name will appear on the toolbar's title bar, as well as on the list of available toolbars.

4. Click **OK**. Notice the new, empty toolbar.

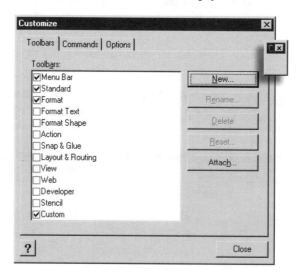

5. Drag the toolbar away from the Customize dialog box so it doesn't disappear when you click another tab in the dialog box. To fill the toolbar with buttons, you drag icons into it. Select the **Commands** tab of the Customize dialog box. Notice that all of Visio's commands are sorted by menu.

6. Drag a command from the Customize dialog box into the new toolbar. For example, under Categories, select **Edit**. Under Commands, drag **Select All** to the new toolbar.

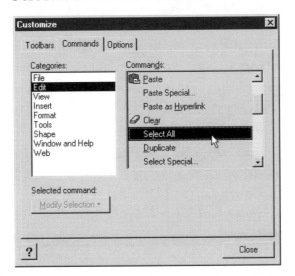

7. To change the properties of the new button, right-click. Notice the shortcut menu.

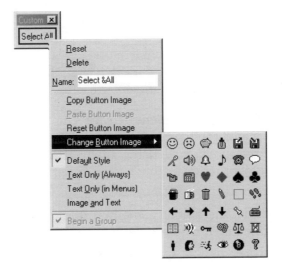

Reset: Resets the button's options.

Delete: Removes the button from the toolbar.

Name: Specifies the name displayed by the ScreenTip and in the menu. The & (ampersand) prefixes the underlined character in menus, such as **Select All**. The underlined character is used with the **Alt** key for shortcut keystrokes.

Copy Button Image: Copies the button's image to the Clipboard.

Paste Button Image: Pastes an image from the Clipboard onto the button.

Reset Button Image: Changes the image back to its original form.

Change Button Image: Selects an alternative image for the icon.

Default Style: Displays text and/or an icon image on the button.

Text Only (Always): Displays text only in menus and in toolbars.

Text Only (in Menus): Displays text only in menus.

Image and Text: Displays icon image and text.

Begin a Group: Defines a group of buttons (a.k.a. flyout).

8. Select the **Toolbars** tab, and click **Attach** to attach the toolbar to the drawing file. Notice that Visio displays the Attach Toolbars dialog box.

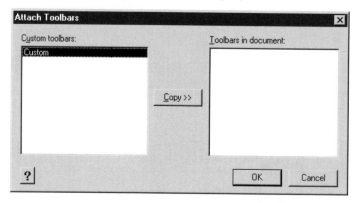

9. Select the toolbar name, then click **Copy**. This step is necessary because customized toolbars are available only on your computer. To make customized toolbars available anywhere the current drawing is opened, the toolbar must be attached to the drawing file.

10. Click **OK**.

11. Select the customized toolbar name in the Toolbars list. Notice that you can now rename and delete the toolbar.

12. Click **Close** to exit toolbar customization.

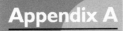

Mouse & Keyboard Shortcuts

> **In this chapter you'll learn about:**
>
> ✓ **Shortcuts by task**
>
> ✓ **Shortcuts by keystroke**

You may find that you work more quickly when you use Visio's shortcut keystrokes and the mouse. In this appendix, you find all shortcuts listed two ways: first in alphabetical order by tool name, then in alphabetical order by keystroke. This list is more complete than that provided by Visio 2000's documentation.

Shortcuts by Task

General Tasks

Use the following mouse buttons and keystrokes to perform general tasks:

Add to or remove from selection set	Shift and click
Customized operation	Double-click
Exit Visio	Ctrl+Q or Alt+F4
Nudge	Select an object, then press cursor keys
Pixel nudge	Select object, Shift, and press cursor keys
Pointer	Ctrl+I
Repeat last command	F4
Select shape	Click
Shortcut menu	Right-click

Pan & Zoom

Use the following shortcut keys to quickly zoom and pan your drawing:

Actual Size (100%)	Ctrl+1
Opens the Zoom dialog box	F6
Pan	Ctrl+Shift and drag while holding down the right mouse button, or press cursor keys when no objects are selected.
Whole Page	Ctrl+W
Zoom in	Ctrl+Shift and click
Zoom out	Shift+F6, or Ctrl+Shift and right-click
Zoom in on an area	Ctrl+Shift and drag a rectangle

Drawing Tools

Use the following shortcut keys to quickly switch between drawing tools:

Arc	Ctrl+7
Connection Point	Ctrl+Shift+1
Connector	Ctrl+3
Crop image	Ctrl+Shift+2
Ellipse	Ctrl+9
Freeform	Ctrl+5
Line	Ctrl+6
Pencil	Ctrl+4
Rectangle	Ctrl+8
Rotation	Ctrl+0 (zero)
Stamp	Ctrl+Shift+3
Text	Ctrl+2
Text Block	Ctrl+Shift+4
Toggle between text edit and selection mode	Select a shape, then press F2

Menu Commands

For many of these shortcuts, you must select a shape first:

Activate the menu bar	Alt or F10
Align Shapes dialog box	F8
Bring selected shapes to front	Ctrl+F
Cascade windows	Alt+F7
Copy to Clipboard	Ctrl+C
Cut to Clipboard	Ctrl+X
Duplicate selected shapes	Ctrl+D
Field dialog box	Ctrl+F9
Fill dialog box	F3
Flip horizontal	Ctrl+H
Flip vertical	Ctrl+J
Font tab, Text dialog box	F11
Glue toggle (on or off)	F9
Group selected shapes	Ctrl+G
Help dialog box	F1
Hyperlinks dialog box	Ctrl+K
Line dialog box	Shift+F3
Macros dialog box	Alt+F8
New drawing (based on current drawing)	Ctrl+N
Open dialog box	Ctrl+O
Page dialog box	F5
Paragraph tab, Text dialog box	Shift+F11
Paste from Clipboard	Ctrl+V
Print dialog box	Ctrl+P
Print Setup tab, Page Setup dialog box	Shift+F5
Redo	Ctrl+Y
Repeat last command	F4
Rotate left	Ctrl+L
Rotate right	Ctrl+R

Save drawing	Ctrl+S
Save As dialog box	F12
Save Workspace dialog box	Alt+F12
Select all	Ctrl+A
Send selected shapes to back	Ctrl+B
Size & Position window	Click the status bar
Snap toggle (on or off)	Shift+F9
Snap & Glue dialog box	Alt+F9
Spelling dialog box	F7
Tabs tab, Text dialog box	Ctrl+F11
Tile windows horizontally	Shift+F7
Tile windows vertically	Ctrl+Shift+F7
Undo	Ctrl+Z
Ungroup selected groups	Ctrl+U
Visual Basic Editor	Alt+F11

Text Formatting

Use the following key combinations to apply and remove formatting on selected text:

Bold	Ctrl+Shift+B
Italic	Ctrl+Shift+I
SMALL CAPS	Ctrl+Shift+Y
Sub$_{script}$	Ctrl+Shift+X
Super^{script}	Ctrl+Shift+Z
Underline	Ctrl+Shift+U

Special Text Characters

Use the following key combinations to add special characters in text:

Beginning double-quote "	Ctrl+Shift+[
Beginning single-quote '	Ctrl+[
Bullet ●	Ctrl+Shift+8

Copyright symbol ©	Ctrl+Shift+C
Discretionary hyphen -	Ctrl+hyphen
Em dash —	Ctrl+Shift+=
En dash –	Ctrl+=
Ending double-quote "	Ctrl+Shift+]
Ending single-quote '	Ctrl+]
Nonbreaking backslash \	Ctrl+Shift+\
Nonbreaking hyphen -	Ctrl+Shift+hyphen
Nonbreaking slash /	Ctrl+Shift+/
Paragraph marker ¶	Ctrl+Shift+7
Registered trademark ®	Ctrl+Shift+R
Section marker §	Ctrl+Shift+6

Text Fields

Use the following key combinations to add fields to text (without accessing the Field dialog box):

Height field	Ctrl+Shift+H or Ctrl+E
Rotation angle field	Ctrl+Shift+A
Width field	Ctrl+Shift+W

Full-screen Navigation

Use these keyboard shortcuts to navigate between Visio and another page when in full-screen view:

Back	Ctrl+left arrow
Forward	Ctrl+right arrow
Next Page	Ctrl+Page Down (not on the numeric keypad)
Previous Page	Ctrl+Page Up (not on the numeric keypad)

Shortcuts by Keystroke

Mouse Buttons

Click	Select shape
Ctrl+Shift and click	Zoom in
Ctrl+Shift and drag	Pan
Ctrl+Shift and drag a rectangle	Zoom windowed area
Ctrl+Shift and right-click	Zoom out
Double-click	Customized operation
Double-click status line	Size & Position window
Right-click	Shortcut menu
Shift + click	Add to or remove from selection set

Function Keys

Alt+F4	Exit Visio
Alt+F7	Cascade windows
Alt+F8	Macros dialog box
Alt+F9	Snap & Glue dialog box
Alt+F11	Visual Basic Editor
Alt+F12	Save Workspace dialog box
Ctrl+F9	Field dialog box
Ctrl+F11	Text dialog box, Tabs tab
Ctrl+Shift+F7	Tile windows vertically
F1	Help dialog box
F2	Toggle between text edit and selection mode
F3	Fill dialog box
F4	Repeat last command
F5	Page dialog box
F6	Zoom dialog box
F7	Spelling dialog box
F8	Align Shapes dialog box

F9	Glue toggle (on or off)
F10	Activate menu bar
F11	Text dialog box, Font tab
F12	Save As dialog box
Shift+F3	Line dialog box
Shift+F5	Page Setup dialog box, Print Setup tab
Shift+F6	Zoom out
Shift+F7	Tile windows horizontally
Shift+F9	Snap toggle (on or off)
Shift+F11	Text dialog box, Paragraph tab

Ctrl Keys

Ctrl+1	Pointer
Ctrl+2	Text tool
Ctrl+3	Connector tool
Ctrl+4	Pencil tool
Ctrl+5	Freeform tool
Ctrl+6	Line tool
Ctrl+7	Arc tool
Ctrl+8	Rectangle tool
Ctrl+9	Ellipse tool
Ctrl+0 (zero)	Rotation tool
Ctrl+A	Select all
Ctrl+B	Send selected shapes to back
Ctrl+C	Copy to Clipboard
Ctrl+D	Duplicate selected shapes
Ctrl+E	Insert height in text field
Ctrl+F	Bring selected shapes to front
Ctrl+G	Group selected shapes
Ctrl+H	Flip horizontal
Ctrl+I	Actual size view (100%)

Ctrl+J	Flip vertical
Ctrl+K	Hyperlink dialog box
Ctrl+L	Rotate left
Ctrl+M	Carriage return (like pressing the Enter key)
Ctrl+N	New drawing based on current drawing
Ctrl+O	Open dialog box
Ctrl+P	Print dialog box
Ctrl+Q	Exit Visio
Ctrl+R	Rotate right
Ctrl+S	Save drawing
Ctrl+U	Ungroup selected groups
Ctrl+V	Paste from Clipboard
Ctrl+W	Whole page view
Ctrl+X	Cut to Clipboard
Ctrl+Y	Redo
Ctrl+Z	Undo
Ctrl+Shift+1	Connection Point tool
Ctrl+Shift+2	Crop image tool
Ctrl+Shift+3	Stamp tool
Ctrl+Shift+4	Text Block tool
Ctrl+Shift+6	Section marker character §
Ctrl+Shift+7	Paragraph marker character ¶
Ctrl+Shift+8	Bullet character ●
Ctrl+Shift+A	Rotation angle text field
Ctrl+Shift+B	**Bold** text format
Ctrl+Shift+C	Copyright symbol character ©
Ctrl+Shift+H	Height text field
Ctrl+Shift+I	*Italic* text format
Ctrl+Shift+R	Registered trademark character ®
Ctrl+Shift+U	Underline text format
Ctrl+Shift+W	Width text field
Ctrl+Shift+X	Sub$_{script}$ text format

Ctrl+Shift+Y	SMALL CAPS text format
Ctrl+Shift+Z	Super^{script} text format
Ctrl+[	Beginning single-quote character '
Ctrl+]	Ending single-quote character '
Ctrl+=	En dash character –
Ctrl+Shift+/	Nonbreaking slash character /
Ctrl+Shift+[	Beginning double-quote character "
Ctrl+Shift+\	Nonbreaking backslash character \
Ctrl+Shift+]	Ending double-quote character "
Ctrl+Shift+=	Em dash character —
Ctrl+- (hyphen)	Discretionary hyphen character -
Ctrl+Shift+- (hyphen)	Nonbreaking hyphen character -

Other Keys

Alt	Activate menu bar
Ctrl+left arrow	Back (hyperlinking)
Ctrl+Page Down (not on the numeric keypad)	Next Page (hyperlinking)
Ctrl+Page Up (not on the numeric keypad)	Previous Page (hyperlinking)
Ctrl+right arrow	Forward (hyperlinking)
Cursor keys (when no objects are selected)	Pan
Select an object, then press cursor keys	Nudge shape
Select object, Shift, and press cursor keys	Pixel nudge

Index

1D shapes, 106, 110
2D shapes, 106, 110

A

address, 353
Adobe Illustrator, exporting to, 294-296
aligning shapes, 164-165
alignment, 140
    changing, 147-148
alignment box, 139
anchor, 355
Arc tool, using, 229-230
areas, 127
    formatting, 127-129
automatic dimensioning, 260-261

B

background, 128
background pages, 33-34
Behavior dialog, 331-335
bitmap, exporting to, 296-298
Boolean operations, 177
Bring to Front, 90, 95
Build Region macro, 178
    using, 180
bullets, 149

C

CAD drawing formats, 371
CAD drawings, importing, 373-376
centering drawing, 95
CGM, *see* Computer Graphics Metafile
changing font, 143-145
Choose Drawing Type dialog, 4
client, 366
closed object, 231

drawing, 231-233
Combine operation, 177-179
compression, 293
Computer Graphics Metafile format, exporting
    to, 298
connecting shapes, 111-112
    automatically, 112-113
    manually, 113
connection points, xviii, 106-107
    adding, 113
connections,
    dynamic, 108
    static, 108
connectors, 105-106, 110
    dynamic, 111
    routable, 111
    types of, 109
control points, 235, 262
converting shapes, 110
Copy command, 118
copying
    graphic objects, 119-120
    shapes, 99-100
    text, 119-120
cropping pictures, 279-280
custom properties, 339
    adding, 345-346
    defining, 341-344
    editing, 344
Custom Properties Editor, 346-348
custom property data, summarizing, 348-352
custom property fields, editing, 346-348
customizing toolbars, 377-382
cut, 118
Cut command, 118

cutting objects, 119

D

Define Custom Properties dialog, 341-344
device-independent bitmap, exporting to, 296-298
DIB, *see* device-independent bitmap
dimension, 258-259
    horizontal, 258
    vertical, 258
dimension lines,
    creating, 244-245, 261-262
    modifying, 262
dimension text, modifying, 264-265
dimensioning,
    automatic, 260-261
    manual, 261-262
display format, 264
displaying pages, 31
distributing shapes, 165-166
double-click behavior, changing, 328
Double-Click tab, 325-328
double-clicking, 326
dragging shapes, 85-86
Drawing Explorer, 317
    using, 318-320
drawing pages, 32
drawing scale, setting, 40
drawing size, setting, 40
drawing tools, 225-226
    using, 228-233
drawings,
    centering, 95
    exporting, 294-309
    opening, 23-24, 28
    saving, 19-20
    sizing, 40
    starting new, 2-3, 7-9
duplicating shapes, 100
dynamic
    connections, 108
    connector, 111
    glue, 107, 109
    grid, 64

E

Edit menu, 117
electronic output, 195-196
Ellipse tool, using, 230-231
e-mailing files, 201-202
Encapsulated PostScript format, exporting to, 294-295
EPS, *see* Encapsulated PostScript
exiting Visio, xiii
export options, 293-294
exporting drawings, 294-309
extension lines, 63
    modifying, 262-264

F

faxing files, 200-201
field, 237
file formats, 274-275, 291-292
fill color, applying, 133-135
fill style, applying, 158-159
finding text, 252-254
Flip commands, 90
flipping shapes, 94
font, changing, 143-145
force justified, 146
foreground, 128
foreground pages, 33-34
Format Painter, 155
Format Shape toolbar, 135
Format toolbar, 135
formatting, 125, 135
    areas, 127-129
    lines, 125-127, 131-133
    local, 153, 156
Fragment operation, 177, 179
Freeform tool, 226

G

GIF, *see* Graphics Interchange Format
glue, 62, 107-109
    converting, 108
    dynamic, 107, 109
    static, 107, 109
    toggling, 66
graphic objects,

copying, 119-120
cutting, 119
pasting, 120-121
Graphics Interchange Format, exporting, to, 299-300
grid, 60
dynamic, 64
setting, 65-66
toggling, 68
group, 173
grouping shapes, 174
groups,
adding shapes to, 174
creating, 174
disbanding, *see* ungrouping
removing shapes from, 174-175
guide points, 61
creating, 68
removing, 68
toggling, 68
guidelines, 61
creating, 67
removing, 67
repositioning, 67
toggling, 68

H
handle, 89
hanging indent, 146
Help menu, 213
horizontal dimension, 258
HTML format, 361
saving Visio drawing in, 363-368
hyperlinks, 353
editing, 357
inserting, 354-357
jumping to, 358

I
IGES, exporting to, 300-301
image maps, 366
importing
CAD drawings, 373-376
non-Visio files, 28-29
indentation, 146

Insert menu, 273
inserting
hyperlinks, 354-357
objects, 277-286
pages, 32
text fields, 240-242
instance, 85
Intersect operation, 177, 179

J
joining shapes, 178
JPEG, exporting to, 301-303

K
keystroke shortcuts, 383-391

L
layers, 31, 38-40
changing properties of, 41-42
creating, 41
removing, 42-43
renaming, 42
laying out shapes, 166-169
line, 125
line style, applying, 158
Line tool, using, 229
lines, formatting, 125-127, 131-133
linked object, placing, 284-286
local formatting, 153, 156
lossy compression, 302, 364

M
Macintosh PICT format, exporting to, 303-304
manual dimensioning, 261-262
margin, 65, 148
master, 85
master shape, 15, 73
metafile formats, 292
mouse shortcuts, 383-391

N
non-Visio files, 25-26
importing, 28-29

O
objects, 231
editing, 286-288

copying, 119-120
cutting, 119
inserting, 277-286
pasting, 120-121
offset copies, 101
one-dimensional shapes, 106, 110
open object, 231
opening drawings, 23-24, 28

P

page
break, 65
orientation, 36
Page command, 118
Page Setup dialog
Drawing Scale tab, 37-38
Page Properties tab, 32-33
Page Size tab, 35-36
pages,
background, 33-34
creating, 32, 43
foreground, 33-34
inserting, 32
rotating, 35-36
sizing, 35-36
pan, 51
Pan & Zoom window, 52-53
paragraph justification, 145-147
paste, 118
Paste as Hyperlink command, 119
Paste Special command, 118-119
Paste Special dialog, 121-122
pasteboard, xvii
pasting objects, 120-121
pattern, applying, 133-135
PC Paintbrush format, exporting to, 304-305
PCX format, exporting to, 304-305
Pencil tool, 226
using, 228-229
PICT format, *see* Macintosh PICT format
picture, inserting, 277-279
pin, 92
placeable shapes, 111
PNG format, exporting to, 305-308
point-to-point, 109

Portable Network Graphics format, exporting
to, 305-308
previewing the drawing, 188-192
print preview, 187
Print Preview command, 187-192
printing, 195
drawings, 197-198
files, 202-203
properties, custom, 339
Properties dialog, 14-15
Property Reporting Wizard, 348-352

R

raster formats, 292
real-time pan, 52
rearranging shapes, 163
Rectangle tool, using, 230
Redo command, 205
redoing, 207
replacing text, 254-255
resizing shapes, 93
Rotate commands, 90
rotating
pages, 35-36
shapes, 94
routable connector, 111
ruler, 59
changing origin of, 68-69
setting, 65-66
ruler origin, 59

S

Save As command, 14
Save As dialog, 16-18
Save command, 13
saving drawings, 19-20
saving files, *see* saving drawings
scale, 37
setting drawing, 40
scaling drawings, 37-38
Select Special, using, 312
selecting, 311
text, 142-143
selection handle, xviii
Send to Back, 90, 95

server, 366
setting tabs, 148-149
shadows, 129-130
Shape Explorer, 73-76
shape extensions, 63-64
Shape menu, 90
shapes, 71
    aligning, 164-165
    connecting, 111-113
    converting, 110
    copying, 99-100
    distributing, 165-166
    dragging, 85-86
    duplicating, 100
    flipping, 94
    grouping, 174
    joining, 178
    laying out, 166-169
    rearranging, 163
    resizing, 93
    rotating, 94
    sizing, 89
    stretching, 93
    ungrouping, 175
ShapeSheet, xii
shape-to-shape, 109
ShapeWare Corp., xix
Size & Position window, 90-92, 95
size, setting drawing, 40
sizing
    drawings interactively, 40
    pages, 35-36
    shapes, 89
SmartShapes, xii
snap, 61-62
    setting, 65
    toggling, 66
solutions, 3-4
spacing, 146
special characters, 239, 253
Special dialog, 335-336
spell checking, 247-249
Spline tool, *see* Freeform tool
starting a new drawing, 2-3, 7-9

starting Visio, xiii-xiv
static connections, 108
static glue, 107, 109
stencil, 71
stencil files, 23, 72
    opening, 76-77
stencil window, adjusting, 77-79
stretching shapes, 93
style, 153
    applying, 155-157
    applying to text, 157-158
    defining, 155-157
sub-address, 354
Subtract operation, 177, 179-180

T
tabs, setting, 148-149
Tagged Image File Format, exporting to, 308-309
template file, 23
text,
    adding, 238-240
    copying, 119-120
    cutting, 119
    finding, 252-254
    pasting, 120-121
    placing, 238-240
    replacing, 254-255
    selecting, 142-143
text block, 139
text box, 238
text field, inserting, 240-242
Text Ruler, 141
text style, applying, 157-158
thickness, changing, 93-94
TIFF, exporting to, 308-309
tiling, 191
    drawings, 198-199
toggle, 59
toggling, 68
toolbar options, changing, 378-380
toolbars,
    creating, 380-382
    customizing, 377-382
tooltip, xv

two-dimensional shapes, 106, 110

U

Undo command, 205
undoing, 207
      more than one action, 207
ungrouping, 175
uniform resource locator, *see* URL
Union operation, 177-178
URL, 353

V

vector formats, 291-292
vertex,
      inserting, 232-233
      moving, 233
vertical alignment, changing, 147-148
vertical dimension, 258
View menu, 51-52, 59
Visio,
      exiting, xiii
      starting, xiii-xiv

Visio Corp. xix-xx
Visio Drawing Viewer, 26-28
Visio editions,
      Enterprise, xiii, 4
      Professional, xiii, 4
      Standard, xii, 4
      Technical, xii-xiii, 4
Visio Help, accessing, 213-217
VML format, 361

W

wildcard characters, 254
workspace file, 23

Z

zero point, 59
      changing, 68-69
zoom, 51
      return to previous, 54
      windowed, 52
zooming in, 54

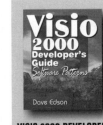

Other Books from Wordware Publishing, Inc.

I don't have time for learning curves.

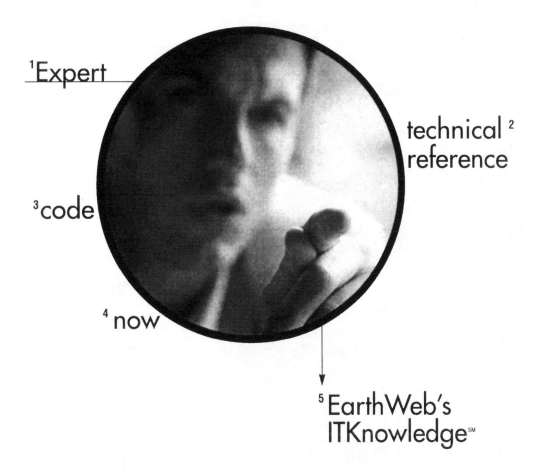

[1]Expert

technical [2]
reference

[3]code

[4] now

[5] EarthWeb's
ITKnowledge℠

They rely on you to be the ❶ expert on tough development challenges. There's no time for learning curves, so you go online for ❷ technical references from the experts who wrote the books. Find answers fast simply by clicking on our search engine. Access hundreds of online books, tutorials and even source ❸ code samples ❹ now. Go to ❺ EarthWeb's ITKnowledge, get immediate answers, and get down to it.

Get your FREE ITKnowledge trial subscription today at itkgo.com.
Use code number 026.

EARTHWEB
Go further *faster*

Visimation

Visual Automation for Visio® Software
Visible Solutions for Business

Add - on Extensions

The best way to boost VISIO productivity
VisiTools are unique extensions to VISIO software for
end users and developers that make VISIO software
even easier to use by automating common tasks.
VisiTools are high value, low cost applications that
work seamlessly with VISIO products to enhance
productivity. Turbocharge your VISIO program for
an out of the box experience!

Development Services

A picture worth 1000 hours of your time
Visimation transforms VISIO software from a general
drawing program to a powerful productivity solution.
We use Microsoft™ technologies and VISIO software to
enhance value, profitability, and communications by
automatically illustrating information. Your data
will spring to life, revealing new opportunities for
revenue growth and quality improvements.

Productive Applications

Draw on our expertise
Visimation builds custom applications that solve
difficult business problems. We tailor VISIO's
acclaimed drawing power and ease of use to
address specific needs in terms that any business
user can understand... creative applications of
VISIO software to simplify complex tasks.

Tools
VisiTools
Shape Manager
Shape Property Tools
VISIO Developer's Kit
VisiNotes

Automation
Custom Applications
Design and Development
End User Training
Developer Training
Consulting

Solutions
Telecommunications
Network Management
Facilities Management
Business Processes
Sales Automation

Visimation, Inc. • 425.557.5990 • www.visimation.com • info@visimation.com